Wordwise Plus

Other books for BBC users

The BBC Micro Advanced Reference Guide
Bruce Smith
0 00 383223 6

The BBC Micro ROM Book
Bruce Smith
0 00 383075 6

Wordwise Plus

A User's Guide

Bruce Smith

COLLINS
8 Grafton Street, London W1

Collins Professional and Technical Books
William Collins Sons & Co. Ltd
8 Grafton Street, London W1X 3LA

First published in Great Britain by
Collins Professional and Technical Books 1985
Reprinted 1986, 1987

Distributed in the United States of America
by Sheridan House, Inc.

British Library Cataloguing in Publication Data
Smith, Bruce
Wordwise plus: a user's guide.
1. Wordwise (Computer program)   2. Wordwise
Plus (Computer program)
I. Title
652'.5'0285425   Z52.5.W6/

ISBN 0–00–383176–0

Typeset by V & M Graphics Ltd, Aylesbury, Bucks
Printed and bound in Great Britain by
Mackays of Chatham, Kent

Also by Bruce Smith

The BBC Micro ROM Book
A highly practical book covering all aspects of using, designing and choosing ROM-based software.
0 00 303075 6

The BBC Micro Advanced Reference Guide
A complete reference guide to all aspects of the BBC Micro including the BBC B+.
0 00 383223 6

Contents

Preface

Wordwise is probably the most popular ROM for the BBC Micro; certainly it has become the most popular word processing ROM available for the Beeb. The arrival of Wordwise Plus with its versatile programming language means that there is almost nothing you cannot do when it comes to the art of processing words!

By rough calculation I estimate that I have written well over half a million words using Wordwise and Wordwise Plus, including the 50000 contained within these covers! Perhaps I may be allowed to say, with a degree of modesty, that many of its intricacies are well known to me!

This book is about both packages. There is a vast amount of information for both Wordwise and Wordwise Plus users herein. The first part of the book is for both of both – where an item is specific to one or other ROM then it is depicted by a flag thus

W Wordwise only
W+ Wordwise Plus only

This will leave you in no doubt as to whether it is of use to you.

Part Two concentrates on the segment programming language; how to use and write segment programs for manipulating text files. While this is, of course, specific to users of Wordwise Plus, it will be of great interest to those of you thinking of upgrading from Wordwise to Wordwise Plus. This section should leave you in no doubt, one way or the other. Finally, Part Three contains a range of useful segment programs ready for you to type in and use.

The title of this book is *A User's Guide*, and this is a most important feature. Throughout, practical worked examples show just what you need to do. If a special sequence of typing actions is required then these are depicted clearly, and in many instances visually. Wherever possible screen-shot dumps are provided to show you just what you should be seeing in front of you.

Users of a cassette-based Wordwise system should not be discouraged from using their word processor to its utmost capability. Anything is possible – indeed the very first book I wrote using Wordwise was saved, loaded and resaved using cassette tapes! The more advanced user will also find much of interest. It is amazing how much you can use Wordwise and still be oblivious of many of its features – including the writing and editing of Basic and assembly language programs! Also contained within are several utility programs that allow you to catalogue your Wordwise programs and restore text that you have accidentally erased.

Owners of Sideways RAM systems will find the writing of machine code utilities to enhance Wordwise and Wordwise Plus well covered, supported by an example sideways RAM program.

I hope, therefore, that *Wordwise Plus – A User's Guide* has just about something for everyone. If not, then you are indeed a hard bunch to please!

Finally some ackowledgements are in order, though that is not necessarily how they are presented here. Firstly to Richard Miles, Janet Murphy and Sue Moore at Collins Publishers, a hard working lot at the best of times who don't always get the recognition they deserve for all their hard work; Computer Concepts for supporting this project, and in particular Charles Moir and Rob Pickering; hints and tips man Martin Phillips for the use of his Epson printer code compilation used in Appendix C, which originally appeared in the February 1985 issue of *Acorn User*, to who I also give thanks; Patrick Quick for use of a couple of his segment programs in the final part of this book; to you the reader for parting with your hard earned cash; and finally to wife and daughter, Tessie and Sarah, to whom I dedicate this book. Thanks chaps.

I am grateful for permission to use extracts from *The Times* and *The Sunday Times* to illustrate Wordwise and Wordwise Plus.

Bruce Smith
New Southgate
July 1985

PART ONE

Chapter One
What's It All About?

Mr Percy Verance
99 Vat Lane
Bottoms Up
Alesford

Dear Mr Verance

You have been selected from all the house owners within your area to take part in our mega 'No Catch' competition.

The staggering prize that you have every chance of winning is £10,000 in cash and all of it tax-free! In addition we will give you a holiday per year for life. Just imagine three weeks, anywhere in the world, every year for the rest of your life?

I think you'll agree, Mr Verance that this is a sensational offer. All that you have to do is to complete the entry form listing the six points listed below, in order of priority, that you feel best sum up the mouth-watering appeal of Charlie's Crisp Canned Carrots. Then, in not more than 10 words, all beginning with the letter C, write a sales slogan for your favourite eat anytime vegetables.

So, Percy, don't delay send your entry off today!

Good Luck,

Yours sincerely

Charles Small
Managing Director
Carrot Corporation

How many times have you received a letter along similar lines, neatly printed and very personalised, using your name several times within the body of the letter? You also know that, although you may be the only person in your immediate area to have received such a letter, thousands of other people all over the country have also received exactly the same letter.

So how are these letters mass-produced? It's unlikely that a pool of typists has been employed to type each letter individually in turn, inserting names at the appropriate places. No, of course not! They use a word processor, and possibly a BBC Micro using Wordwise or Wordwise Plus itself!

This is just one of many time-saving features that a word processor allows. You type your text at the keyboard and it's stored within the memory of the BBC Micro. Your typing is displayed on the screen which becomes a sheet of electronic typing paper. Changing names, words and addresses can be performed automatically and easily.

Look at the letter once again. It has another feature that distinguishes it from a traditionally typed letter. Notice how the last letter in the last word on each line all line up – there are no ragged edges. This has been quite deliberate on my behalf. I could have specified for Wordwise not to do this and instead produce a ragged edge. This *justification*, as it is termed, gives the whole letter an air of professionalism.

Once a letter or some text has been typed in, we'll use the word 'document' or 'text' to refer to all possibilites in future. You can also save it to cassette or disc, whichever you have. This allows you to retrieve it at a later date; tomorrow, next week, next month or even next year. You can alter it if you require (a process known as *editing*) and then print it onto a sheet of paper. Using a traditional typewriter, you would have to retype the whole lot once again – a waste of time if your document is several pages in length!

If you want several copies of your document, then simply print them – a copy for you, a copy for your file and a copy to the person concerned. (Get rid of the photocopier!)

The whole purpose of Wordwise is that it allows you to convert your Beeb into a sophisticated word manipulator, and word processing is all about flexibility.

The equipment

Let's look at what you will need to get your Wordwise word processing station into action. You probably have most of the equipment already. Obviously, there is the BBC Micro and a monitor. A television is quite adequate for most purposes though it does have some minor drawbacks over a proper computer monitor. I use a colour medium resolution monitor and find that this is quite easy on the eyes for prolonged use. Many people find a green screened monitor (a monitor which gives white text on a green background) preferable. This is not a view I would generally subscribe to but 'to each their own', as the saying goes.

To save your documents you will need either a cassette recorder or a disc drive (Figure 1.1). Both perform the task of loading and saving documents

Figure 1.1. Disc drives speed up the whole word processing process, but are not essential.

admirably, but there can be no argument that a disc drive is much much quicker. A maximum-sized Wordwise file takes under two seconds to load from disc compared with three or four minutes from tape. For home use this is no real drawback as the features and conveniences of using Wordwise more than compensate. The very first book I wrote using Wordwise in 1982, I actually saved all 40000 words onto several cassette tapes!

If you are using Wordwise for more serious applications – perhaps a mailing list or for your business – then a disc drive would be much more efficient. Any BBC-compatible disc drive will work with Wordwise; no extra programs are necessary. If you are undecided as to what disc drive to purchase I would refer you to magazines such as *Acorn User* to look for advertisements and, more importantly, reviews. Many new disc drives may well be on the market when you read this – but whatever brand name you buy I would strongly recommend that it is a 40/80 track switchable drive. This will give you the best value for money and the most disc space onto which you can save your documents.

A printer is also a very desirable item (Figure 1.2). You will need to print your documents onto paper (this is often referred to as the 'hard' copy) so that you can distribute them to other parties. However, for limited use a printer may not be essential. Remember that you can save and load your text onto a magnetic medium, so provided the receivers of your document have Wordwise installed within their Beeb, they can load it in and read it!

The choice of printer will depend on your application. Daisywheel printers give a very professional typeface and are particularly suited for business applications. Good printers of this sort can be quite expensive, but they allow you to change the typeface simply by inserting a new character font – just as you would on a standard golf-ball typewriter, for instance.

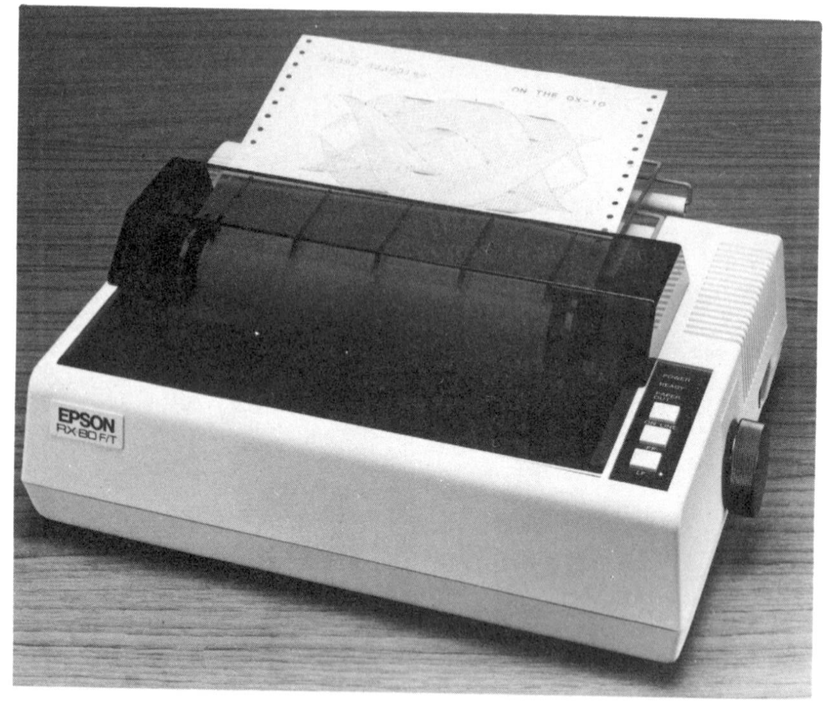

Figure 1.2. Choose a printer to suit your own needs.

If you wish to produce text that contains features such as underlining, italics, emphasised print, double print, and perhaps graphics dumps all rolled into one, then you should be on the look-out for a dot matrix printer. These also tend to be reasonably priced.

Again, in both instances, look in magazines for reviews. My own preference is for the dot matrix type of printer. The most common printer of this sort is the Epson printer, and most other printers tend to be Epson-compatible. Many of the features within Wordwise are set up for Epson-compatible printers so this is worth bearing in mind. Most of the newer range of Epson-compatible printers offer a feature that is known as NLQ, which stands for Near Letter Quality, and allows you to print text to a very good quality approaching that of a daisywheel printer.

How you arrange your Wordwise word processing station is up to you and, to a great extent depends on the equipment you are using. Figure 1.3 shows my own set-up. The BBC Micro is adorned by a second processor (more on this and Hi-Wordwise in Chapter 12). The colour monitor perches above easily accessible twin disc drives, while my dot matrix printer sits purposely out of the way, leaving plenty of room for reference books, magazines and cups of coffee!

Figure 1.3. The Wordwise word processing station.

Installing Wordwise

The final piece in the jigsaw is, of course, Wordwise itself. Wordwise is the program that is stored within the ROM chip that you will find inserted into a small area of black foam within the packaging. This assumes that a dealer has not already fitted it for you, in which case you can skip over the rest of this chapter if you wish (though you might find it informative reading!).

To install your Wordwise chip you'll need to take the lid off of the BBC Micro. This is in reality quite a simple procedure, provided some ground rules are followed. These are outlined below, but consult an Acorn dealer if you are in any doubt.

> **Warning**: If your BBC Micro is still under guarantee then any tampering around inside it will invalidate your guarantee.

BBC B+ owners should refer to Appendix A for a summary of this installation process as the internal layout of the board is completely different from that described below.

To perform the surgery to your Beeb you'll need a cross-point screwdriver, some room to manoeuvre and just a dash of confidence (no problem). Step by step this is what you do.

1. First switch off your micro and unplug it from the mains. Also turn off all devices connected to the Beeb, such as disc drives, printers and monitor or TV.
2. Turn you micro upside down and locate the two screws marked 'FIX'. Remove these and place them somewhere safe (not on the floor!).
3. Turn your Beeb the right way up but with the back towards you. You will see two similar fixing screws in the top two corners of the black plastic fascia sheets. Remove these and place them with the other two screws.
4. Turn your Beeb around so that the keyboard is facing you and remove the lid of the Beeb by lifting it up from the edges. If you lean over your Beeb then you should be able to see the sideways ROM sockets, partially obscured by the left-hand side of the keyboard.
5. The next step is to loosen the keyboard. Depending on which issue board you have, there will be two or three nuts and bolts to remove. Place your hand under the Beeb at the front and lift the front up, so that the micro is almost on its 'hind legs', as it were. Locate the two or three cross-point heads, within the black plastic fascia sheet, and loosen these so they are easy to turn. Place the Beeb flat and loosen the remaining nuts by hand. Place the nuts and bolts plus shakeproof washers (if present) safely with the other screws.
6. Take the keyboard in your hands, one on each side, lift it up a couple of centimetres and then pull it forward a few centimetres to expose the sideways ROM sockets. You might need to turn the keyboard at an angle slightly, to do this. The ribbon cable connecting the keyboard to the main board will be long enough to allow you to do this. If you have to disconnect this cable then you should have no trouble reconnecting it.

Four!

If you now look to the lower right-hand side of the Beeb's interior you should see a row of four chips and/or sockets depending on what ROM chips you have installed (these are called the sideways ROM sockets and are shown clearly in Figure 1.4). For example, if you only have Basic installed there will be two chips and two empty sockets; if you also have a disc interface fitted you will have an extra ROM and only one empty socket. If all of these sockets are in use then you must have an extra ROM in position, which you should know about! You will need either to remove this to insert the Wordwise chip or purchase a ROM expansion board to enable you to use extra ROMs in your BBC Micro. In this case, consult a local computer dealer.

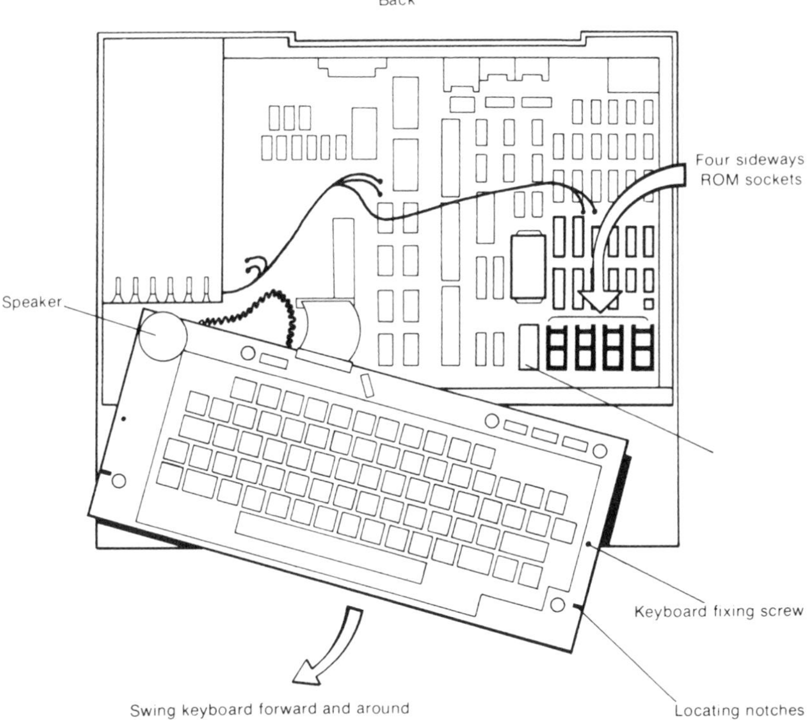

Figure 1.4. The sideways ROM sockets (adapted from Acornsoft's ROM-fitting instructions, with permission).

Getting your priorities right

Before you insert the Wordwise chip into your Beeb, there might be a need for you to rearrange any other ROMs already present, depending on the priority you wish to give Wordwise. Are you likely to use Wordwise almost all the time, or at least much more frequently than, say, Basic? If the answer is yes, then it is worth inserting the Wordwise chip in such a way that Wordwise is automatically selected each time you turn on the Beeb – just as Basic is normally selected, for example. Alternatively, you can insert Wordwise so that it has to be specifically selected by you with a command once you have turned on the Beeb.

Figure 1.5 shows the priority of the four sideways ROM sockets. Socket number 15 is the highest priority and if you insert Wordwise here then it will be selected when you switch on. If you place Basic here with Wordwise in socket number 12, 13 or 14 then Basic will be selected as normal. Figure 1.6 shows these configurations for use with or without a DFS (Disc Filing System) ROM fitted.

Inserting Wordwise into its socket requires care. The process should not

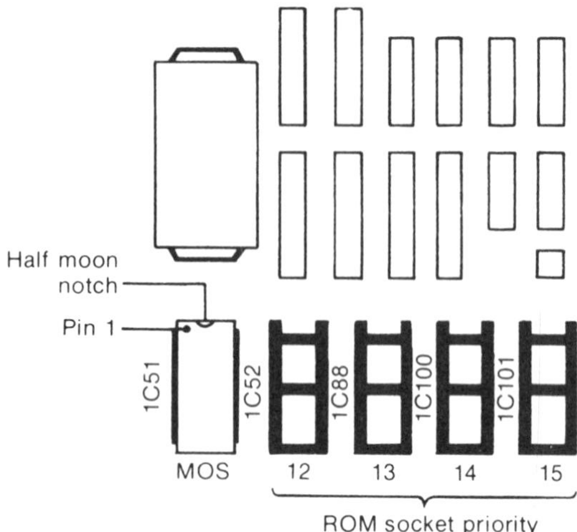

Figure 1.5. ROM priorities (adapted from Acornsoft's ROM-fitting instructions, with permission).

a) Wordwise has priority

b) BASIC has priority

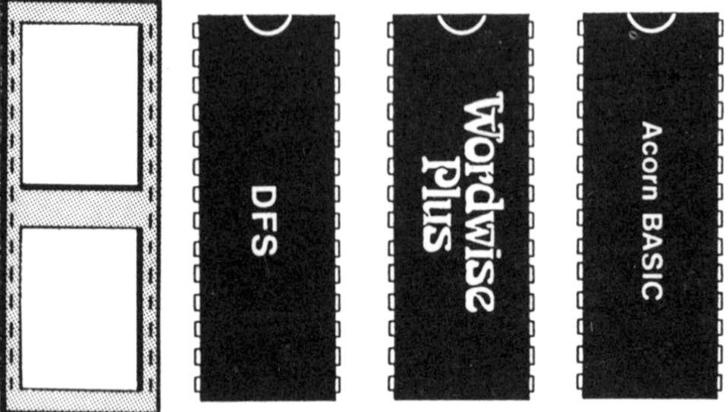

Figure 1.6. Wordwise positioning combinations.

be rushed and each stage should be double-checked. The Wordwise ROM is susceptible to damage from static electricity, so handling the chip must be performed *only* after you have earthed yourself to discharge any accumulated static electricity. This can be performed by touching any metallic surface that is earthed itself. Certain surfaces will act as accumulators and build up a static charge on your body. Nylon carpets are prime culprits so avoid working on these. The screen of a monitor or TV also accumulates such a charge so avoid contact with these, too.

Follow these procedures step by step:

1. Open up your Beeb and locate the sideways ROM sockets as described above. Decide which sideways socket you are going to use.
2. Earth yourself to discharge any static electricity, as this can be damaging to the chip. You can do this by touching some metal apparatus that is earthed (a water pipe, for example).
3. Before removing Wordwise from the black foam, identify the half moon to one end of the chip (see Figure 1.7)

Figure 1.7. Identifying the top end of the Wordwise chip.

4. Remove the chip and hold it between thumb and forefinger and line it up over the ROM socket. Pin 1 and the half moon notch should be pointing towards the back of the case.
5. Now slowly apply firm pressure and push the pins into the corresponding receptacles of the socket, ensuring that all legs are located and are not splayed or bent.
6. The legs on the Wordwise chip may not line up correctly, sitting straddled across the socket. You will need to be bend them inwards slightly but *do not use your fingers!* Instead, find a firm table surface and, holding the chip at an angle, press the pins along one length against the table, bending them in slightly (Figure 1.8). Repeat this for the pins on the other side of the chip. The chip should now fit into the socket easily.
7. Push the chip firmly home.
8. Reassemble your Beeb by reversing the dismantling instructions given earlier.

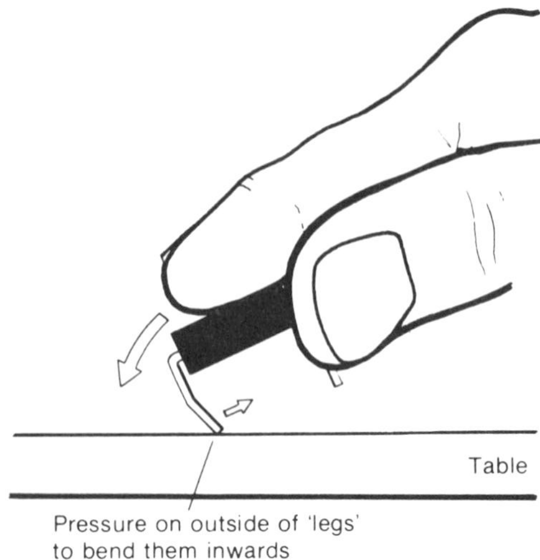

Figure 1.8. Bending the chip's legs.

Wordwise rules

If you decide that you wish Wordwise to be the priority ROM you may well need to remove any existing ROM situated in socket 15. This ROM is likely to be the Basic ROM. To remove the ROM you will need to have a small flat-bladed screwdriver to hand. Following the above precautions, locate the chip you wish to remove and, using the flat-bladed screwdriver, gently prize up each end, a bit at a time as illustrated in Figure 1.9. Once the chip is free, being careful not to touch any of the silver 'legs', lift it from the board using thumb and forefinger and place it on a clean surface away from any electrical devices that might cause damage. Then place the ROM into a lower priority socket following the instructions above, and complete the task by inserting Wordwise into socket 15.

To reassemble the Beeb, reverse the disassembly process. When it comes

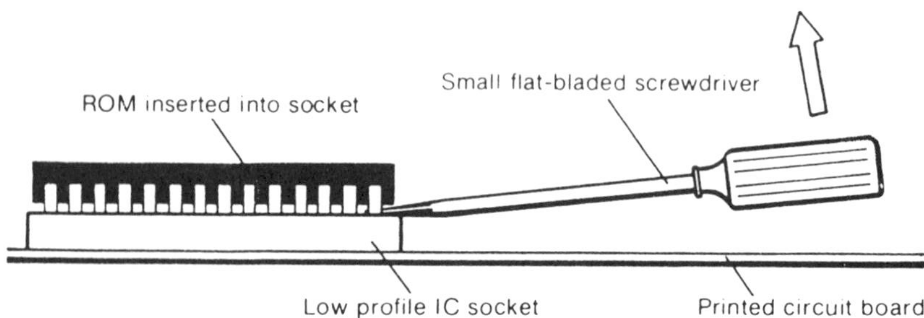

Figure 1.9. Easing a ROM out of its socket.

to positioning the keyboard you will notice that the board holding the keys has a small notch on each side about 4 cm up from the bottom. It is important that these notches are located about the oblong raised mouldings on each side of the main case – thus ensuring that the keyboard is correctly positioned. Finally, when it comes to assembling the main lid, ensure that the three small red lights (LEDs) at the lower right-hand corner locate correctly in the corresponding three holes in the case itself. Finally, reconnect your monitor, printer, etc.

Into Wordwise

With the Wordwise chip installed we approach the moment of truth; the testing! Plug in and turn on the power. If Wordwise has priority then you should get the main Wordwise Plus menu displayed as shown in Figure 1.10. If you are using the standard Wordwise you will be prompted (see Figure 1.11) with the question

Old Text (Y/N)?

in which case tap the 'Y' key to get to the menu. This is illustrated in Figure 1.12.

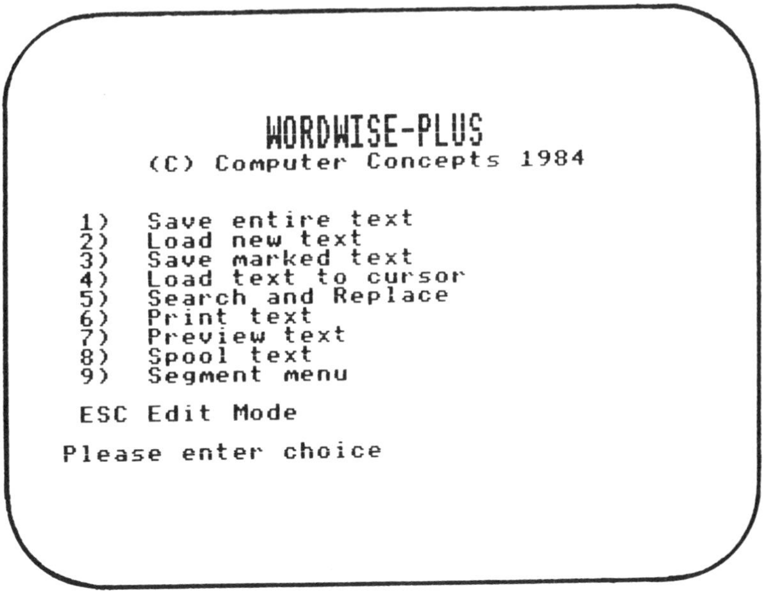

```
            WORDWISE-PLUS
     (C) Computer Concepts 1984

 1)   Save entire text
 2)   Load new text
 3)   Save marked text
 4)   Load text to cursor
 5)   Search and Replace
 6)   Print text
 7)   Preview text
 8)   Spool text
 9)   Segment menu

 ESC  Edit Mode

Please enter choice
```

Figure 1.10. The Wordwise Plus main menu.

If Basic has priority, enter the following command

*WORDWISE

and press return to get the menu or message.

```
            WORDWISE
   (C) Computer Concepts 1982

Old text? (Y/N)
```

Figure 1.11. Wordwise kicks off with a question.

```
            WORDWISE
   (C) Computer Concepts 1982

 1)  Save entire text
 2)  Load new text
 3)  Save marked text
 4)  Load text to cursor
 5)  Search and Replace
 6)  Print text
 7)  Preview text
 8)  Spool text

 ESC Edit Mode

Please enter choice
```

Figure 1.12. The Wordwise menu.

If, when you switch on, you get a blank screen or the error message

Language?

switch off your micro, unplug it and reopen the case. This error is caused because the Beeb cannot find a ROM that contains a suitable language it can present to the user (i.e. Basic or Wordwise). (These types of ROM are termed 'language ROMs', as they handle your communication with the BBC Micro.) This problem has most likely arisen because you have not inserted a chip correctly. So unbolt the Beeb's lid and go through all the above checks once more.

Chapter Two
Introducing Edit Mode

With Wordwise installed and selected you are in what is known as the 'menu' mode. If you look you will see that you are presented with a list or menu of options that may be chosen simply by pressing the corresponding key. For example, the bottom line of the menu reads

ESC Edit Mode

If you press the <ESCAPE> key you enter the Edit Mode, shown in Figure 2.1.

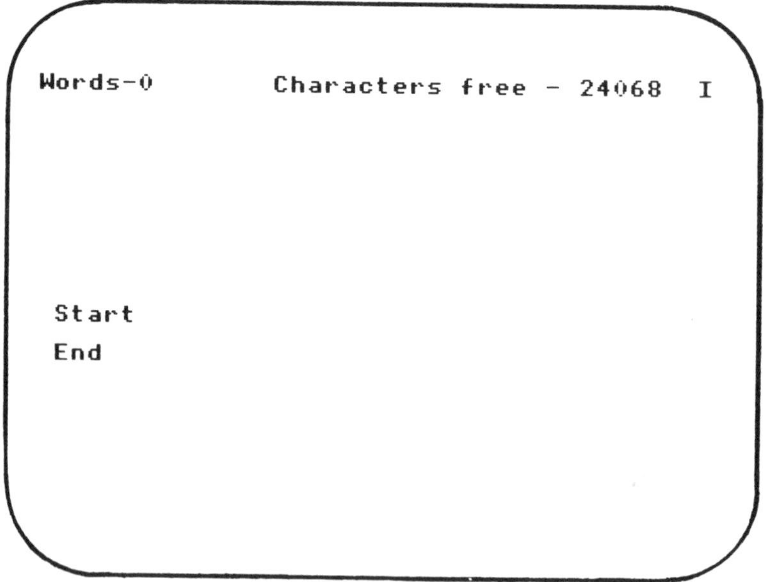

Figure 2.1. The Edit Mode screen.

Edit Mode is where all the text we wish to enter and edit is stored. There is already some 'text' on the screen. Sitting firmly in the middle left of the screen is a small flashing line. This is called the text cursor or 'cursor' for short. Immediately above and below the cursor are the words *Start*, and *End* respectively. If you have a colour monitor or TV you'll know that these are red in colour; I'll use italics for these to distinguish them from text.

At the top of the screen we have the status line. This, as its name implies, presents details on the current state of Wordwise memory otherwise known as the *text space*. 'Words' is followed by a blank space. As we shall see shortly, as we enter text, this gap is used to display the number of words in the current document. 'Characters free' is followed by a large number – 24068, in fact. Don't worry if the number you have is slightly different. The value will differ from machine to machine depending on which ROMs you have installed, if any. This number relates to the number of character spaces free within the text space for us to place characters in. Every time you type a character at the keyboard this number will decrease by one. This is useful when it comes to very long documents as it gives you an indication of the amount of space remaining. Finally at the end of the status line there is a green-coloured letter 'I'. I'll describe the function of this shortly.

To get back to the main menu at any time, simply press <ESCAPE>. This key can be used to 'toggle' between Edit and Menu Modes as required and has absolutely no effect on any text stored within Wordwise – so use it as you please.

To complete the installation of the Wordwise chip, place the function keystrip under the plastic keystrip above the red function keys if you haven't already done so.

Entering text

As mentioned above, to enter text into your word processor you first need to be in Edit Mode – then you just type it in! So, first ensure that you are in Edit Mode, toggling the screen modes as required with <ESCAPE> and then try typing in the words

WORDWISE PLUS

To get the space between Wordwise and Plus, simply tap the space bar at the appropriate point (see Figure 2.2).

The status line has now changed. It reads

Words-1 Characters free-24055 I

According to this, we have entered just one word, when we know that we have actually entered two! Wordwise only recognises a new word when it has a space placed after it. This is not exactly the truth, however, as it is possible to obtain a completely accurate word count as we shall see. Tap the space bar once to see what happens. The cursor moves one place across the screen, and the Words count is now 2. Notice also that the Characters free count has been decremented by one and now reads 24054. A space is also seen as a character by Wordwise. This is quite reasonable, as even a space must be stored within the text space in memory so that Wordwise knows it is

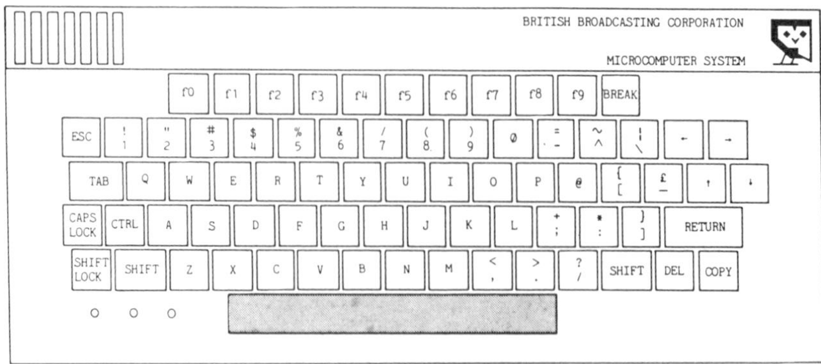

Figure 2.2. The space bar.

there. Type in 'WORDWISE PLUS' once more, followed by a solitary WORDWISE. The text cursor is now sitting almost at the end of the screen, so what happens when we enter some more text that goes beyond the end of the line? Let's see. Tap the space bar and then type in PLUS. As you press the 'U' key, the entire word moves down onto the next line. Typing 'S' completes the word and Figure 2.3 shows what you should have visible on the screen.

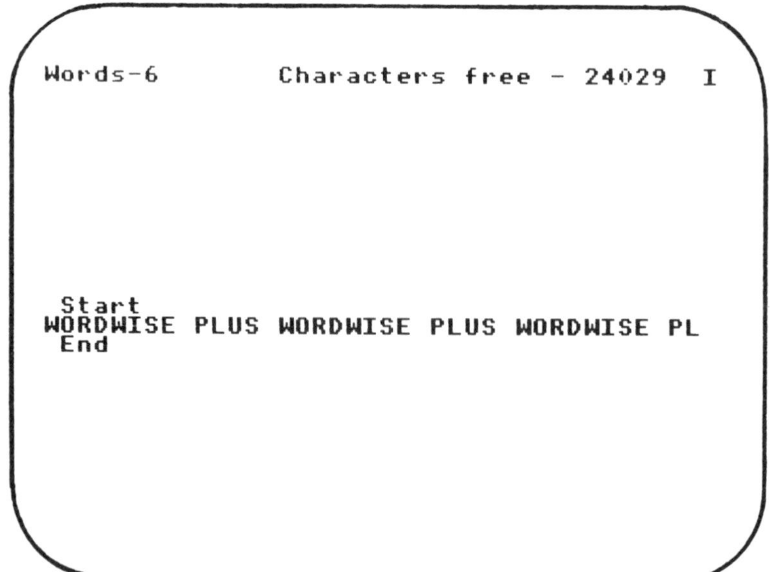

Figure 2.3. Wordwise ensures that no words are split across two text lines: (a) before (b) after.

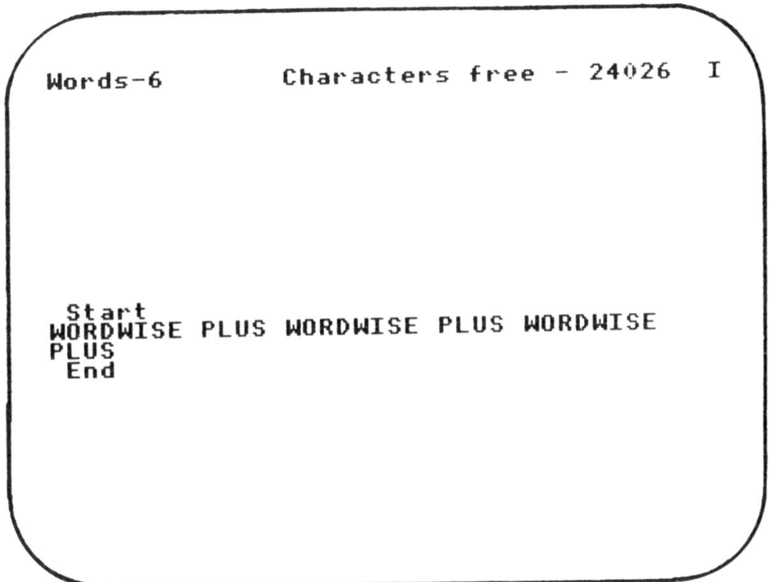

Erasing text is very simple, and can be done using the DELETE key (Figure 2.4). Press <DELETE> once and the text cursor will move back a single space and erase the S from PLUS.

All the keys on the keyboard have an auto-repeat facility. This means that if you hold a key down it will continue to print that particular character. Holding the DELETE key down will have the effect of continually deleting characters from the screen. Try it and see; hold it down until all the text has been erased. When the cursor gets to its origin position (that's the point where we started entering text) there are no more characters to delete and so a bleep is made by Wordwise through the Beeb's internal speaker.

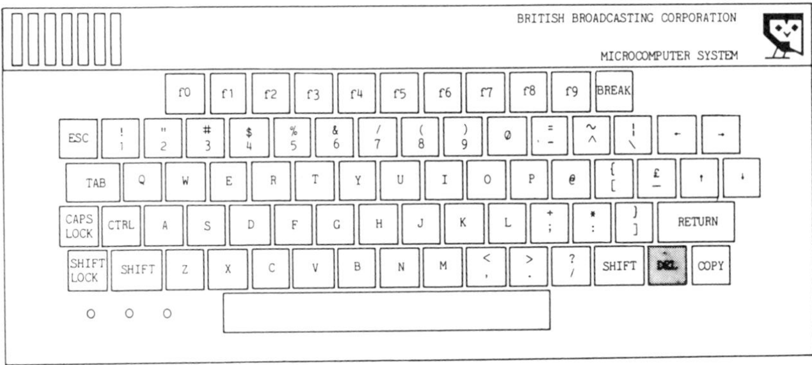

Figure 2.4. The DELETE key.

Changing case

The text we have just entered, and deleted, was all in upper-case characters. Obviously for most purposes we would normally wish to enter text in lower-case and then occasionally shift to upper-case to type in capitals. We can do this by pressing the CAPS LOCK key on the extreme left of the keyboard (Figure 2.5). As you press this, the middle light of the

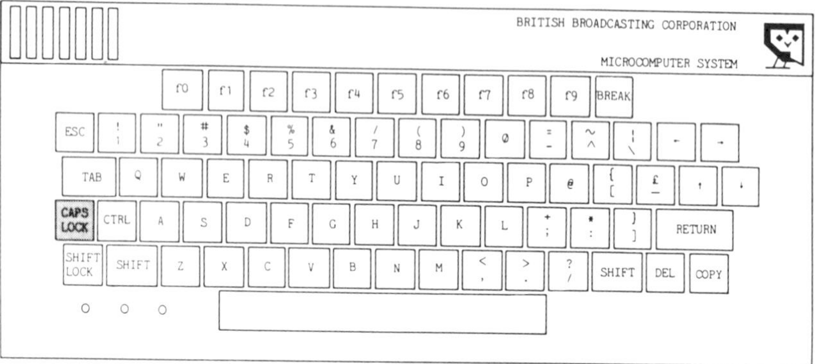

Figure 2.5. The CAPS LOCK key.

three to the left of the space bar will be extinguished. Any text entered now will be displayed in lower-case. If upper-case is required, hold down the shift key (there is one on each side of the bottom row of keys – see Figure 2.6) and press the alphanumeric key you want.

Let's try it, this time we'll enter

Wordwise Plus

To get 'W' hold down SHIFT, press the W key and then release the SHIFT key. In future I'll refer to this type of sequence as SHIFT-W. The 'W' should appear. Now enter 'ordwise' in lower-case. Enter a space then SHIFT-P to get the upper-case 'P' followed by lower-case 'lus'.

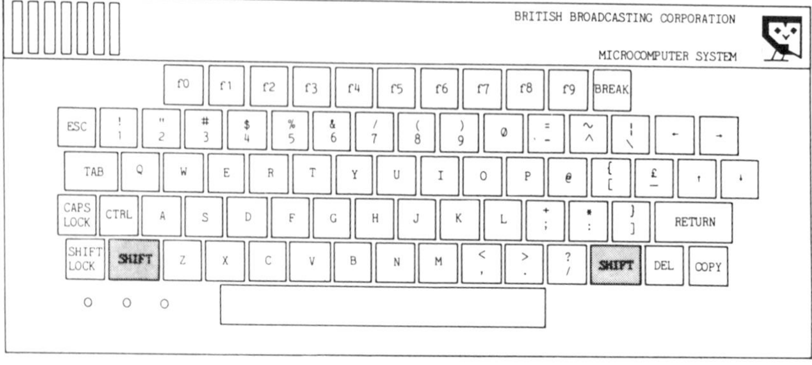

Figure 2.6. The SHIFT key.

The roving cursor

There will be times when you wish to start entering text on a new line, perhaps when starting a new paragraph. This new line can be generated by pressing the RETURN key (Figure 2.7). Before you do this, ensure that you have not entered a space after the 'Plus'. If you have, erase it with <DELETE> so that the cursor is immediately after the 's' of 'Plus'. The Word count should show 1.

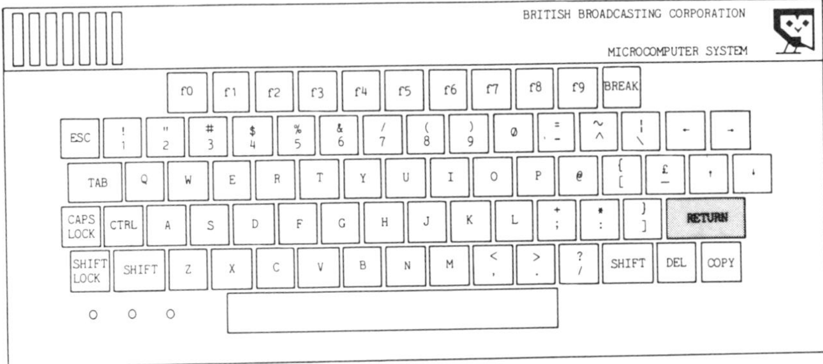

Figure 2.7. The RETURN key.

Now press the RETURN key and a new blank line will be inserted between the *Start* and *End* markers, with the cursor sitting directly below the 'W'. Note here that the Words count has not been incremented; it still shows 1. On the other hand, the Characters free count has been decremented by one. Remember that Wordwise only recognises words for counting purposes when they are ended with a space character. In most instances, the actual word count is not very important, so don't feel obliged to press the space bar after every word. However, if an accurate word count is needed it is quite simple to obtain, as we shall see towards the end of this chapter.

Why did the Characters free count decrement? The answer, just in case you hadn't already guessed, is because the <RETURN> key stroke must also be recorded by Wordwise, and it is there although you can't actually see it on the screen.

Type in three more lines containing 'Wordwise Plus', remembering to hit <RETURN> at the end of each line. Figure 2.8 shows what you should end up with.

Suppose we now wish to type in a line of text at the very beginning of the example. To do this we need to place the text cursor at the start of the text and insert a blank line by pressing <RETURN>; but how do we get the cursor to the top of the text?

If you look at the extreme right-hand corner of the keyboard you will see four keys arranged in a slightly offset square and all marked with an arrow, pointing left, right, up and down (Figure 2.9). These are the cursor control

```
Words-8          Characters free - 24013   I




 Start
Wordwise Plus
Wordwise Plus
Wordwise Plus
Wordwise Plus
 End
```

Figure 2.8. Four lines of text in Edit Mode.

keys and they control the movement of the text cursor around the Edit Mode screen. Try pressing them a few times and experiment in positioning the cursor under a certain letter. To move the text cursor straight to the beginning of the text press the up arrow key four times, or simply hold it down and let the auto-repeat feature do it for you!

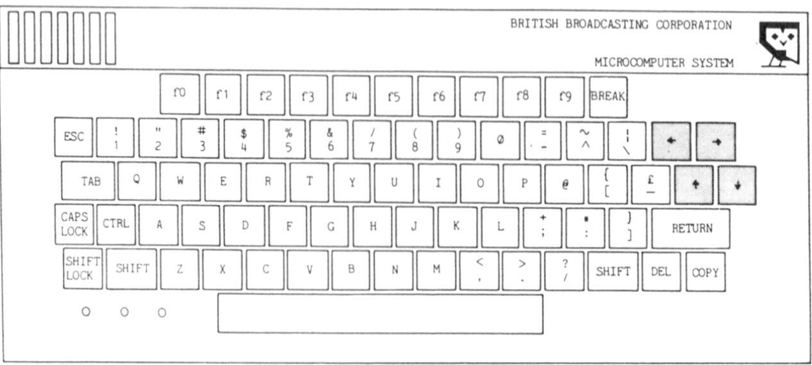

Figure 2.9. The cursor control keys.

Once you are confident that you can move the cursor around fairly readily, position it under the first 'W' and press <RETURN>. A blank line will be inserted between the *Start* marker and the first line of text. The text cursor still remains under the 'W'. Before entering our additional text, we need to move the cursor up a line using the up arrow key. Now we can type in some more text (use the SHIFT key for the apostrophe):

A User's Guide to<RETURN>

Do not enter <RETURN>. Instead, when you see this, press the RETURN key – anything inside triangular brackets will normally mean 'press this particular key'. This will generate a new blank line, leaving the text on the screen looking like this:

```
  Start
 A User's Guide

 Wordwise Plus
 Wordwise Plus
 Wordwise Plus
 Wordwise Plus

   End
```

We can also enter blank lines in between each line of text simply by moving the text cursor to the start of the first word on the line *below* where we wish to enter the new blank line. Pressing RETURN will then insert the blank line immediately above the cursor position.

To place a new line between the first and second lines of 'Wordwise Plus', move the cursor to the second 'W' and press RETURN. Try inserting the other blank lines yourself.

When you edit long documents you may often want to move from the end of the text to the very beginning and vice versa. Even when using the auto-repeat feature on the up and down arrow keys, this will take several seconds to perform. The cursor can, in fact, be moved in a single stroke – well, two, actually, by using <SHIFT↑> and <SHIFT↓>. Try it on your text. Similarly, by using <SHIFT←> and <SHIFT→> the text cursor can be moved to the beginning and end of each line. First move the cursor to the top of the first line so that it sits under the letter 'A'. Now press <SHIFT→>. The cursor should now be sitting directly under the 'e' in Guide. Move the cursor back to the start of that line and then down a single line so that it is sitting at the start of a blank line. Try using the <SHIFT→> now; nothing happens. This is because the line is literally a blank line and contains nothing other than a single RETURN character – therefore it is at the start and end of that line!

Controlling ASD

The DELETE key is useful for erasing characters from your text. However, it works backwards – that is, from right to left across the screen. This is fine if the cursor is positioned at the right-hand end of the word or sequence of letters you wish to delete. However, sometimes the cursor is underneath the first letter of those you wish to rub out. In such cases it is desirable to erase characters working from left to right across the screen. This is possible. To do this we need to bring the CTRL key into the action (you can read CTRL as ConTRoL). This is next to the letters 'A' and 'S' on the keyboard (Figure 2.10) and it works rather like the SHIFT key in that you depress it with another key to get the desired effect. To erase the character above the cursor use CTRL-A (i.e. press the CTRL and A keys together). Move the cursor to the beginning of a line, and try rubbing out the entire line by holding down CTRL-A. Like all other keys, this combination has an auto-repeat function, so be careful as you could delete wanted text if you are not judicious with its use.

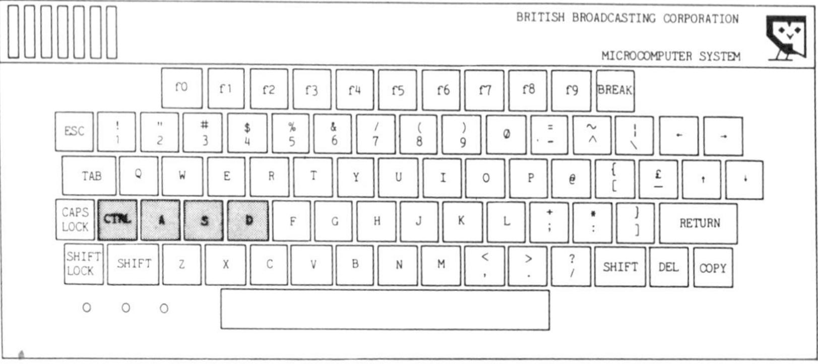

Figure 2.10. The ASD control keys.

Another useful CTRL key action is when it is combined with the 'S' key. This will swap the case of the character above the cursor. For example, 'W' would become 'w' and 'o' would become 'O'. Again, try it for yourself. Move the cursor to the start of a line containing the words 'Wordwise Plus' and hold down CTRL-S. As the cursor passes below each letter, its case is swapped. The whole line changes to 'wORDWISE pLUS'. By passing the CTRL-S character through the line again the original format will be resumed. This technique is often referred to as 'case toggling'.

Invariably, when deleting text from Wordwise, we will be interested in rubbing out whole words rather than just the odd character or two. Using a CTRL-D action the word above the cursor is deleted. It doesn't matter where the cursor is positioned within the word, it will be deleted. To see this in action, move the cursor to the start of a text line containing 'Wordwise Plus', placing the cursor under the 'W', now press CTRL-D; 'Wordwise' disappears. The text cursor remains in the same position, but the word 'Plus' has been moved left to fill up the gap. Now move the text cursor so that it is sitting under the 'u' and press CTRL-D again. The word 'Plus' is erased.

For purposes of definition, a word is any collection of characters, i.e. letters, numbers and punctuation, that is separated by a space or return character from another word. Try experimenting and getting used to using all these CTRL functions. Effective use of these can save you a good deal of time when it comes to editing larger documents at a later stage.

To insert or not?

So far all the text we have been typing in has been inserted into each blank line. To see this more clearly move the text cursor so that it is sitting on a line directly underneath the 'P' in 'Plus'. Now type in

'is a'

The entire line should now read

Wordwise is a Plus

The two words have been inserted into the line, and the text to the right of the cursor has been shoved along to the right to make room for each new letter we have entered. When Wordwise operates in this manner it is said to be in Insert Mode, and this is signified by the yellow coloured 'I' in the top right-hand corner of the screen, on the status line.

We can enter text other than by inserting it. This is performed by overwriting text and is therefore known as Overwrite Mode. To get into Overwrite Mode you need to press function key 0, *f0*, which is the first red key at the top right-hand side of the keyboard. The function keys as shown in Figure 2.11 all have very special functions, as we shall see, and for this reason the keystrip placed above them earlier is used to indicate the function of each key. You'll see that the wording above *f0* is.

INSERT
or
OVER

Move the cursor to the beginning of a line containing some text. Press *f0*. (You hear a high pitched tone to inform you of the change.) Note that the yellow 'I' has now been replaced by a yellow 'O' on the status line. A glance at the status line will always tell you exactly what mode of text entry is currently in use. Now enter some text; you might like to start typing in the

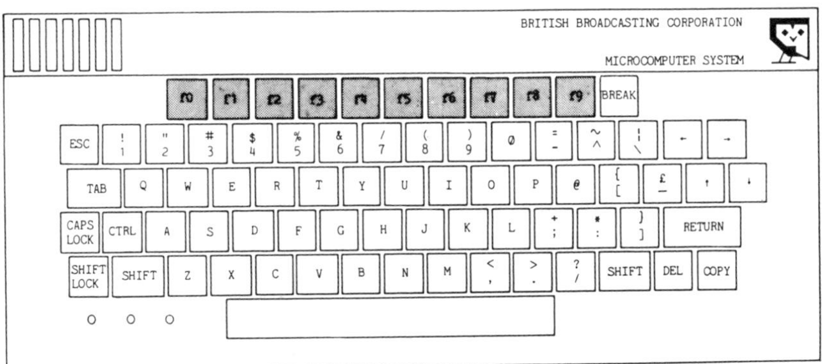

Figure 2.11. The function keys, *f0* to *f9*.

alphabet. What happens as you tap each letter in turn is that it overwrites the character which was formerly there. When the end of the line is reached and there are no more characters, keep on typing. As you press each key, Wordwise sounds a bleep to let you know that there is no text to be overwritten. Your new text is still entered, however.

This mode of text entry should always be used with caution. I can recall numerous occasions when I have been happily tapping away at the keyboard only to look up and find that I have overwritten a paragraph or two of text, where I should have been entering a new paragraph before the one I had just erased! I much prefer to use Insert Mode only, and simply rub out any redundant text afterwards, but that's my choice and not necessarily yours!

To get back to the relative safety of Insert Mode, just press *f0* once again to restore the yellow 'I' to the status line.

Counting on words

To finish this chapter, let us return to the subject of the word count. You'll remember that when text is being entered into Wordwise, the 'Words' count is updated only when the space bar is pressed after a word has been entered. An accurate word count can be obtained, however, to take account of all words that do not end with a space – those at the end of the line, for example. For Wordwise Plus users this can be performed by typing CTRL-W (see Figure 2.12). Erase all of your existing text using CTRL-A and/or DELETE, and then type in 'Wordwise Plus' three times. The text area will look like this:

```
 Start
Wordwise Plus
Wordwise Plus
Wordwise Plus

  End
```

The Words count will show 3, but in reality there are 6 words. To update Words press CTRL-W and the revised word count of 6 will be installed. This CTRL-W feature is only available on Wordwise Plus. Standard Wordwise users will need to employ a slightly different technique, but one that is useful to Plus users as well. Looking at *f5* we can see the words

WORD
COUNT
TO?

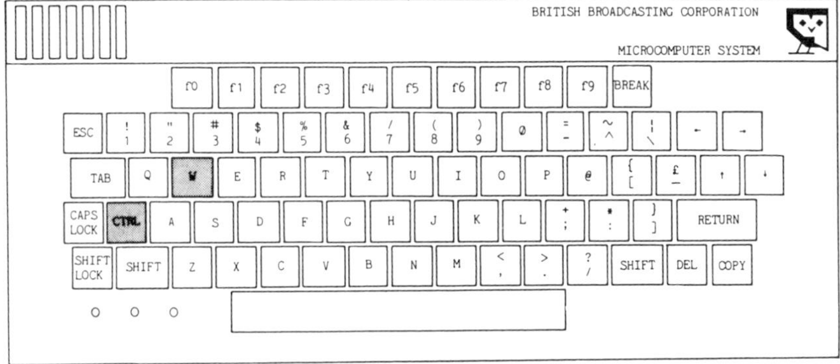

Figure 2.12. The CTRL-W keys.

on the strip above it. By pressing *f5*, an accurate word count can be obtained from the current text cursor position to any other specific letter in the text. To do this, first move the cursor to the very end of the text and then type a letter that has not been used within the body of the text. In these cases I tend to use the character '@' as this is rarely used. Now move the cursor to the top of the text and press *f5*. A bleep will be sounded and the status line will show the question

word count to?

flashing on and off. Now press the @ key. The word count will be updated to 6 and the status line will return to normal. All that now remains is to delete the @ character.

Chapter Three
Wisewords

Now that the text cursor has been mastered, let's move on to to some more serious applications of Wordwise Plus and learn how to use more of the main menu options and those provided by the function keys while in Edit Mode.

One small step...

First, clear the Edit Mode screen to ensure that there is no text held within Wordwise. You can do this in one of two ways: erase it with DELETE or CTRL-A or simply turn off the BBC Micro for a few seconds and then switch it back on.

The next stage is to enter some text to practise on. Type in the following, but don't worry if you make any mistakes – hopefully by the end of this chapter you'll be a dab hand at editing out your mistakes! Where you see <RETURN> in the text, simply press the RETURN key, otherwise just keep typing and don't worry if what appears on your screen is formatted differently from what follows:

```
The Times Sunday July 21 1969
<RETURN>
<RETURN>
   Neil Armstrong became the first
man to take a walk on the moon's
surface today. The spectacular
moment came after he had inched his
way down the ladder of the fragile
lunar bug Eagle while collegue
Edwin Aldrin watched his movements
from inside the craft. <RETURN>
The landing in the Sea of
Tranquility, was near perfect and
the two astronauts on board Eagle
reported that it had not tilted too
```

```
far to prevent a take-off. The
first word from man on the moon
came from Aldrin: "Tranquility
base. The Eagle has landed"
<RETURN>
```

The first rule, once you have entered some text into Wordwise, is to save it for safety's sake just in case there is a power cut or someone accidentally pulls out the plug. Don't utter that old cliché: 'No, won't happen to me', because you can be assured that it will at some stage. Take it from someone who knows! The stage at which you make the first text backup is entirely your choice. I normally save and resave my files about every 500 words or so. If you are using disc then the time factor for a save is negligible, but for tape users it can become tedious to wait while you save. In that case you should weigh up the time saved versus possible retyping time.

To save the text, first place a new, *unused* disc (already formatted) into your disc drive, or alternatively an unused tape into your cassette player, making sure that it is fully rewound and any tape counter set to zero. Then press ESCAPE to return to the main menu. The first two options provide the facility for saving and loading text respectively, so to save the text press key 1, which is immediately to the right of the ESCAPE key (Figure 3.1). As soon as you do this the

'Please enter choice'

line will disappear and be replaced by

'Please enter filename'

Wordwise Plus has now prompted you to enter the name under which you wish to save your text. For disc users this means any name up to 7 characters in length, or 10 characters in length if you are using tape. We'll discuss the use of filenames in a while, but for now just type in

DEMO

Figure 3.1. The 1 key, selects option 1.

and then hit the RETURN key. The file will then be saved to disc or to tape after you have been prompted to press record in the normal manner. Don't forget to press stop on the tape recorder when the text has been saved. The completion of the save is almost instantaneous on disc, but tape users will need to wait about 15 seconds. Saving text is as simple as that!

The next step is to know how to load your text back in. To do this we need to clear the text memory space. You can switch off the BBC Micro for a few seconds and then on again to do this. Of course, there are ways to get Wordwise to do this for us, but let's leave that to a future chapter. Before you switch off, remove any discs you have in your disc drive. When you switch back on, reinstate Wordwise and select option 2 on the main menu by pressing key 2. Once again you will be asked to

Please enter filename

so just type in

DEMO

and press RETURN. If you are using tape, make sure you remember to rewind it to just before the start of the saved file. The program will load, completion of which is signified by the return of the

Please enter choice

prompt. Press ESCAPE to get into Edit Mode and see your newly loaded text!

Menu Mode revisited

Return to the main menu (using<ESCAPE> if need be) and scan down the list of options available. A brief description of each of these options follows, just to give you a better overview of the capabilities of Wordwise. Each will be discussed in detail, though not in the order they are presented on your screen.

We can see that options 3 and 4 are also concerned with the saving and loading of text, but in slightly different ways. Option 5 is labelled Search and Replace, and this allows certain words to be sought out and exchanged with new words. Option 6 allows documents to be printed to a printer, providing you with hard copy. Option 7 allows us to 'look' at the final text as it will appear when printed with option 6. This is not as silly as it seems and I will be coming to this subject next. Option 8 is another way of saving your Wordwise text which allows you to do a variety of things, such as sending letters to your friends who do not own Wordwise! Finally, users of Wordwise Plus have an extra option available to them, option 9. This is not available to standard Wordwise users, so I'll say no more at this point other than it's covered in Chapter 14.

Preview time

By now you will be familiar with the wraparound effect you get in Wordwise when you are entering text, whereby words move onto the next line if there is not enough room for them to be stored on the same line. If you count the spaces across the screen in Edit Mode you will see that there is room for 40 characters.

When it comes to producing a document, this width is quite small. For example, the words you are reading now are all arranged in this book at a count of about 80 characters per line. Wordwise also works to this 80 characters per line format, though it would not seem so at present. Option 7 invokes this, so to see it in action just press key number 7 (in Menu mode).

```
The Times Sunday July 21 1969


   Neil Armstrong became the first man to take a walk on the moon's surface
today. The spectacular moment came after he had inched his way down the ladder
of the fragile lunar bug Eagle while collegue Edwin Aldrin watched his movements
from inside the craft.
The landing in the Sea of Tranquility, was near perfect and the two astronauts
on board Eagle reported that it had not tilted too far to prevent a take-off.
The first word from man on the moon came from Aldrin: "Tranquility base. The
Eagle has landed"

Press any key_
```

Wordwise has switched into an 80-column screen mode and displays the text exactly as it would appear if we had printed it out onto the printer. To return to the main menu, press the space bar.

If you have a printer connected and switched on you may like to try printing your text (or 'copy' as it is often called). To do this simply press 6 while in Menu Mode. Again, the preview facility will be selected but this time as the text is printed onto the screen it will also be sent to your printer to be printed.

At this stage you might find that there are a couple of problems; I'll describe the most common ones. First, after printing a couple of lines onto the screen, everything 'stops' and nothing appears to be happening at the printer. In this case there is almost certainly a problem at the printer. Check that it is switched on correctly, has some paper and the connections between BBC Micro and printer are all correct. Second, if you are using an Epson printer it might all be printing on the same line. This is because the printer does not 'recognise' the carriage returns Wordwise is sending to it. To counteract this press <ESCAPE> and then, while in Menu Mode, type

```
*FX6
```

and press return. You will be asked to press another key (use the space bar) and then try pursuing option 6 once again. This problem does not occur with all printers; the Star printer, for example, does not need you to issue this command before you use it. You need only enter the command once; all subsequent printing will 'remember' that you have previously entered this command. Press option 6 in Menu Mode to get your hard copy.

The printed copy reflects exactly what we originally saw on the screen by previewing the text with option 7. The trouble is that the text is somewhat messy, filling the entire width of the paper with no margins. What we need now is to format the text to give it a more acceptable output, and this is performed by embedding commands within the text itself.

Embedded commands

An embedded command is exactly what you would think it is – a command that is placed within a document that Wordwise will recognise and act upon. Embedded commands will not appear as part of your text; they will be ignored and not shown on the screen or printed. However, the effect that they have will be clearly visible.

To insert an embedded command into the text you will obviously need to be in Edit Mode. Move the cursor to the top left-hand corner of the screen (you can use <SHIFT↑>) and then press the <RETURN> key. This will insert a blank line at the very top of the text into which we can place some embedded commands.

Let us now decide what we wish to do to the text. First we wish to provide a line margin, say of eight characters, and reduce the total number of characters on a line to 60 characters. Therefore we want:

Line Margin = 8
Line Length = 60

The Wordwise embedded commands are, in virtually all instances, simply mnemonics of what we want. For example, the embedded command for Line Margin is LM and the embedded command mnemonic for Line Length is LL; this makes it very easy to remember them. The number we wish to set each to is placed directly after each mnemonic. Therefore the two embedded commands are written thus:

Line Margin 8 is LM8
Line Length 60 is LL60

The commands are now ready to be inserted into the document at the top on the blank line. They cannot, however, be entered just as they are because they will not be recognised as embedded commands. An embedded command must always be preceded by pressing the function key *f1* and terminated by pressing the function key *f2*. If you look at the keystrip you will see that the titles for these two keys are given as

f1 GREEN embedded command
f2 WHITE embedded command

An embedded command always appears green on the Edit Mode screen.

Okay, now enter the two embedded commands, pressing the following keys in turn:

f1
L
M
8
f2
f1
L
L
6
0
f2

When you press *f1* the cursor will move one space to the right. Although it looks as if a space has been inserted into your text, it hasn't! Pressing *f1* causes Wordwise to insert a special 'control' character that it recognises as marking the start of an embedded command sequence. This control character just happens to 'look' like a space character. This same 'space' character will appear when you press *f2* to mark the end of an embedded command sequence. Take care not to insert any true spaces within the body of an embedded command sequence as this will have an effect on the operation of the command – it probably won't work correctly!

The commands themselves will appear green in colour. Although I have used upper-case characters above, it is quite legitimate to use lower-case characters and still obtain the correct effect. Thus LM8 and LL60 are the same as lm8 and ll60.

To see the effect of the embedded commands press <ESCAPE> to return to the main menu and select option 7 to preview the text. The output should look like this:

```
The Times Sunday July 21 1969


   Neil Armstrong became the first man to take a walk on the
moon's surface today. The spectacular moment came after he
had inched his way down the ladder of the fragile lunar bug
Eagle while collegue Edwin Aldrin watched his movements from
inside the craft.
The landing in the Sea of Tranquility, was near perfect and
the two astronauts on board Eagle reported that it had not
tilted too far to prevent a take-off. The first word from
man on the moon came from Aldrin: "Tranquility base. The
Eagle has landed"

Press any key_
```

Again, you can produce a hard copy to look at simply by choosing option 6.

By previewing text, you can see if it is to your liking. If it is not then you can readjust the embedded commands, by editing them, and preview the text once again until you get it right. For example, the original text as it appeared in *The Times* that day was printed to a character width of 40, and it was also justified. This simply means that both edges appeared smooth and not ragged. To get the character width to 40 we simply adjust the line length from 60 to 40. To do this, return to Edit Mode, move the cursor to the 6 of 60, press CTRL-A to erase it and then type 4 to give 40. To turn Justification On the embedded command is JO (or jo). Move the cursor to the end of the line by pressing <SHIFT→> and type

f1
J
O
f2

Preview the text again to see the difference:

```
The Times Sunday July 21 1969


   Neil  Armstrong  became the first man
to take a walk  on  the  moon's  surface
today. The spectacular moment came after
he had inched his way down the ladder of
the   fragile   lunar  bug  Eagle  while
collegue  Edwin   Aldrin   watched   his
movements from inside the craft.
The  landing  in the Sea of Tranquility,
was near perfect and the two  astronauts
on  board Eagle reported that it had not
tilted too far to  prevent  a  take-off.
The first word from man on the moon came
from   Aldrin:  "Tranquility  base.  The
Eagle has landed"

Press any key_
```

When you wish to enter several embedded commands one after the other (i.e. to form an embedded command string) it is not really necessary to enter the *f2* character. This need only be entered at the end of the entire string. Thus

*f1*Lm8*f2f1*LL40*f2*

would reduce to

*f1*Lm8*f1*LL40*f2*

To distinguish embedded control sequences from text, in future I'll be adopting the following style:

<*f1*LM8*f1*LL40*f2*>

As before, the italic characters refer to the function key to be pressed and the triangular brackets denote a sequence of key presses as opposed to text to be typed in.

You might like to try saving this on your tape or disc under the program title 'DEMO2'. The embedded commands will also be saved with the text, so that when you come to load it at a future date these will be preserved.

Star commands

All the normal operating system star commands such as:

*HELP
*CAT
*OPT

etc. are available for use from the Menu Mode screen only. To use a star command ensure that you are in Menu Mode and simply press the '*' key followed by the command that you wish to enter. For example, to list the ROMs present in your screen simply type:

*HELP

```
        WORDWISE-PLUS
   (C) Computer Concepts 1984

 1)  Save entire text
 2)  Load new text
 3)  Save marked text
 4)  Load text to cursor
 5)  Search and Replace
 6)  Print text
 7)  Preview text
 8)  Spool text
 9)  Segment menu

 ESC Edit Mode

Please enter choice

*HELP
```

Figure 3.2. Executing a star command.

This is shown in Figure 3.2, then press <RETURN> to see the result.

Disc users

The Disc Filing System commands are all prefixed with a star and can therefore be used readily from Menu Mode. Do exercise care when using the 'dangerous' disc commands. By dangerous I mean the ones that actually transfer data from and to the surface of the disc; examples include:

*COMPACT
*COPY
*BACKUP
*LOAD

These commands will always *destroy* your current document. If you have to use them, *always* without fail, save the current text you are working on to another disc.

All other disc commands can be considered 'safe' in that they do not destroy current Wordwise contents. However, commands such as *DESTROY and *DELETE and *WIPE must be used with a degree of caution.

Once you have saved a file to disc, *always* lock it with

*ACCESS PROG L

This will prevent you accidentally saving a new file over an old one.

The Can't Extend message is quite a common occurence in Wordwise, less so in Wordwise Plus. This will normally happen when you are trying to resave a document to which you have added more text. Wordwise will try to fit this in the same space on the disc and then issue the Can't Extend' message when it finds there is not enough space to insert the new file. To get around this simply *DELETE the file from the disc and then resave it. An even better way would be to save the file under a slightly different filename, *DELETE the old one and then *RENAME the new file.

Once you have saved a file the best way to verify that it has been saved correctly is to *DUMP it from the disc to the screen. If the DFS can perform this task correctly then you do not have a file that is corrupted in any way. To do this simply insert the disc into the disc drive and type:

*DUMP PROG

in Menu Mode, where PROG is the name of the text file.

Tape users

Saving and loading to and from tape is normally quite straightforward. The main difference is that you will need to be on-hand to answer the Cassette Filing System prompts such as

RECORD then RETURN

It is possible to verify a tape saving by loading the text back in over the MOS. Because the MOS is in a ROM it cannot be corrupted – this also keeps any text in Wordwise safe. To do this you need to type

*LOAD PROC C000

Note that you use a star command to verify, *not* option 2. If a tape file does become corrupted then you can try to 'force' it to carry on loading by issuing an

*OPT 2,0

command. If you are using Wordwise you might find that this is still not good enough. In this instance save any current document and then return to Basic using

*BASIC

and then type

*OPT 2,0

*LOAD PROG 2000

where PROG is the filename. Then you can use the DUMP utility provided in Chapter 11 to reclaim areas of text.

Wordwise Plus users will find that it is more forgiving. If it cannot make sense of bits of the tape file it will insert a ¦ character into the appropriate position in the text. All you have to do later is to delete the ¦ s and edit in the missing text.

Chapter Four
Markers and Searching

Wordwise has a pair of markers which, as their name suggests, allow you to mark a section of text, be it just a few characters or a few hundred lines of characters. A marker is represented by a single white square, and is obtained by pressing function key 3, *f3*. The key strip has this marked upon it. Markers can be used for a variety of purposes, such as to allow you to find your way back quickly to a certain point in a large document; to allow you to move a section of text from one part in a document to another; to allow you to copy a repetitive section of text quickly and simply; and to allow you to delete a section of text. As you can see, the markers can play a very big role in effective word processing.

Moving text

The ability to move sections of text around within a document is one of the main features of a word processor such as Wordwise. For instance, you might wish to move a paragraph from the start of a letter to its very end. Using a normal typewriter you would probably have to retype the whole letter. With Wordwise you simply place a marker at the start and end of the section text in question, move the cursor to the point in the text where you wish the marked section of text to be moved and then press the 'Move Marked Text' function key, *f8*. And it really is as simple as that!

Let's have a go. If you have either the previously saved DEMO1 or DEMO2 in position, okay – otherwise load in DEMO2 using option 2 on the main menu. We can try moving the entire contents of paragraph one so that it comes after paragraph two.

Enter Edit Mode and move the cursor to the start of the first sentence positioning it just before 'Neil'. Then press <*f3*>, upon which a white block should appear on the screen – this is a marker. In addition, a small red block should appear on the end of the status line. The block will flash and is placed here to remind you that there is one marker in use at present. Now move the cursor to the end of the second sentence which is also the end of the first paragraph (the last word being 'craft.') and press <*f3*> once again to place the second marker into position; a second red block will appear on the status line. Both markers are now in position, but what if we try to add a third marker? Try it by pressing <*f3*> once again. A bleep is make by the Beeb and the message

MARKERS!

appears in the centre of the status line. Only two markers are allowed at any one time. To get rid of the message, press the space bar.

The next step is to move the cursor to the end of the second paragraph, which is also the end of the text, so this can be performed with <SHIFT↓>. Next press <RETURN> to insert a new blank line, and we're ready to move the text. To do this just press <*f8*>. This function key is marked

```
 Move
Marked
 Text
```

on the key strip. The marked text will be repositioned, almost instantaneously, at the position of the cursor. The markers will also be deleted. The two red blocks will vanish from the right end of the status line.

If you now preview the text it will look somewhat like this, using embedded commands <*f1*LM8*f1*LL40*f2*>:

```
The Times Sunday July 21 1969


The landing in the Sea of Tranquility,
was near perfect and the two astronauts
on board Eagle reported that it had not
tilted too far to prevent a take-off.
The first word from man on the moon came
from Aldrin: "Tranquility base. The
Eagle has landed"
Neil Armstrong became the first man to
take a walk on the moon's surface today.
The spectacular moment came after he had
inched his way down the ladder of the
fragile lunar bug Eagle while collegue
Edwin Aldrin watched his movements from
inside the craft.

Press any key_
```

Copying text

Copying text is performed in a similar manner to that above. It differs from moving text, however, in that the original marked text is not deleted after it has been copied elsewhere. This facility is most useful if you wish to insert a repetitive piece of text into one, two or more points in a long document.

We could add a title to our current document by copying a few words from within the text to the top. The words I have in mind can be found at the end of what is now the first paragraph:

Tranquility base

Position the markers by moving the cursor to the correct position and pressing <*f3*>. This requires the cursor to be placed under the 'T' (to exclude the quotes) and under the full-stop after 'base' (to exclude the full-stop). That particular line of text should look rather like this on the screen in Edit Mode:

Aldrin: "*f3* Tranquility base *f3*. The

The *f3* is represented by a white marker on the screen.

As before, you simply need to move the cursor to the position where you want the text copied. Press <SHIFT↑> to move the cursor to the top of the text and then insert a single blank line by pressing <RETURN> to insert an extra blank line. All that remains to complete the transfer is to press the function key *f9* marked as

```
 Copy
Marked
 Text
```

The text will now be copied across, and previewing it with option 7 from the main menu will show

```
The Times Sunday July 21 1969

Tranquility base

The landing in the Sea of Tranquility,
was near perfect and the two astronauts
on board Eagle reported that it had not
tilted too far to prevent a take-off.
The first word from man on the moon came
from Aldrin: "Tranquility base. The
Eagle has landed"
Neil Armstrong became the first man to
take a walk on the moon's surface today.
The spectacular moment came after he had
inched his way down the ladder of the
fragile lunar bug Eagle while collegue
Edwin Aldrin watched his movements from
inside the craft.
```

Unlike deleting text, a text copy operation does not remove the markers. This is quite deliberate as it allows us to copy the same section of text again or as many times as we like. However, we might well wish, to remove them at some stage so how is this done?

With Wordwise Plus this is really quite simple. Just press <CTRL-R> and this will Remove the markers from the text. This must be performed while in Edit Mode. Unfortunately, this does not exist in the standard Wordwise prior to issue 1.17. If you use the standard Wordwise you can check the issue number by returning to the Menu Mode and typing

*HELP

A reference to Wordwise will appear (along with references to any other ROMs plugged into your BBC Micro) and will be followed by the issue number. For example, the response might be:

```
*HELP

DFS 1.20
  DFS
  UTILS

WORDWISE 1.10
```

Here issue 1.10 of Wordwise is present. In this instance the markers would need to be deleted 'by hand'. This means moving the cursor so that it is positioned under each marker in turn and pressing <CTRL-A>. There are easier ways of deleting markers in the standard Wordwise and I'll be looking at these in a future chapter.

Deleting text

When dealing with small pieces of text it is normally convenient to use <DELETE> or <CTRL-A> to erase redundant sections of text from a document. However, this is a tedious and time-consuming approach if the text is no more than a few dozen words long. By using markers and <*f7*>, sections of text can be deleted quickly.

Try deleting the second paragraph in this way. Place a marker at its start and end and then press <*f7*>. Because the section of text is quite long, Wordwise will ask you if you are quite sure that you wish to delete the marked section of text. It does this by displaying the message

Are you sure?

on the status line. Pressing the 'Y' key will confirm the fact and the marked text will be erased including the markers. Pressing any other key will cause the deletion to be aborted leaving both your text and markers intact.

Previewing the text will show you that only a single paragraph of our original text remains in memory.

```
The Times Sunday July 21 1969

Tranquility base

The landing in the Sea of Tranquility,
was near perfect and the two astronauts
on board Eagle reported that it had not
tilted too far to prevent a take-off.
The first word from man on the moon came
from Aldrin: "Tranquility base. The
Eagle has landed"

Press any key_
```

As with copying text, the Words count and Characters free count on the status line will be adjusted accordingly.

DIY markers

Markers are also useful when it comes to marking a particular point in a document that you might want to find rapidly, rather than searching by scrolling through it. However, the restriction to two markers means that once you have used one, you are unable to use them for copying, moving or deleting purposes. This is where the DIY marker comes into play.

A DIY marker is simply any character that you are not using in your text. For example, the '@' character is very seldom used, similarly characters such as $, ^, {, and }, use one of these to mark a position in a piece of text. Try it by placing an @ somewhere in the text we are currently working on. Anywhere will do.

When you wish to find your way to that particular point, first move the cursor to the top of the Edit Mode screen with <SHIFT↑> and then push <*f4*>. This function key is marked

CURSOR
TO?

on the keystrip. As you press *f4* the status line will display the message

Move Cursor to?

All that you have to do now is press the character that you wish to move to, in this case the '@' key. As soon as you do Wordwise will search the current text for the specified character and position the cursor underneath it. Note that Wordwise will always search for the character from the current position of the cursor, and that is why you should normally move the cursor beforehand to the very start of the document, unless you know that the character is below the current cursor position. If two or more of the characters being searched for exist, the cursor will stop at the first one it encounters. However, a second or third similar marker could be sought out by performing the *f3* sequence again, but without repositioning the cursor at the top of the screen!

Deleting to a marker

Markers can also be used as part of a

DELETE
  TO?

sequence in conjunction with the function key *f6* in Edit Mode. This deletion is performed by placing a marker at the end of the section of text to be deleted. A section of text can be of any length. You can use an *f3* marker or a DIY marker, whichever you please. Once the end of your text has been marked, try using an *f3* marker, and then reposition the cursor at the start of the section to be deleted. As an example, try deleting all the text you are currently editing. Use <SHIFT↓> to reach the end of the text, then press <*f3*>. Move to the top of the text with <SHIFT↑> and then press <*f6*>. If the text to be deleted is more than a 250 characters in length, the message

Are you sure?

will appear on the status line. As before, pressing 'Y' will execute the delete action; pressing any other key will cause the function to be aborted. This is obviously a useful way of clearing text from memory in readiness for a new document, and is preferable to turning the Beeb off and then back on.

Text can be deleted up to the next <RETURN> character by pressing <RETURN> when you are prompted with the message 'Delete to?'.

Saving marked text

Markers can be used to mark out a section of text of any length within a document, that can be saved independently from the entire text. The procedure for doing this is straightforward. First place the markers at the start and end of the section of text you wish to save. Next <ESCAPE> to the main menu and select option 3 which is labelled

3) Save marked text

If you select this option without having inserted both markers, the message

MARKERS!

will be shown on the screen.

Wordwise will then prompt you to enter the filename that you wish to use to save the marked section of text. Wordwise Plus will also display the name of any previous filename that you used to save text under. Saving will then proceed as previously described.

Once you have saved your marked section of text, it can be used however you wish at a later stage, just as though you had originally saved it by utilising option 1. The following example shows where the markers would need to be placed within our current practice text to save man's first words from the surface of the moon.

```
The Times Sunday July 21 1969

Tranquility base

The landing in the Sea of Tranquility,
was near perfect and the two astronauts
on board Eagle reported that it had not
tilted too far to prevent a take-off.
f3The first word from man on the moon
came from Aldrin: "Tranquility base. The
Eagle has landed"f3
```

As before, *f3* is the key press required to insert the marker. <ESCAPE> to the main menu and save the marked text as described above. Use the filename TBASE; we'll put this to use later.

Beware of BREAK

Figure 4.1 shows that the position of the BREAK key is right slap bang at

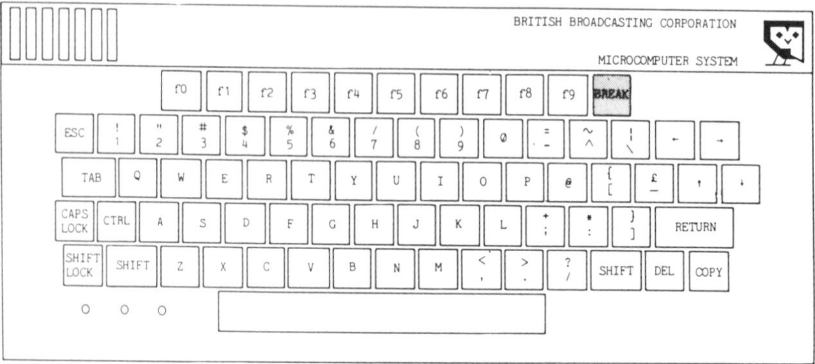

Figure 4.1. The BREAK key.

the end of the line of red function keys. This is not really a problem as long as you do not get careless in your attitude towards the function keys and inadvertently press the BREAK key instead of, say, *f9* or perhaps *f8*. Pressing BREAK in Wordwise Plus is not a problem as you simply return to the main menu. However, it will not do this on the standard Wordwise. Instead, it will return you to the 'start up page' (see Figure 4.2) and prompt you with the message:

Old Text? (Y/N)

If you have text that you wish to keep, you *must not* press the 'N' key. If you do, your text will be erased irrevocably from memory and will be lost forever. Pressing the 'Y' key will return you you to the main menu and keep your text intact.

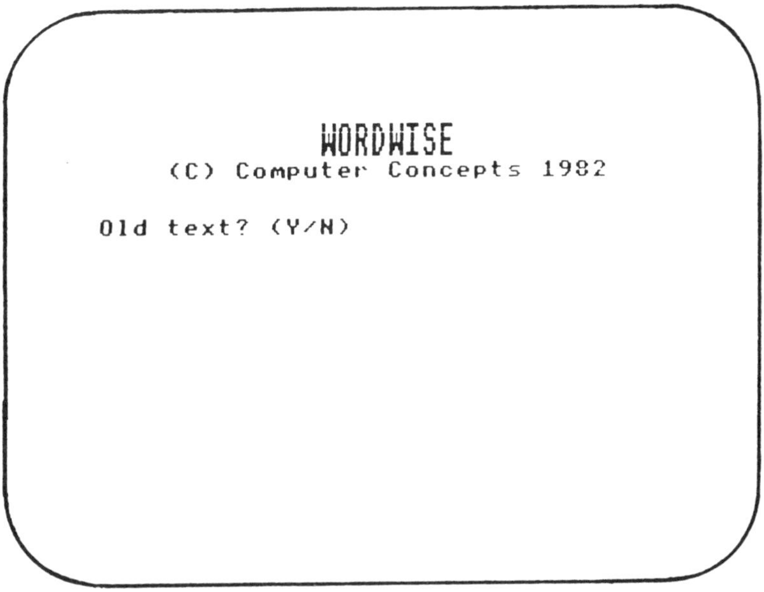

```
                 WORDWISE
      (C) Computer Concepts 1982

 Old text? (Y/N)
```

Figure 4.2. The standard Wordwise start-up page.

Another pitfall that standard Wordwise users should avoid, is pressing the BREAK key when previewing text with option 7. This will confuse Wordwise and you will be unable to use it correctly without turning the micro off and then back on. You will, of course, lose all your text. So beware of BREAK!

Replacing with search

The ability to replace one word or a series of words with another is very useful, and is provided by main menu option 5

5) Search and Replace

We can enter some new text now to see just how this option works. If you have not already done so, delete any existing text as outlined above using *f6*. Now enter the following text exactly as shown

```
This is a for line demonstration.
This is not line number for.
This is for demo only.
This is line number for!
```

Note that I have deliberately spelt the number four as 'for' within the text! Before you go any further, save a copy of this text using option 1 on the main menu; call the file FOUR.

Suppose we now wished to alter all 'fors' that should actually be 'four'. These occur in line numbers one, two and four. Any search and replace will be performed from the current position of the cursor so it is necessary to move the cursor to the top of the text if we wish it all to be searched. Do this by pressing <SHIFT↑>. <ESCAPE> to main menu and press option 5. The

Please enter choice

line will now be replaced with the message

Global or selective? (G/S)

```
WORDWISE-PLUS
(C) Computer Concepts 1984

1)  Save entire text
2)  Load new text
3)  Save marked text
4)  Load text to cursor
5)  Search and Replace
6)  Print text
7)  Preview text
8)  Spool text
9)  Segment menu

ESC Edit Mode

Global or selective? (G/S)G

Please enter search string
for

Please enter replace string
four
```

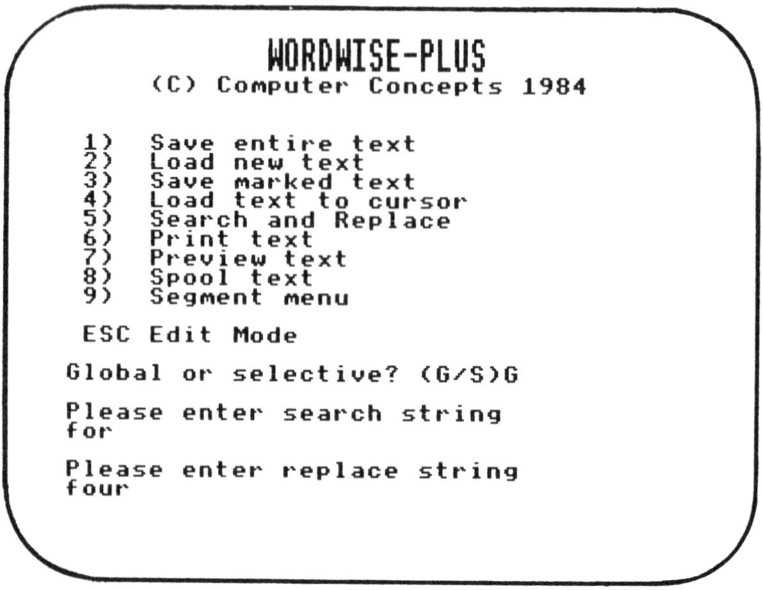

Figure 4.3. Entering Search and Replace details.

Press 'G' for now. A new message will appear below:

Please enter search string

The search string is the word or words that we wish to replace – in this case the word 'for' – so simply type in for. (Note that it should be typed using lower-case characters.) Press <RETURN> and the message

Please enter replace string

will now appear. This is asking you to type in the word that you wish to use as a substitute for the previously entered word. In this case type in

four

and then press <RETURN>.

Figure 4.3 shows how the screen will look just prior to pressing <RETURN>. The screen will seem to blink momentarily and the

Please enter choice

message will reappear. The search and replace has been completed. Press <ESCAPE> to enter Edit Mode and you should see

```
This is a four line demonstration.
This is not line number four.
This is four demo only.
This is line number four!
```

Indeed all fors have been replaced by four. However, the 'for' in the third line has also been replaced, and this was not desired. This has been replaced as we originally chose to use a 'Global' search and replace (remember – we pressed 'G' when prompted earlier on). Wordwise interprets Global to mean everytime you encounter a 'for' replace it with a 'four'. Even if Wordwise found a word such as 'forgive' it would change it to 'fourgive'. The moral here is 'if in doubt use a selective search and replace'.

Let us try again. Load in the previously saved file called FOUR. To do this, select option 2 on the main menu. If you are using Wordwise Plus there will be a slight pause, a bleep will be emitted on the Beeb's speaker and you will see the message

Are you sure? (Y/N)

displayed. This is a safety net, so that you do not accidentally load in a new document, destroying the existing one, without having saved it first. Unfortunately, this safety net is not present on the standard Wordwise so you will need to do your own double-checking. Take care – the keys to select options 1 and 2 are next to each other on the keyboard and they have opposite effects. Inadvertently pressing the wrong one by mistake could prove most annoying! So, press 'Y' in response to the question (any other key will return you to the main menu with no side effects) and enter the filename (followed by <RETURN>) to reload the FOUR file. With the cursor at the top of the text, return to Menu Mode and press option 5, and this time press 'S' in answer to the message

Global or selective? (G/S)

Now enter your search and replace words as before, i.e. 'for' and 'four'.

This time, as Wordwise finds an occurrence of the search word within the text it will stop, clear to Edit Mode, bleep and leave the cursor sitting under the first letter of the search word. A message will be displayed on the status line:

Replace? (Y/N)

Pressing the 'Y' key will allow Wordwise to replace that particular occurrence with the replacement word you specified. Press the 'N' key and Wordwise will not replace that word and leave it alone. In both instances, the next occurrence of the search word within the text will be sought. To get the text correct you will need to press 'Y' in response to the first two prompts; then 'N' to skip the 'for' in the third line; and finally 'Y' in the fourth line. The final text will look like this:

```
This is a four line demonstration.
This is not line number four.
This is for demo only.
This is line number four!
```

The best way to learn how to search and replace is to practise. Bear in mind the following three points:

1. The search will always start from the position of the cursor. To search through an entire document you must move the cursor to the top using <SHIFT↑>. If you wish only to search from a particular point in the text then simply move the cursor to that point.
2. The search and replace is case-dependent, so FOR, For and for are all different from one another.
3. All occurrences of a string will be sought, thus searching out 'for' will also find the 'for' in 'forgive' and 'whatfor'.

Searching for a point

The search and replace facility can be used to good effect to find your way to a particular point in some text, providing it has the first occurrence of a unique word. First select option 5 and choose a selective search. Enter your unique search word and then just press the <RETURN> key when prompted for the replacement string. Once Wordwise has found the word you are looking for, press <ESCAPE>. This will abort the search, returning you to the main menu but leaving the cursor sitting under the word which is sought.

If the word is not unique then you can, of course, simply press 'N' on each similar word that Wordwise encounters until the particular one you are seeking shows its head.

Savers plus W+

We saw above that when you load in new text over old, Wordwise Plus will ask if you are quite sure – the safety net. Wordwise Plus will also ask you the same question if you try to save a file using a filename that already exists (disc users only, this one). When you save or load, Wordwise Plus will always give you the name of the last file you saved or loaded (though not on the first file you load or save!).

If Wordwise Plus locates a similar filename on disc it will first prompt

Replace old file? (Y/N)

Again, this is a safety net that will ensure that you don't overwrite the wrong file (well – that's the theory!). Pressing 'Y' will execute the save, and pressing any other key will abort it and leave you in Menu Mode.

Unfortunately, these safety net features are not available in the standard Wordwise so *always* double check each save and load as you do it. Options 1 and 2 are next to each other but have totally opposite and irreversible effects!

Loading text to cursor

Option 4 of Menu Mode allows us to load text into a current document without overwriting what is there; a sort of insert more than anything. All the text below the position of the cursor will be moved down to make room for the new text that is to be inserted. This is providing there is enough room left to insert the new text, otherwise the message:

NO ROOM!

will be displayed and the text will not be loaded in.

You can try this now with the section of marked text we saved earlier called TBASE. Simply move the cursor to the point where you want to insert the text, and select option 4. Of course, you can do this to the same document as many times as you like providing there is room.

Chapter Five
Formatting Text

So far we have had a look at some of the 46 embedded commands that Wordwise Plus supports and the 32 that the standard Wordwise supports. In this chapter I'll be dealing with the embedded commands that are common to both versions of Wordwise and, in particular, those that have a direct effect on the formatting of the text.

Indents

The dictionary defines an indent as a depression. In Wordwise terms this means a depression into the normal flow of the text from the left-hand side. The following section of text shows how part of a document would look which has had an indent of 5 characters added to part of it:

```
Despite intense efforts by the World Government police the
People's International Terrorist Services (PITS) seized the
Lunar ferry, Selene. The two conditions for its release and
the 210 passengers on board are:

     1: Free all PITS members from detention camps
     throughout the Greater Republic.
     2: The payment of 2M credits into a Selenian bank
     account.

The deadline for fulfilment of these terms was given as 1200
GMT today.

-Global  Bulletin News
 1 December 2089
```

Points 1 and 2 within the transcript have been made much clearer and distinct from the main body of the text by indenting them by five characters.

As with all embedded commands, the indent command takes two characters to represent its mnemonic followed by the character count itself. The mnemonic for INdent is IN. To indent the above text by 5 characters the following command was used:

<*f1*IN5*f2*>

Indents are cancelled with the Cancel Indent command, CI. This does not expect to find a numeric value after it as it resets the left-hand margin to the default value or the value you assigned to it at the start of the document with LM.

The CI command is simply

*<f1*CI*f2>*

Because I chose to insert a spacing line between the main body of the text and the two indented items, the embedded commands were inserted into this line. The embedded commands therefore sit like this within the text:

```
<f1LM10f1LL60f2>
Despite intense efforts by the World Government police the
People's International Terrorist Services (PITS) seized the
Lunar ferry, Selene. The two conditions for its release and
the 210 passengers on board are:
<f1IN5 f2>
     1: Free all PITS members from detention camps
     throughout the Greater Republic.
     2: The payment of 2M credits into a Selenian bank
     account.
< f1CIf2>
The deadline for fulfilment of these terms was given as 1200
GMT today.

-Global  Bulletin News
1 December 2089
```

Occasionally you will want to indent just a single line. Rather than having to use two embedded commands for this (i.e. IN and CI). Wordwise supplies a single Temporary Indent command that acts only on the line that immediately follows it. The TI command is followed by a numeric value defining the number of spaces that the line is to be indented.

Using TI we can temporarily indent the date given in the text above, so that it appears to the right-hand side of the text, by indenting it 45 characters. The final two lines, in terms of keyboard strokes, would go like this:

```
-Global  Bulletin News
<f1TI45f2>1 December 2089
```

On preview the final text would appear thus:

```
Despite intense efforts by the World Government police the
People's International Terrorist Services (PITS) seized the
Lunar ferry, Selene. The two conditions for its release and
the 210 passengers on board are:

     1: Free all PITS members from detention camps
     throughout the Greater Republic.
     2: The payment of 2M credits into a Selenian bank
     account.
```

```
The deadline for fulfilment of these terms was given as 1200
GMT today.

-Global  Bulletin News

                                            1 December 2089
```

Wordwise Plus users have a further indent facility available to them. This is Fully Indent, FI, and this justifies text to the right-hand margin, leaving the left-hand margin ragged. On the above example I had to count the number of characters by which the last line had to be temporarily indented to produce a near smooth edge, for the TI command to work effectively. The Fully Indent command will do this for you. Like TI, FI works on a single line at a time. As an example, we could fully indent the last two lines of the text by preceding each with a FI embedded command. Including the embedded commands we have this:

```
<f1 FIf2>-Global  Bulletin News
<f1 FIf2> 1 December 2089
```

The preview option would then show the effects of the fully indent command

```
Despite intense efforts by the World Government police the
People's International Terrorist Services (PITS) seized the
Lunar ferry, Selene. The two conditions for its release and
the 210 passengers on board are:

     1: Free all PITS members from detention camps
     throughout the Greater Republic.
     2: The payment of 2M credits into a Selenian bank
     account.

The deadline for fulfilment of these terms was given as 1200
GMT today.

                                      -Global  Bulletin News
                                             1 December 2089
```

Fully Indent will work even if you now change the line length value, unlike Temporary Indent which would require a recalculation.

Centre line

Documents can be headed in a number of fashions. One that is quite useful is to place the heading so that it is centred above the main body of the text. This could be useful for producing your own letters which have a name and address equi-spaced about the centre. The embedded command to perform this is CE, standing for CEntre. The value which follows CE will determine how many lines that follow will be centred by a single embedded CE command. The maximum number of lines that may be centred is 200.

Consider the following address:

```
Royalty Incorporated
Buck House
Number 1 The Mall
London
SW1 1ER
```

Here we have five lines that we wish to centre above the text. The command stroke sequence is therefore:

```
<f1CE5f2> Royalty Incorporated
Buck House
Number 1 The Mall
London
SW1 1ER
```

Previewing, or printing this would give

```
Royalty Incorporated
     Buck House
 Number 1 The Mall
       London
      SW1 1ER
```

and it would be positioned exactly around the centre of the current line length, i.e. at the 30 character mark if the line length was set to 60.

Note that the CE5 command is entered on the same line as the first line to be centred. It is quite permissible to enter the CE on a separate blank line before the text to be centred. However, you will need to increment by one the line count, as CE starts counting from the line on which it appears. Thus, CE5 would become CE6.

Spaced out

When you write a letter to a loved one by pen, typewriter or word processor you normally do so by writing or typing one line after the other, perhaps just leaving an odd blank line here and there when you start a new paragraph. Previewing a document in Wordwise also shows the text on concurrent lines. However, when producing draft documents that might require editing and room for your comments, changes and alterations, it is quite useful to be able to insert a blank line between each line of text. This is called 'double-line spacing', and is of particular use to me, as the manuscript for this book was printed using double-line spacing ready for the editing process.

The following printed output was performed using double-line spacing:

```
Come on let's talk about it,

There's no secrets kept in here.

Forgive me for asking

Now wipe away your tears

- China Crisis
```

Of course, we are not limited to double-line spacing. We can also use triple, quadruple and so on, right up to 50-line spacing! The embedded command for Line Spacing is LS, followed by the number of lines. For example, LS2 would produce double-line spacing; LS3 would give triple-line spacing and so forth.

The key sequence for the above text to give double-line spacing was

<*f1*LS2*f1*>

and this would be placed at the very start of the text like this:

```
<f1LS2f1>

Come on let's talk about it,

There's no secrets kept in here.

Forgive me for asking

Now wipe away your tears

- China Crisis
```

Any number of line spacing commands can be mixed within a document; they will simply affect all the text following the embedded command in the specified manner. To cancel the extra line spaces, the Single Spacing embedded command is used:

<*f1*SS*f2*>

This has exactly the same effect as LS1.

If you wish to leave several blank lines within the body of a document, perhaps to insert a diagram of previously prepared tables, the most obvious way to do this is to press <RETURN> a few dozen times. While being quite permissible, it does make your text look messy and, more importantly, you cannot see the text you have just entered without the aid of a preview or scrolling back and forth. An embedded command allows a specified number of SPace lines to be printed using the mnemonic SP. For example, to insert

10 space lines use the key sequence:

<*f1*SP10*f2*>

The current setting of line spacing will affect this command. If SP10 was used in conjunction with LS2, for example, the extra line spaces created by LS2 would also be output.

Pages of text

When you preview or print text from Wordwise, it does so continually without any breaks. However, for most instances, we will want a printed copy at some stage and therefore need to take into account the paper we are using. Fanfold paper comes in a large box, and can be torn along perforations when the printed copy has been completed. A4 paper is in single sheets and needs to be inserted as you go through the printing process. Clearly, it would be nice if it was possible to format text into pages of printable sheets to take account of the paper we are using. Well, it is possible with the Enable Paging (EP) embedded command. To use this you just insert it at the very top of your document *before* any text, thus

<*f1*EP*f2*>

Now all text will appear as a sequence of pages.

The number of lines on a page can be set with the aid of an embedded command. Unless you change it, Wordwise assumes that the number of lines per page will be 66. This number is chosen specifically to enable you to deal with standard fanfold printer paper, as we shall see later on. These pages of text also appear as such on the screen in preview mode. To see them, enter some text very quickly. The easiest way to do this is to enter the alphabet and some numbers a couple of times, simply hitting <RETURN> after each character, thus:

A<RETURN>
B<RETURN>
C<RETURN>
.
.
.
Z<RETURN>
1<RETURN>
2<RETURN>
etc.

When you have around 70 lines or so inserted, press <ESCAPE> and select the preview option from the main menu (number 7). Now watch as the screen scrolls. After generating the 66th line a page break occurs. On

Wordwise Plus this is clearly visible thus:

```
-----------------------PAGE BOUNDARY-----------------------
```

It is a little less clear on the standard Wordwise, however, showing just as a large gap between the end of the text on one page and the start of it on the next page.

Using the Page Length (PL) embedded command, the number of lines on each page can be altered as desired. To set the page length to 50 lines the keystrokes would be:

<*f1*PL50*f2*>

In fact, if you look carefully at the number of lines you will see that there are about 12 fewer printed lines than the number you have specified. This is to allow space between the top and the bottom of the text so that the perforations in fanfold paper can be jumped over. Of course, it also looks much neater. Few people who type letters start at the very top and progress to the last line of the typing paper.

With a default page length of 66, you get 54 printed lines of text per page. If you really did want 66 lines of printed text per page you would need to set PL to 66+12 or 78 – and get some very long paper into the bargain!

In addition to printing the PAGE BOUNDARY message on the screen (though not to the final printer output) Wordwise Plus will also number each page. If you preview the text again you will see printed at the bottom of the screen (and sheet of paper if outputting to the printer) the word:

PAGE n

where n is the page number. This is useful for collating pages of text and keeping them in sequence. Users of the standard Wordwise also have this feature available but it must be turned on first of all at the top of the document using the Print Page embedded command, PP:

<*f1*PP*f2*>

To see just how the page number is incremented and printed at the bottom of the page, try setting the page length to some small figure, such as PL25, and then preview the text.

Forcing pages

A new page can be forced by inserting the embedded command BP into the text at the point where you wish the new page to start. BP, standing for Begin Page, will only work if you have previously enabled paging. As an example, using the futuristic news report given at the start of this chapter, the two conditions could be printed on a separate page by inserting the embedded command

<*f1*BP*f2*>

before and after them. Here are all the keystrokes to show how its output was formatted:

```
<f1 LM10f1LL60f2>
Despite intense efforts by the World Government police the
People's International Terrorist Services (PITS) seized the
Lunar ferry, Selene. The two conditions for its release and
the 210 passengers on board are:
<f1 BPf1 IN5f2>
1: Free all PITS members from detention camps throughout the
Greater Republic.
2: The payment of 2M credits into a Selenian bank account.
<f1BPf1INOf2>
The deadline for fulfilment of these terms was given as 1200
GMT today.

                              <f1 FIf2> -Global  Bulletin News
                                     <f1 FIf2>1 December 2089
```

New pages can also be enabled conditionally. For example, suppose you have a document that spreads over two pages, and contains a table within it. When previewing the text with paging enabled, you see that the table is split over two pages thus:

```
LM   -   Left Margin
LL   -   Line Length
IN   -   INdent
TI   -   Temporary Indent
CI   -   Cancel Indent
PL   -   Page Length


                       PAGE 1

---------------------PAGE BOUNDARY-------------------



JO   -   Justification On
NJ   -   No Justification
LS   -   Line Spacing
SS   -   Single Spacing
EP   -   Enable Paging
```

By carrying the table onto the next sheet it loses its impact, and the continual need to flick backwards and forwards across two sheets of paper becomes tedious. By inserting a Conditional Page embedded command at the onset of the table, a new page can be generated if there is insufficient space on the existing page to insert all of the table. The numeric value that follows the CP command should reflect the number of lines contained within the table (including titles, etc.). The above table contains 11 lines to run continuously, therefore the embedded command is simply

<*f1*CP11*f2*>

When Wordwise encounters this embedded command it checks to see how many lines are left on the current page. If there are less than the number plus 1 (i.e. 12) then a new page will be generated and the whole table will be printed on the new page.

Sheet by sheet

I mentioned earlier the need to insert an Enable Paging command at the beginning of a document if it is to be printed on sheets of paper. If fanfold paper is being used then there are no problems as the printer will simply skip onto the next sheet. However, if you are using single sheet stationery, such as headed notepaper for a letter, then this continual output of pages is not desirable because you will be unable to insert them as quickly as they are needed! For this purpose, always include the Enable Messages, EM, embedded command when using single sheets of paper, thus:

<*f1*EM*f2*>

Now when you print or preview text, as each page is printed the message

PAPER!

will be printed on the base of the screen (but not to the printer). Wordwise will also sound a bleep. Now you can remove the printed sheet from the printer and insert a new sheet. The next page can be printed simply by pressing the space bar. This process can be repeated for each page of text in turn. I always find it best to omit the EM command from the text until I am ready to print the final draft, as this does not hinder the previewing process during general use.

The counter command to EM is DM for Disable Messages:

<*f1*DM*f2*>

Tab stop

If you have ever used a typewriter you might possibly understand the function of the TAB key. Tabs – or to give them their full name – tab stops, are predefined positions on the carriage of the typewriter, say every ten characters along. Pressing the TAB key moves the carriage along so that the next character typed will be at the position of the typewriter head, making it a simple task to tabulate tables or lists of figures.

The BBC Micro also has a TAB key, as shown in Figure 5.1, and Wordwise uses this in a similar manner. Pressing it will 'move' the text cursor along the text by ten spaces. Figure 5.2 shows the position of several tab stops with respect to the screen position.

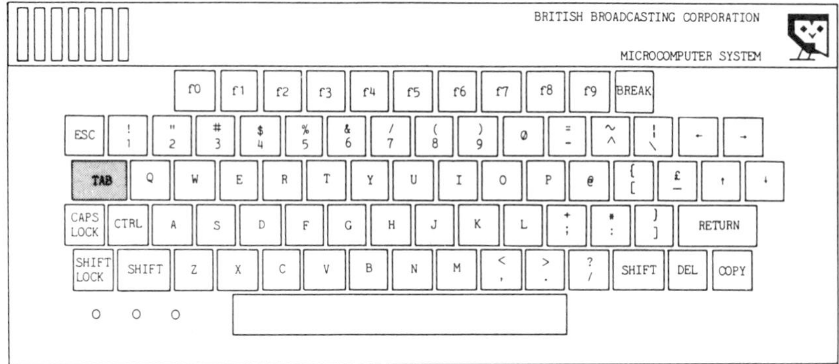

Figure 5.1. The TAB key.

As with all the other aspects of Wordwise, the best way to learn the ins and outs of embedded command actions is to experiment freely with them. This is certainly the case with the action of the TAB key. So, delete any text from your current operation to leave a blank Edit Mode screen. Now press '1' followed by <TAB> (press the TAB key). The cursor does not actually 'move' ten spaces to the right; instead, it places a right-arrow on the screen. This is correct and, again, is to prevent your text occupying more space than necessary. Now add a few more numbers pressing <TAB> in between each, thus:

1<TAB>2<TAB>3<TAB>4<TAB>5

Now preview the text and you will see that the tabs have been effected and the five numbers are spaced ten characters apart from one another:

1 2 3 4 5

All columns of tabs are arranged justified on the left-hand side – in other words, the left edge is the smooth edge and the right edge is the ragged edge. To see this in action, change back to Edit Mode and move onto the next line underneath the line of numbers and insert the following text:

11<TAB>22<TAB>33<TAB>44<TAB>55<TAB><RETURN>
111<TAB>222<TAB>333<TAB>444<TAB>555<TAB><
RETURN>
1111<TAB>2222<TAB>3333<TAB>4444<TAB>5555<TAB>
<RETURN>

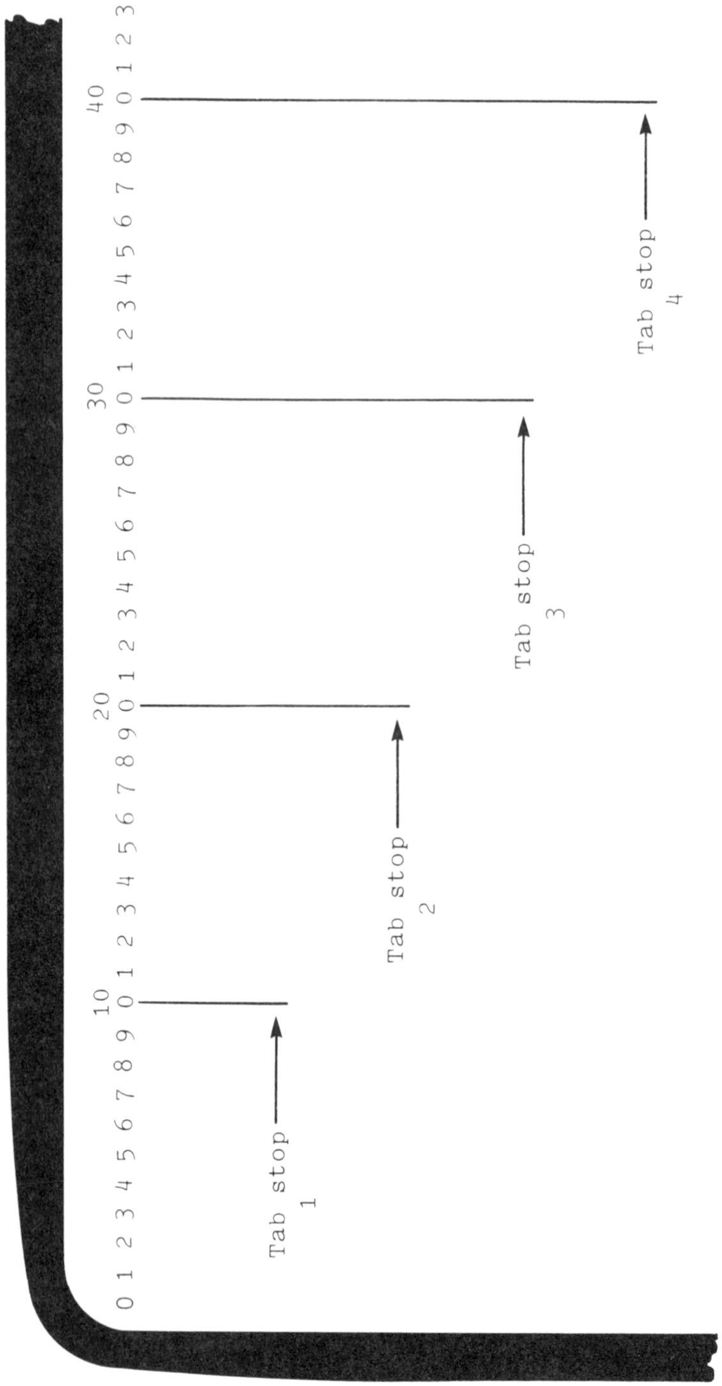

Figure 5.2. Positions of some default tab stops (represents the top left-hand corner of the screen).

Now preview the text to see:

1	2	3	4	5
11	22	33	44	55
111	222	333	444	555
1111	2222	3333	4444	5555

The ten character tab stop positions are the default ones, i.e. the ones used by Wordwise when you have not specified any others. As you may now have guessed, it is possible to set the tab stop positions using the Define Tab stop embedded command, DT. The command is followed by a series of numbers, all separated from one another by a comma. These numbers relate to the new positions of the tab stops. For example, to set the first 5 tab stops to character positions 6, 9, 13, 18, and 24, use

<*f1*DT6,9,13,18,24*f2*>

Figure 5.3 shows these tab stop positions relative to the screen.

Delete the previous set of numbers to leave just the first line of figures, 1 to 5. Then insert this embedded command sequence at the start of the above table of numbers and preview to see its effect. Again try experimenting with various columns of figures and data. If you try adding a string of characters that overspill from one tab stop position to another you will find that the data becomes confused as Wordwise tries to seek out the next tab stop position. To see what I mean try re-entering and previewing the previous number example in its entirety!

Wordwise Plus allows up to 14 tab stops to be defined with the DT command; the standard Wordwise allows 9. In both cases the character range is from 0 to 200.

As a final point, although the Define Tab stops embedded commands are the same in both Wordwise Plus and Wordwise, there is a very subtle difference in the numbering used in conjunction with the tab stop position. In Wordwise Plus, in the command sequence

<*f1*DT6*f2*>

the first tab character will be positioned in the seventh column. Thus, Wordwise Plus moves seven spaces then prints the character. In the standard Wordwise the same command would result in the character being positioned at the sixth character position. Thus Wordwise would leave five spaces then print the character. The reason for this change is to allow the INdent command to match exactly the character position of the Define Tab stop command – in other words, DT7=IN7. In the standard Wordwise one has to be added to the DT count to allow exact matching.

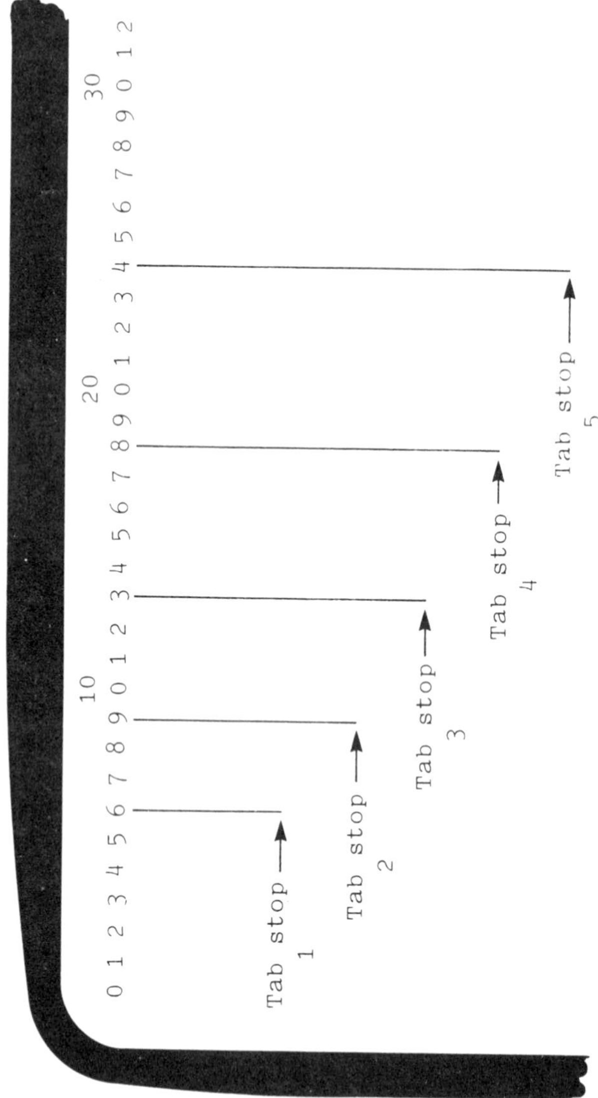

Figure 5.3. Positions of the redefined tab stops (represents the top left-hand corner of the screen).

Chapter Six
Printer Control

This chapter is devoted to using embedded controls within Wordwise to control special printer effects. Although you may not have a printer yet, you will find it an invaluable asset for your word processor at some later stage. Even now you may be sending your documents through the post on disc or cassette to people who do have a printer and who might wish to produce a hard copy. By inserting these special printer-controlling embedded commands you can still give your document and text the added effects that you want from it.

Printer's choice

There is a huge variety of printers available for the home user to choose. As mentioned in Chapter 1, I would refer you to the various reviews appearing in the pages of magazines if you still looking to purchase one. The most popular variety is the dot matrix type that is Epson-compatible. This is the type of printer I will assume you have, for the purposes of description here. Even if you have a different type of printer however, the principles are exactly the same; it is simply a matter of referring to your printer manual for the correct printer control codes. More about this in a moment.

The Epson printer, because of its popularity, has become a sort of unofficial standard for dot matrix printers. (A useful practical book is *Get More from the Epson Printer* by Susan Curran published by Collins.) The Star printer is Epson-compatible as are other printers such as the Canon range and the Taxan Kagas. Theoretically, all the codes and effects presented in this chapter should work on the above printers with no modification.

Dot matrix printers can produce a wide variety of print types and special effects. For example, Figure 6.1 shows the whole range of characters and effects possible on my Star Delta printer. As you can see, there are various different styles of letter print (or character fonts, as they are more generally called). Examples include italics, pica, and elite. In addition, text can also be produced in an enlarged form, condensed, emphasised and underlined.

```
 !"£$%&'()*+,-./0123456789:;<=>?@ABCDEFGHIJKLMNOPQRSTUVWXYZ[\]^_`abcdefghijklmno
pqrstuvwxyz{|}~
 !"£$%&'()*+,-./0123456789:;<=>?@ABCDEFGHIJKLMNOPQRSTUVWXYZ[\]^_`abcdefghijklmnopqrstuvwxyz{|}~
 !"£$%&'()*+,-./0123456789:;<=>?@ABCDEFGHIJKLMNOPQRSTUVWXYZ[\]^_`abcdefghijklmnopqrstuvwxyz{|}~
 !"£$%&'()*+,-./0123456789:;<=>?@ABCDEFGHIJKLMNOPQRSTUVWXYZ[\]^_`abcdefghijklmno
pqrstuvwxyz{|}~
 !"£$%&'()*+,-./0123456789:;<=>?@ABCDEFGHIJKLMNOPQRSTUVWXYZ[\]^_`abcdefghijklmno
pqrstuvwxyz{|}~
```

Figure 6.1. The character set of the Star Delta printer (Epson-compatible).

Other codes enable the printing of subscripts and superscripts. In addition, you can set the fraction of an inch which the paper is advanced when you wish a new line to be printed.

Sending the code

Wordwise has a special printer embedded command that is used to send codes to the attached printer. The code is called the Output Control, and as such the mnemonic taken for the embedded command is OC. Wordwise expects to find a sequence of numbers, separated by commas, after this command, which it interprets as the codes to be sent to the printer. Let's take a very simple example for starters. First ensure that your printer is connected and switched on. Wordwise should be completely free of any text and waiting for keyboard input in Edit Mode. Now type

<*f1*OC12*f2*>

What this command will do is to send the code 12 to the printer. In Basic terms this relates directly to the command

VDU12 or PRINT CHR$(12)

– in short, a form feed. A form feed shows itself as a screen clearing in Basic or the ejection of a whole sheet of paper on the printer. To see it work, <ESCAPE> to the Menu Mode and select option 6:

6) Print text

All being well, a sheet of paper will be ejected from the printer.

A less drastic move would be to advance the paper by just a single line – do a line feed in other words. The control code for this is 10, therefore the complete embedded command becomes

<*f1*OC10*f2*>

You could simply delete the 2 from 12 and insert the 0 in its place. Selecting option 6 from Menu Mode will show the command's effect. A much simpler way to perform a line feed on the printer in normal everyday use would be just to insert a <RETURN> into the text!

As mentioned earlier, some printers do not have an automatic line feed facility so you might need to enable line feeds on the printer by typing

*FX6

from Menu Mode.

Character fonts

To select the style in which we wish to print text means looking at the printer manual to extract the necessary codes. This is not as painful as it seems. You'll find that Appendix B contains a list of typical printer control codes, namely the standard FX Epson codes, plus the slightly different codes for the RX and MX Epson range of printers. Also, to help you extract the correct codes from your manual, especially if you do not have an Epson-compatible printer, I will work through examples from the manual of my own Star Delta printer. (Remember – these are Epson-compatible, so Epson, Canon and Taxan printer owners can use them exactly as they see them!)

First, find the chapter on functional control codes, and in particular those used to control print style. If you have trouble locating these, refer to an index or contents page. When you find the relevant pages you will find that they will be laid out in a similar style, for ease of reference. What we now need to search for are the ESC or CHR$ codes. In my experience, all printer manuals have both, so concentrate on the row of CHR$ codes. For example, in my Star Delta manual the table to select the italic ASCII character set (i.e. to print in italics) looks like this:

```
Font style controls

CODE : ESC 4
     PURPOSE     : Select the italic character set
     FORMAT      : CHR$(27)   CHR$(52)
     REMARKS     : This command causes the printer to
                   select the italic ASCII character set.
```

All the information needed to produce Wordwise text in italics is here!

The line we are really interested in is the line marked FORMAT:

FORMAT : CHR$(27) CHR$(52)

Indeed, all we have to do is take the two numbers given in that line –

27 and 52

– and place them into an OC embedded command. And that is all there is to it! So, delete any text in Wordwise and enter the embedded command

<*f1*OC27,52*f2*>

The 27 comes directly after the OC, is followed by a comma and finally by the 52. Obviously, if your printer is not Epson-compatible you will need to extract the relevant codes from your own printer manual and insert them instead.

To see the command take effect, we need to enter some text into Wordwise so that it can print it in italics. Hit <RETURN> and add the following

A line of text in italics

Now print the text to your printer using option 6 on the main menu. What you get should be

A line of text in italics

If you find that your printer manual does not contain these CHR$ values then it will certainly have the ESC character sequences which you can quite easily convert into CHR$ values. In the above example, the italic font was also specified as

CODE : ESC 4

ESC relates to ESCAPE. The ASCII code for ESCAPE is 27, similarly the ASCII code for 4 is – yes, you guessed it – 52. So ESC 4 is 27,52. To help you deal with the ESC code sequences Appendix C contains a list of ASCII character values.

Up to a point

Once a style or character font has been selected with an output control sequence, the printer will continue to act on it until it is switched off or it is cancelled by another command. Figure 6.2 shows my printer manual definition of 'Select the standard ASCII character set'. Normally this is selected by default when the printer is switched on.

```
Font style controls

CODE : ESC 5
     PURPOSE    : Select the standard character set
     FORMAT     : CHR$(27)  CHR$(53)
     REMARKS    : This command causes the printer to
                  cancel the italic character set and
                  select the standard ASCII character
                  set.
```

Figure 6.2. Select standard ASCII character set.

So, to cancel the italic text and get back to normal upright characters, the embedded control code will be:

<*f1*OC27,53*f2*>

Enter this in your text after the single line of text now present and add the following:

No more italics, just plain uprights!

In terms of keystrokes your Edit Mode screen will look something like this:

```
<f1 OC27,52f2>
A line of text in italics
<f1 OC27,53f2>
No more italics, just plain uprights!
```

<ESCAPE> to Menu Mode and select option 6. Your printed copy will contain italics and plain text mixed, thus:

A line of text in italics

No more italics, just plain uprights!

More text per line

If you want to get more text on a line of printer paper then there are several ways to go about it, depending on how many characters you want per line. Pica-sized Mode prints text at the rate of 10 characters per inch. Figure 6.3 shows the printer manual notes referring to Pica-sized Mode.

```
CODE : ESC B 1
    PURPOSE    : Set the print pitch to pica-sized mode
    FORMAT     : CHR$(27)  CHR$(66)  CHR$(1)
    REMARKS    : After this command is sent to the
                 printer, subsequent printing is done in
                 pica-sized mode, with 10 characters
                 per inch.
```

Figure 6.3. Pica-sized character set.

Straight away you will probably notice that we now have three CHR$ values rather than the two we have dealt with so far. This is not problematic; you just send all three. The Pica-sized Mode select embedded command is

<*f1*OC27,66,1*f2*>

However, in the case of three control codes the ESC control sequences are slightly different. You only convert the *first two* codes to their ASCII equivalent; the third code is used as it is. In this case the ESC sequence is

ESC B 1
ESC becomes 27
B becomes 66

but the 1 remains as a 1, to give

27,66,1

Try the code by tagging it plus some suitable text onto the end of the text currently present, thus:

```
<f1 OC27,52f2>
A line of text in italics
<f1 OC27,53f2>
No more italics, just plain uprights!
<f1 OC27,66,1f2>
Pica-sized mode print - 10 characters per inch
```

The printed output of this shows the Pica-sized Mode text:

```
A line of text in italics

No more italics, just plain uprights!

Pica-sized mode print - 10 characters per inch
```

Elite-sized mode provides 12 characters per inch while condensed print squeezes in 17 characters per inch. The control codes for each are

Elite : 27,66,2
Condensed : 27,66,3

Adding these to our growing demo text shows the effects they have:

```
A line of text in italics

No more italics, just plain uprights!

Pica-sized mode print - 10 characters per inch

Elite-sized mode print - 12 characters per inch

Condensed print - 17 characters per inch
```

You can see from the output that the text produced by elite and condensed print starts further to the left-hand side than before. This is because I have chosen an indent of 5 characters for printing purposes – as the character width changes with respect to the number of characters printed per inch, so does the position of the print.

Underlined and double-sized

Double-sized characters are possible with dot matrix printers and provide an excellent way to head the start of a document. This is also referred to as Enlarged Printing Mode. Underlining text allows you to add emphasis to what you are saying; it is also a good way in which to make subheadings within a document stand out. The printer output codes for double and underlining text on Epson-compatible printers are:

Double-sized on : 14
Underline on : 27,45,1

Note that enlarged print is enabled without the ESC character. Turning off double-sized and underlining modes is done with the following codes:

Double-sized off : 20
Underline off : 27,45,0

Delete any existing text from Wordwise and try entering the following text:

```
<f1 OC14f2>
This is double-sized text
<f1  OC20f2>
<f1OC27,45,1f2>
Underlining makes text more prominent
<f1OC27,45,0f2>
```

Printing this text will produce the following on your printer paper:

```
This is double-sized text

Underlining makes text more prominent
```

Of course, it is possible to combine printer control codes to allow you to combine printed effects. For example, you could produce double-sized text that is underlined and then italicise the lot as well, as the following printer output shows:

```
Underlining big text

Underlining big italic text!
```

Super-sub

If you are processing documents that contain mathematical material then the abilty to print superscript and subscript numbers will be invaluable.

Superscript Mode is enabled with the output control sequence

27,83,0

and may be used with the italic font as well as normal print, also in pica, elite and condensed pitches. They may not be used in Enlarged Print Mode. The following output shows superscripts in action:

```
Fifty six to the power of thirty is written
as : 56³⁰
```

To ensure that only the 30 is printed in superscript it must be placed directly after the 56, as illustrated below:

```
Fifty-six to the power of thirty is written as : 56
<f1OC27,83,0f2>30<f1OC27,84f2>
```

The code

OC27,84

is used to cancel superscript and subscript printing. Of course, it is possible to print entirely in Superscript Mode – suitable for producing the 'small' print that nobody ever reads!

And you agree to pay me three months

salary per year for life

Subscript Mode works by printing text on the bottom of the line, as the following example clearly shows:

This is superscript mode printing

The output code to enable subscript printing is:

27,83,1

Emphasising a double strike

Finally there are two other useful printing effects well worth employing. In Emphasised Print Mode the text is printed twice in the same position; this means that it looks much bolder and darker. In Double Strike Mode the characters are printed once and then the printer advances the paper by 1/144th of an inch before printing the line again. The codes involved for both are

Emphasised print on : 27,69
Emphasised print off: 27,70
Double strike on : 27,71
Double strike off : 27,72

See if you can spot the difference between the two in the following printer output:

This is emphasised print
This is double strike print

Printer plus W+

All the information given so far in this chapter is effective for both Wordwise and Wordwise Plus. As one might expect, the latter has several additional niceties when it comes to controlling printer output.

Top of the list is the Output Print Sequence embedded command, OPS. In all there are ten OPS commands but only four are defined on default, and these four enable and disable underlining of text and double strike printing. The commands and their function are:

OPS0 – Underline on
OPS1 – Underline off
OPS2 – Double strike on
OPS3 – Double strike off

Therefore in Wordwise Plus it is even more simple to underline text. You would simply use the embedded command sequence

<*f1*OPS0*f2*>

Underlining is useful, but I am not such a fan of double strike printing. I much prefer to use emphasised printing. An embedded command allows these four OPS commands and the other six (i.e. OPS4 to OPS9) to be redefined. The command is RPS, Redefine Print Sequence, and it expects to be followed first by the OPS number to be redefined and then by the CHR$ (or ESC) values. For example, the control codes for emphasised print on and off are 27,69 and 27,70. To program these into OPS2 and OPS3 simply use the sequences

<*f1*RPS2,27,69*f2*>

and

<*f1*RPS3,27,70*f2*>

It would be possible to define all your standard printer sequences with RPS first in Wordwise and then save this as a file, perhaps called START. Then all you need do is load in the START file when you want to use Wordwise and avoid all unnecessary typing!

A set of commands that have the same effect on printed output as OPS0 to OPS3 are also available, and are listed below:

DS – Double-strike start
DE – Double-strike end
US – Underline start
UE – Underline end

These commands are affected by any reprogramming using RPS. Thus if emphasised print was programmed into OPS2 the DS would produce emphasised print. The real advantage of using these commands comes when you preview your text. In such cases, any underlined text shows as being underlined on the screen. Similarly any text affected by DS will be shown in inverse video – that is, printed as black text on a white background.

Try previewing the following bit of text to see how it looks:

<*f1*US*f2*>This text is underlined in preview<*f1*UE*f2*>
<*f1*DS*f2*>And this text is in inverse video!<*f1*DE*f2*>

Escaped W+

We saw earlier that some printer manuals do not always provide the CHR$ values to be used directly within an OC command, or similar, but are presented purely as ESC sequences. It is a straightforward matter to convert these into CHR$ values, but Wordwise Plus provides a special embedded command that allows you to enter ESC sequences just as they are printed in the manual and with no need for conversion. The embedded code to do this is ES. For example, placing

<*f1*ES*f*>

within your text would cause the ASCII code 27 to be sent to the printer. Letters, which must be enclosed within quotes, i.e. "Q", and numbers may also follow the ES command, separated from one another by commas in the normal way. For example, in an earlier discussion of ESC control codes we saw that the ESC sequence for selecting the italic character font was

ESC 4

Rather than converting this to the CHR$ values 27, 52 we could simply use the ES sequence

<*f1*ES,"4"*f2*>.

In fact, you can combine just about any number into an ES code. Take this imaginary control code

<*f1*ES,"A",1,&23,%10101010,@123*f2*>

Breaking this down into simple parts we have

ES – the ESC send command
"A" – ASCII 'A' i.e. 65 decimal
&23 – hexadecimal value &23
%10101010 – binary value 10101010
@123 – octal value @123

In case you are not familiar with some of the above terms, a hexadecimal number is calculated to a base 16 (hexadecimal is very common in computer use); a binary number is calculated to base 2 (again very common); and finally an octal number is calculated to a base of 8 (not very common this one!).

Many of the embedded commands we have covered in this chapter are rather long-winded to keep typing in every time you wish to use one or two of them. You will be relieved to hear that there is a much easier way in which these commands can be entered using the red coloured function keys – a subject that we'll look at in some detail in Chapter 9.

Chapter Seven
Headers and Footers

In Chapter 5 we saw that not all of the lines on a page are used. For example, you will remember that in a standard page of 66 lines, 12 are left blank, six at the top and six at the bottom. In addition to making a nice gap between the bottom of the text, the paper perforations and the top of the text on the next page, these gaps also make housings for additional lines of information. These 'lines of information' are called the footers or headers depending on whether they are printed at the bottom or the top of the text. Typical examples of footers and headers respectively are

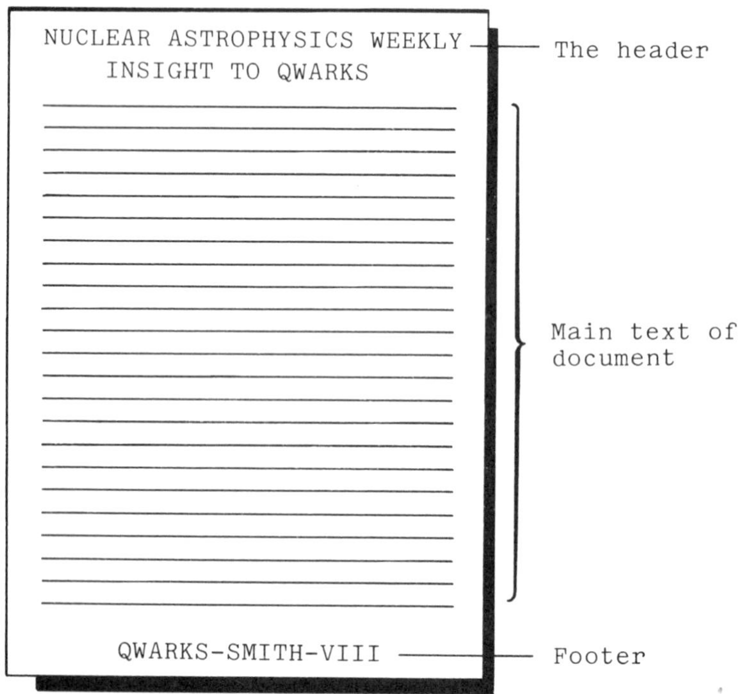

Figure 7.1. A typical document page with headers and footers.

Wordwise Plus – Chapter 7 : Page 86

and

Wordwise Plus – A User's Guide

The latter is clearly seen at the top of page 74, for example. Figure 7.1 shows a typical page layout with footers and headers included.

As always, a worked example makes things much clearer, so let's now do just that.

Footers

Figure 7.2 shows a typical page out of my manuscript for this book. I've used just single line spacing in this instance just to make it quite clear where the footer falls within the 'gap' at the bottom of the page. As you can see from the figure I've numbered the last dozen lines or so for your convenience. The lines that form the blank 'gap' are numbered 61 to 66 inclusive. Wordwise will, unless told otherwise, always place a footer on line number 63. To define the nature of the footer the embedded command DF is used. The DF

```
54  Footers
55  Figure  7.2  shows  a  typical page out of my manuscript for
56  this book. I've  used  just  single  line  spacing  in  this
57  instance  just to make it quite clear where the footer falls
58  within the 'gap' at the bottom of the page. As you  can  see
59  from the figure I've numbered the last dozen lines or so for
60  your  convenience.  The  lines that form the blank 'gap' are
61
62
63                Wordwise- Chapter 7 : Page 89
64
65
66
-----------------------PAGE BOUNDARY-------------------------
 1
 2
 3
 4
 5
 6
 7  numbered 61 to 66  inclusive.  Wordwise  will,  unless  told
 8  otherwise,  always  place  a  footer  on  line number 63. To
 9  define the nature of the footer the embedded command  DF  is
10  used.  The  DF command is entered in the normal way, however
11  the text that is to  form  the  footer  follows  immediately
12  after  the white embedded command, the f2 in otherwords. The
13  footer text can be anything that can fit onto  the  line  up
14  until a <RETURN>. For example to define the footer
15       Wordwise - Chapter 7
16  the following embedded command would be entered
```

Figure 7.2. A footer as used in the manuscript for this book.

command is entered in the normal way, however the text that is to form the footer follows immediately after the white embedded command, the *f2* in otherwords. The footer text can be anything that can fit onto the line up until a <RETURN>. For example to define the footer

Wordwise – Chapter 7

the following embedded command would be entered

<*f1*DF*f2*>Wordwise – Chapter 7<RETURN>

In short, the embedded command is entered, the footer text is typed directly after it, and the whole line is terminated with a single <RETURN>.

To see this in action for yourself, you'll first need to enter some text into Wordwise. The quickest way to do this is just to enter each letter of the alphabet, pressing <RETURN> after each one. Alternatively, if you have some 'real' text saved on tape or disc, just load it in and use the markers and *f9* to copy it within your text several times to expand it to a suitable length (about 70 lines). The next thing to do is to move to the top of your text using <SHIFT↑> and insert the enable paging embedded command – footers (or headers) will not be produced if paging is not enabled. To do this enter:

<*f1*EP*f2*>

This can be placed either before, after or on the same line as the footer itself. I always start all my documents with EP at the very top as the first embedded command. It's worth adopting some form of habit or style just so you don't forget it.

Right, assuming you have enough text switch to Menu Mode and preview the text with option 7. As the preview scrolls through the screen, halt it as you get to the page break. To do this, simply hold down the CTRL and SHIFT keys together (Figure 7.3). This works in both Wordwise Plus and standard Wordwise so long as you keep CTRL-SHIFT depressed; as soon as you let go, scrolling will continue. Wordwise Plus users can stop scrolling altogether in Preview Mode simply by pushing the space bar once. To re-

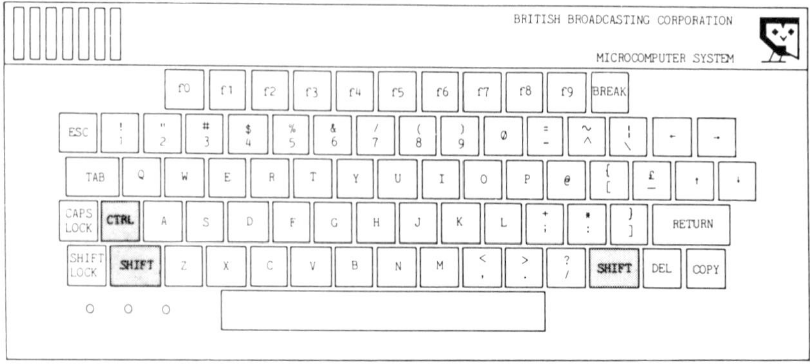

Figure 7.3. The CTRL and SHIFT keys.

enable scrolling, simply tap the space bar once again. At the page break boundary you should see the footer sitting to the very left-hand margin, as shown in Figure 7.4

```
This is line number fifty-eight of the figure
This is line number fifty-nine of the figure
This is line number sixty of the figure



Wordwise - Chapter 7



----------------------PAGE BOUNDARY--------------------




This is the first line of the next page
This is the second line of the next page
This is the third line of the next page
```

Figure 7.4. The footer.

The footer has clearly been produced. Wordwise Plus users might also have noticed that the PAGE footing and the number of the page have been omitted. This is because Wordwise Plus recognises that you wish to define your own footer and assumes that you will make your own page numbering arrangements – but more on this in a moment.

The footer as it stands is justified to the left-hand margin. I prefer to centre footers on the page using the CE (CEntre) embedded command. This can simply be added to the footing definition after the DF command thus:

<*f1*DF*f1*CE*f2*>Wordwise – Chapter 7

```
This is line number fifty-eight of the figure
This is line number fifty-nine of the figure
This is line number sixty of the figure



                   Wordwise - Chapter 7



----------------------PAGE BOUNDARY--------------------




This is the first line of the next page
This is the second line of the next page
This is the third line of the next page
```

Figure 7.5. A centred footer.

When you preview the text now you will see that the footer is at the centre of the page,as in Figure 7.5.

Wordwise Plus users could even fully indent their footers by substituting the embedded command, FI, in place of CE.

Page numbers may be added by following the footer with the Print Page embedded command PP. I like to add the word 'Page' before the PP command – though it's not really necessary. Edit your existing footer so that it reads

<*f1*DF*f1*CE*f2*>Wordwise – Chapter 7 – Page <*f1*PP*f2*>

Previewing your text will now show the whole footer as in Figure 7.6.

```
This is line number fifty-eight of the figure
This is line number fifty-nine of the figure
This is line number sixty of the figure


            Wordwise - Chapter 7 - Page 1


---------------------PAGE BOUNDARY--------------------



This is the first line of the next page
This is the second line of the next page
This is the third line of the next page
```

Figure 7.6. The centred footer with page number incluced.

When you are producing a very long document, it is quite likely that you will not be able to store it all within Wordwise at one time. Instead, you will want to write the document in easy to manage sections of say 2500 words or so. In such cases it becomes difficult to number pages consecutively as Wordwise will always start off with page 1, followed by pages 2,3,4 and so on. To get around this problem, an embedded command, PN, allows you to give the Page Number that you wish to start off with. The command should be followed by the page number that you wish to commence with. This should follow directly after the PN mnemonic, so that it appears in green; the *f2* white embedded command should follow the page number. As an example, suppose we wished to start the next sheet of text at line 89. The embedded command sequence would then be:

<*f1*PN89*f2*>

Adding this to the front of the footer would produce the output shown in Figure 7.7.

```
This is line number fifty-eight of the figure
This is line number fifty-nine of the figure
This is line number sixty of the figure


               Wordwise - Chapter 7 - Page 89


---------------------PAGE BOUNDARY-------------------


This is the first line of the next page
This is the second line of the next page
This is the third line of the next page
```

Figure 7.7. Footer with selected page numbering.

Keep it tidy

The last few examples of embedded command lines have all been rather long. It is good practice to get into the habit of keeping your embedded command lines relatively short. As a general rule of thumb, an embedded command line should never spill over two lines of the Edit Mode screen. If a line is approaching this sort of length, break it down into shorter parts. For example, consider the last footer with its associated commands; we could quite happily break this down as follows, with no adverse effects:

```
<f1EPf2>
<f1PN89f2>
<f1 DFf1 CEf2>Wordwise - Chapter 7 - Page
```

Very often, the document you are printing will finish some way down a sheet of paper, not at its very end, which will mean that the footer you have produced will not appear on the very last page of the final printed document. It is possible, however, to force a footer to be produced at the bottom of the last page, should it stop short. This is performed with the Begin Page command, BP. When you end a document with a BP command, in which you are using headers (an explanation of these will follow) it should stop abruptly. It should not be followed by <*f2*> or a RETURN, otherwise the next header will be printed on the next page. A final page eject then should simply be

<*f1*BP>

Headers

A header is defined with the DH embedded command and is followed by a line of text which you wish to be printed in the top 'gap' of a sheet of paper. It works exactly like the production of a footer except that the header is placed on line 3 of each page by default. You can include page numbers if you so wish, as already described, and headers may be left justified, centred or, in Wordwise Plus, fully indented.

To define the header

Wordwise Plus – A User's Guide

the sequence would be

<*f1*DH*f1*CE*f2*>Wordwise Plus – A User's Guide

As with footers, the actual header text must be terminated with a <RETURN>. If a Print Page command is also embedded, the page number will be printed out and incremented at the end of the page. This ensures that page numbers specified in headers and footers on the same page are the same!

Normally a header will not be printed on the very first page. This allows you to print your own title page heading. However, you may be binding your document and as such it will have a titled cover. In such instances it would be desirable to produce the header at the top of the first sheet of your document, and this is possible. To do so, the Enable Paging command must appear with the Define Heading command as the first line of the document thus:

<*f1*EP*f1*DH*f1*CE*f2*>Wordwise Plus – A User's Guide

Adjusting footers and headers

As we have seen, once a footing or heading has been defined it is printed in the third line of the 'gap' at the top and bottom of the printed page. These positions can be adjusted to suit your own needs by redefining the footing and heading positions with FP (Footing Position) and HP (Heading Position). Both embedded commands should be followed by a numeric value that can be anything between 0 and the number of lines in the top and bottom spaces. For example, to print a header on the first line of the 'gap' and the footer on the last line of the 'gap' (i.e. the first and sixty-sixth lines of a standard sheet of paper) the following command sequences could be used:

```
<f1HP1f2 >
<f1FP6f2 >
<f1DHf1 CEf2>This is the header
<f1DFf1 CEf2>This is the footer
```

So far I have been referring to the top and bottom 'gaps' of a page. These are more correctly known as the 'top' and 'bottom' spaces, and each consists of six line spaces. Like most other things in Wordwise, these are variable in length and may be adjusted to suit using the Top Space (TS) and Bottom Space (BS) embedded commands. Basically both may be assigned any value in the range 0 to 50, but to keep pages balanced, whatever you add to or subtract from TS and BS will be reflected in the number of actual printed lines on each page. For example, the Wordwise defaults PL, TS and BS are

Page Length = 66
Top Space = 6
Bottom Space = 6

By adding BS and TS together and subtracting them from Pl we have the number of lines that are actually printed on, which is

66−(6+6)=54

So, if the values of TS and BS were increased by two

<f1TS8f2>
<f1BS8f2>

the number of printable lines reduces by four

66−(8+8)=50

Similarly, if TS and BS are decreased by two

<f1TS4f2>
<f1BS4f2>

the number of printable lines are increased by four

66−(4+4)=58

If you have no need for footers or headers and wish to cram as much text as possible onto a single sheet of paper then TS and BS can be set to zero:

<f1TS0f2>
<f1BS0f2>

Should you try to assign a value greater than 50 to TS or BS then the standard default value of 6 will prevail.

Plus numbers W+

Wordwise Plus includes a line numbering embedded command that is useful when it comes to calculating exacty where you want your footers and headers to appear. The LNS and LNE commands stand for Line Number Start and Line Number End respectively. With LNS selected Wordwise Plus will print three figure line numbers down the left-hand side of the screen in Preview Mode. The numbers start at 001 and carry on until the value of PL, 066 on default, whereupon a new page and a new sequence of line numbers begin. This command should be used in Enable Paging mode; if you have some text *in situ* then place

<*f1*LNS*f2*>

at the top of the text and then preview it.

Chapter Eight
Final Command

There are several embedded commands and an additional main menu option that we have not yet covered. We can correct that now by examining the function of each in turn. All of the commands that follow are available on Wordwise Plus; several were implemented on later versions of Wordwise, though not on the early versions. If you are using the standard Wordwise, check in the back of your Wordwise manual under the section 'Embedded Commands Summary' and tick off those that do apply to your version of Wordwise.

Spooling text

One item that does apply to both Wordwise Plus and Wordwise is option 8 on the main menu. This is given as

8) Spool text

Spool is a form of saving your text. However, rather than simply saving it as a text file including all the embedded control codes and so forth, it actually saves the formatted state, in other words how the final version will look. When you preview text using option 7 you see your document as it will appear when printed – this is the formatted state and the manner in which a spooled file is saved. This can be useful if you do not have a printer and wish to send a letter to a friend who also has a BBC Micro, but not Wordwise. The file can be read simply by executing

*TYPE <filename>

on a disc system.

With the standard Wordwise, printer codes, such as those to produce emphasised print or italics, are not saved as part of the spooled file. This is not the case with Wordwise Plus; control codes are spooled and will produce the desired effect if the file is subsequently printed.

Pound of flesh

One of the most annoying aspects of using printers in conjunction with Wordwise is that most printers are not set up to print the pound sign. Look at your keyboard and you will locate the pound sign to the top left of the <RETURN> key (Figure 8.1). If you press this key in Edit Mode (you'll

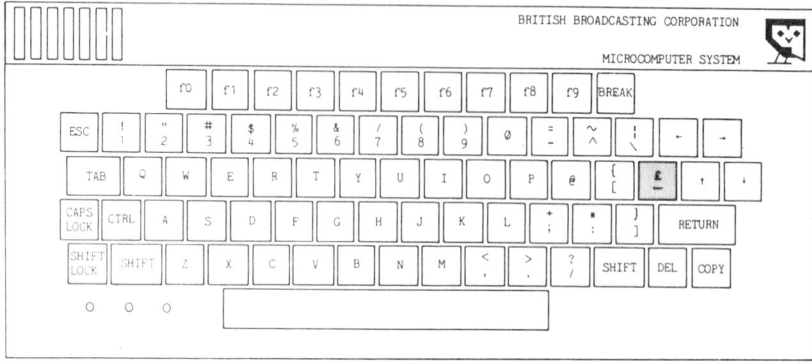

Figure 8.1. The £ key.

need to press SHIFT at the same time to get it) you will indeed see the £ sign on the Edit Mode screen. However, when you come to print your text it may not be shown; instead it will be replaced by a tick, or ' if you prefer. I am now, of course, referring to Epson-compatible printers; if you are using another form of printer you may possibly be able to use the pound sign correctly without any fuss – consult your printer manual and then try it!

Back to the Epson-compatible FX printer. The albeit unofficial standard way to print a pound sign is to redefine the hash symbol (Figure 8.2) which shares the '3' key. To do this use the following embedded OC commands:

<*f1*OC27,82,1*f2*> – enable pound sign
<*f1*OC27,82,0*f2*> – disable pound sign

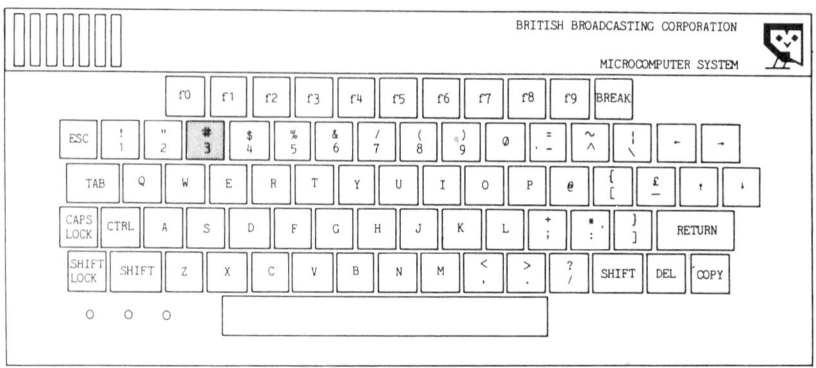

Figure 8.2. The hash, #, shares the '3' key.

Star printers are slightly different in this respect as they must have the following sequences sent to enable and disable the pound sign:

<*f1*OC27,55,1*f2*> – enable pound sign on Star
<*f1*OC27,55,0*f2*> – disable pound sign on Star

An alternative on Epsons would be to send the ES sequence

<*f1*ES“R”,1*f2*>

to enable the pound, and

<*f1*ES“R”,0*f2*>

to disable it.

The Define Pound (DP) embedded command allows you to select just which character you would like to be sent to the printer when Wordwise encounters the pound sign. The examples above show how the hash sign can be used to generate a pound sign. The hash sign has an ASCII code of 35, so by issuing the embedded command

<*f1*DP35*f2*>

Wordwise will send the hash character to the printer whenever it encounters a £ in the text. In other words, you can have your cake and eat it – pound signs on the Edit Mode screen and on the printer!

Padding out

When using the JO (Justify On) embedded command, Wordwise will always jiggle your text around so that the left and right-hand margins are straight and neat, justified in other words. It does this by inserting spaces between words when you preview or print your document. For most instances this is fine; the insertion of extra spaces (purely in the final preview or print, not into the actual file) is not really of any concern. However, there will be occasions when you wish two words to appear side by side on the preview or hard copy, but because of the justification they are split across two lines, the first word at the end of one line, the second word at the start of the next. To ensure that both words appear on the same line we can insert a *pad character* between the two words *instead* of the normal typed space. The default tab character on Wordwise is ¦ shown in Figure 8.3; to obtain this you will need to use the SHIFT key. Note that this will appear as two short parallel lines in Edit Mode, thus ||.

Suppose we wished to ensure that the words

Wordwise Plus

were not split across two lines. Instead of tapping the space bar between the

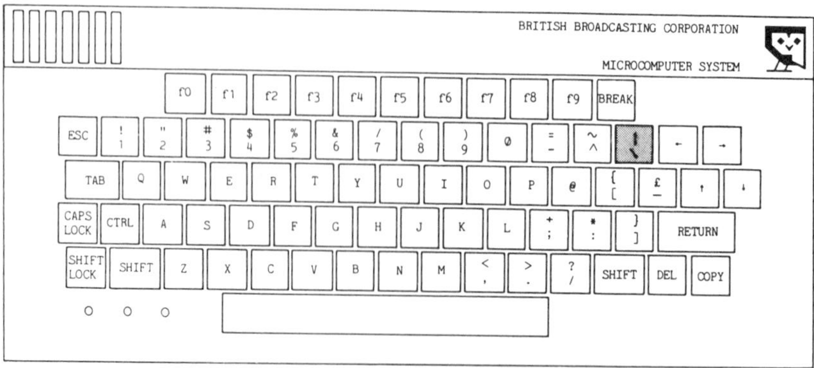

Figure 8.3. The pad character key.

words Wordwise and Plus we should use the pad character instead, thus

Wordwise¦Plus

Of course, we are not limited to using the pad character between two words; in fact we could use it to string a sentence of words together to ensure that the lines are not split, thus

Wordwise ¦ Plus ¦ rools ¦ okay

Obviously we can only fit so many words onto a single line, and this factor will be determined by the number of words already on the line and the length of the line as set by LL.

It is also quite legitimate to place more than one pad character after another, for example if we wished to ensure that the numbers

23   34   45   56

appear on the same line. Here there are four spaces between each number; simply use four pad characters instead:

23¦¦¦¦34¦¦¦¦45¦¦¦¦56

The ¦ key is the default pad character. It can, of course, be set to any other character you wish by redefining it with the embedded command PC, should you wish to use ¦ in your text. For example, to define the @ key as the pad character the following command should be embedded into your text:

<*f1*PC"@"*f2*>

Note that the @ is enclosed within quotes. These should be omitted on the standard Wordwise. The @ character can now be used as the pad character in the normal manner, i.e.

A@new@pad@character@is@now@in@use!

Calling the operating system

The operating system of the BBC Micro is often referred to as the Machine Operating System, MOS or OS if you prefer. The commands that are associated with it are recognised by the fact that they are preceded by an asterisk. Examples include

*TAPE
*DISC
*NET
*ROM

ROMs other than the MOS, but ROMs that are not language ROMs such as Wordwise, i.e. Caretaker and Toolkit, also contain asterisk-based commands. Any asterisk-based command can be accessed from within Wordwise Plus and later versions of Wordwise using the embedded command OS. For example, try the following in Edit Mode. Information about the contents of ROM sockets can normally be obtained with the *HELP command. To place this information into our text we could type the following sequence into Edit Mode:

I have the following ROMs in my BBC Micro:
<*f1*OS"HELP"*f2*>

Figure 8.4 shows what the preview or printout of this would show. In fact, Figure 8.4 was itself produced using the Computer Concepts Printmaster

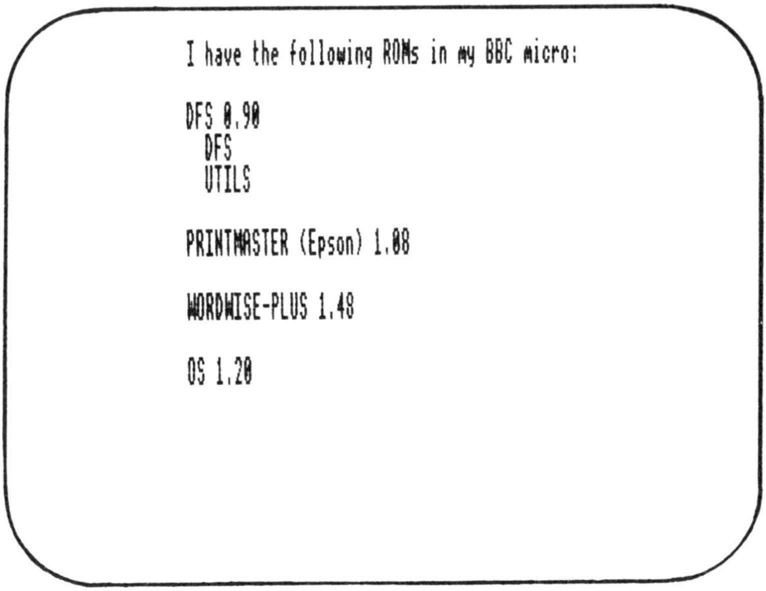

```
I have the following ROMs in my BBC micro:

DFS 0.90
  DFS
  UTILS

PRINTMASTER (Epson) 1.08

WORDWISE-PLUS 1.48

OS 1.20
```

Figure 8.4. Executing an operating system command from within Wordwise.

ROM simply by inserting an extra OS command, thus

<*f1*OS"GDUMP"*f2*>

where *GDUMP is the Printmaster command to dump the graphics screen to the printer!

You will have noticed that when passing a command to the MOS the asterisk is omitted; also the command is enclosed within quotes and should appear green in Edit Mode. Further points to bear in mind when using OS is that Wordwise Plus cannot keep track of the number of lines output while control is with the MOS, thus any paging will probably be ruined.

File by file

Wordwise includes two commands that allow you to use files stored on disc or cassette from within your current document. The commands are Get File and Print File; their corresponding embedded commands are, GF and PF. The two differ in that GF will simply read in the file while PF will read it in and act on any embedded command. I should clarify the term 'read-in' in this instance. The file in question is not read in and inserted into your text at the appropriate point – instead it is read straight from disc or cassette directly to your screen or printer.

The syntax of the two embedded commands is as follows:

<*f1*GF"FILE"*f2*>

<*f1*PF"FILE"*f2*>

As with the OS command, the filename FILE in the above examples should be enclosed within quotes and appear green in Edit Mode.

Let's try a couple of examples. Enter the following in Edit Mode:

These are the ROMs in my BBC Micro:
<*f1*OS"HELP"*f2*>

and save this on tape or disc using option 1 under the filename

HDEMO

Now delete this text and enter the following new text:

This is an example of the Get File command:
<*f1*GF"HDEMO"*f2*>

Ensure that the disc containing the file HDEMO is in the drive, or that your cassette tape has be rewound to just before the point where the file is saved. Now preview the text; Figure 8.5 shows roughly what you should get. As you can see the text including the OS"HELP" has been printed.

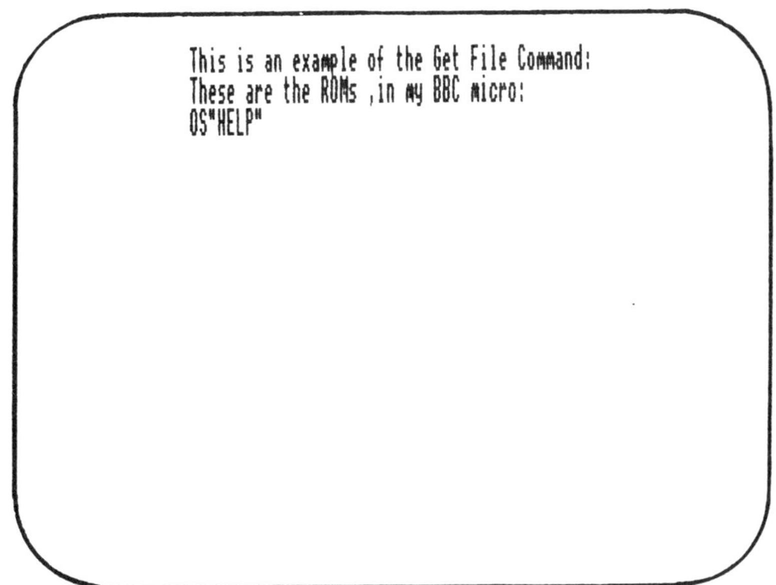

Figure 8.5. Implementing the GF command.

Now add the following text and commands so that Edit Mode contains this:

> This is and example of the Get File command:
> <*f1*GF"HDEMO"*f2*>
> This is an example of the Print File command:
> <*f1*PF"HDEMO"*f2*>

Previewing or printing this with options 6 or 7 will produce the output depicted in Figure 8.6. The Print File command has now actually been executed to present a list of the ROMs in my BBC Micro when the file was printed!

The Print File is of particular use when it comes to performing a repetitive task. For example, if you wished to mail all your friends with details of a forthcoming event, perhaps a party, you could have all your addresses on a Wordwise-compatible database, such as Beebugsoft's Masterfile, and simply read them in at the top of your letter ready for printing. Typically your Edit Mode text might run along the following lines:

```
<f1LM8f2 >
<f1LL60f2 >
<f1PF"ADDR1"f2 >


Hello mate!

Don't forget to come to my birthday party on the 25th
December will you?
```

The instructions to get here are as follows:

<f1PF"MAP1"f2 >

See you then!

Regards,

Bruce

The file MAP1 might be one of a series of MAP files that have directions from various points in town – the appropriate one can be edited in and printed depending on where the person is coming from.

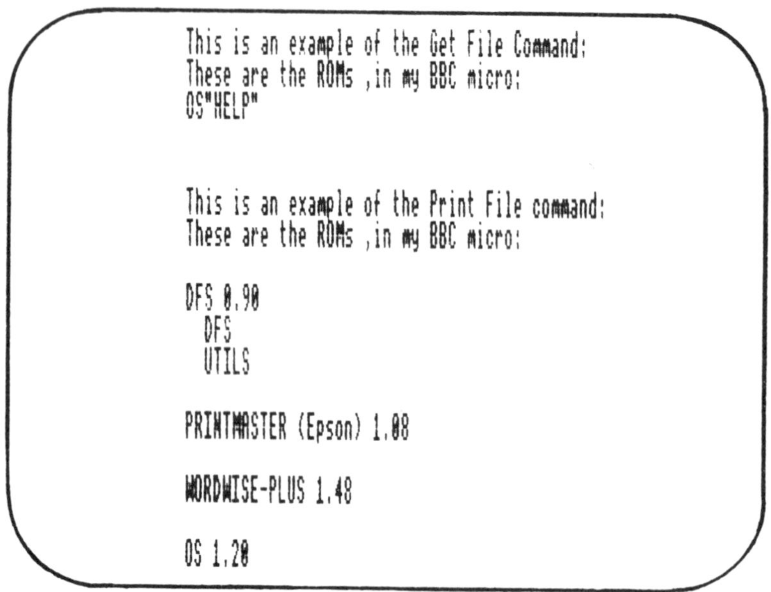

Figure 8.6. Implementing the PF command.

Pause for thought W+

The PAuse command, PA, is available in Wordwise Plus, and provides a useful way of stopping Wordwise Plus performing what it was doing, until such time as the space bar is pressed. This command can be simulated in later versions of the standard Wordwise which have the OS command implemented, simply by using the *FX call *FX138,0,32 thus:

<*f1*OS“FX138,0,32”*f2*>

Although you may not think so at first, the ability to cause Wordwise's actions to pause really is very useful. For example, you might wish to change sheets of paper during printing, or the colour of the printer ribbon, or even the daisywheel if you are using this type of printer. All you do is insert the OS command into the text, or Wordwise Plus users can insert the embedded command

<*f1*PA*f2*>

into the text at the appropriate point. On printing (or previewing), Wordwise will pause at the point at which it encounters this command, issuing a bleep. It will only recommence when you tap the space bar – you can do whatever you wish in the interim!

Strings and things W+

Wordwise Plus has many extra facilities other than 'standard' word processing commands. One of these extra facilities is the ability to use string variables within embedded command sequences. If you have even a small amount of Basic programming ability you will probably know exactly what a string variable is. A string variable, in the case of Wordwise Plus, is simply any single upper-case letter followed by a dollar sign. Examples include

A$, B$, C$

etc., twenty-six in all, i.e. A$ through to Z$. String variables are used to hold strings of characters, thus

W$="Wordwise Plus"

In the above example the character string "Wordwise Plus" has been placed 'into' W$, the string variable. Note that the character string is enclosed within quotes.

Many of the Wordwise Plus embedded commands allow you to use string variables as the argument to the command; the Reference Manual shows these. One such embedded command which depends solely on the use of string variables is the Print String command, PS. This command will simply insert the contents of the specified string variable into the text that is being previewed or printed. To see this in action return to the Menu Mode and type in at the keyboard

:W$="Wordwise Plus"

Don't forget the colon at the very beginning otherwise the keyboard will not accept what you wish to type. Figure 8.7 shows you what will appear on the screen. Now press <RETURN> after which you will be invited to 'Press any key'. Now return to Edit Mode and enter the following embedded command

<*f1*PS W$*f2*>

```
                WORDWISE-PLUS
      (C) Computer Concepts 1984

    1)  Save entire text
    2)  Load new text
    3)  Save marked text
    4)  Load text to cursor
    5)  Search and Replace
    6)  Print text
    7)  Preview text
    8)  Spool text
    9)  Segment menu

    ESC Edit Mode

   Please enter choice

   :W$="Wordwise Plus"
```

Figure 8.7. Assigning a string in Menu Mode.

Now preview or print your text. When Wordwise Plus encounters the command in the text it will insert the contents of W$ (Wordwise Plus in this case) into the text.

Wordwise Plus only allocates a total of 613 spaces within its workspace to hold all the string variables. This can be eaten up rather quickly if you are using them extensively within your text. If you try to define a string variable and the error message

No $ Room

is returned, then you have eaten up too much. You can find out just how many spaces are left for your character strings by entering the following while in Menu Mode:

:PRINT VARFREE <RETURN>

Remember to press the <RETURN> key at the end. Now Wordwise Plus will display the number of spaces free. If you try it after defining W$ as described above, then 597 should be returned. Try defining other strings and use PS to print them within your text. The maximum length of any string that can be placed into a string variable is 255 characters.

The only string variable you should steer clear of is P$, as this is used to hold the last filename that you used to save or load with. Try this in Edit Mode if you have loaded or saved since switching on:

The last filename you used was:
<*f1*PS P$*f2*>

You can clear the contents of any string variable simply by inserting a null string into it. To clear W$ you would type

:W$=""

in Menu Mode.

Variable variables W+

Many embedded commands within Wordwise Plus may also use numeric variables as their argument. A numeric variable is rather like a string variable, however it is used to hold a number rather than a character string. Like a string variable, a numeric variable consists of any single upper-case letter, but is followed by a percent sign thus:

A%,   X%,   S%

When you enter Wordwise Plus these numeric variables are all set to zero, but they can be made to hold any number in the range 0 to 65535. In other words, they can hold only positive numbers and none greater than 65535.

Numeric variables can be set in Menu Mode in a similar fashion:

:A%= 10<RETURN>

If A% was defined as above, it could be used, for instance, to set the indent thus:

<*f1*IN A%*f2*>

When the IN command is encountered the value of A% is taken as the number of characters for the indent!

In all, then, there are a possible twenty-six numeric variables. However, Wordwise Plus 'uses' two of these to store information so that it is easy to get at. W% is used to hold the current word count as displayed on the status line, and P% is used to hold the current page number when it is being printed, previewed or spooled.

Entering numeric and string variables in Menu Mode as described above is a long-winded approach. You'll be pleased to know that there is a much easier method using the segment menus, as we shall see in Part Two of this book.

Chapter Nine

A Key Function

If you have programmed in Basic at any time you will probably be aware that you can define the red function keys to perform certain tasks for you simply by pressing the appropriate function key. Try this in Basic to see what I mean. Type

*BASIC

to leave Wordwise and then type in the following line, pressing <RETURN> at the end of the line:

*KEY0 *WORDWISE ¦ M

What we have done is to place the command *WORDWISE into the function key *f0*. Now whenever we press *f0* it will have the same effect as if we had just typed in that particular command. Try it; press *f0* and you'll be switched into Wordwise straight away.

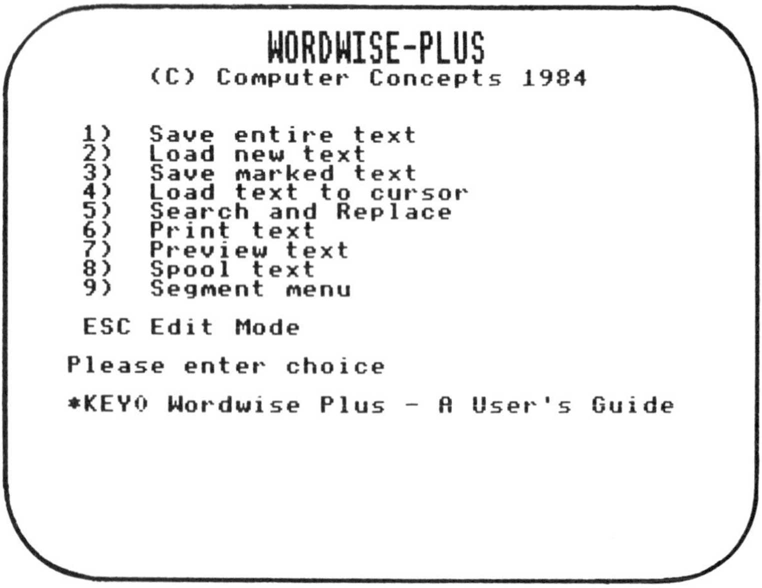

```
                 WORDWISE-PLUS
        (C) Computer Concepts 1984

   1)  Save entire text
   2)  Load new text
   3)  Save marked text
   4)  Load text to cursor
   5)  Search and Replace
   6)  Print text
   7)  Preview text
   8)  Spool text
   9)  Segment menu

   ESC Edit Mode

  Please enter choice

  *KEY0 Wordwise Plus - A User's Guide
```

Figure 9.1. Defining a function key can be performed in Menu Mode.

Wordwise uses the function keys to allow us to use many of the word processing facilities marked on the function keystrip. However, despite this it is still possible to program the function keys for our own use. Now that you are in Wordwise Menu Mode enter the following:

*KEY1 Wordwise Plus – A User's Guide

Quite a long one this. Note that the ¦ and M are not included at the end of this definition, but don't forget <RETURN> at the end. Figure 9.1 shows the Menu Mode screen at this stage. Now <ESCAPE> to the Edit Mode and hold SHIFT and CTRL down together; then press *f1* and release all the keys together. As all the keys are pressed together the string typed 'into' *f1* a moment ago will appear on the screen as shown in Figure 9.2. Therefore to get at any text or commands placed into the function keys we must hold down SHIFT and CTRL together and then press the appropriate function key. This facility is available only in Edit Mode and will not work in Menu Mode.

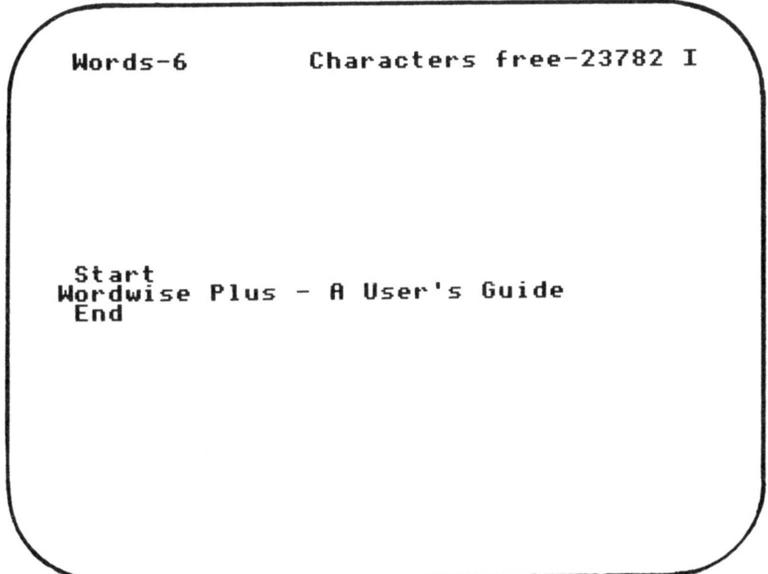

Figure 9.2. Pressing *f1* in Edit Mode inserts the key string.

Key commands

The programmability of the function keys allows us to program embedded command sequences into the function keys for use. Thus commands which are longish or tedious to type in can be available from a single (well, triple!) keypress. Take underlined text, for example. On Epson-compatible printers this is obtained with the embedded command OC27,52 and cancelled with OC27,53 on the standard Wordwise or with US and UE on Wordwise Plus.

Let us take the former example for the time being, as it is somewhat longer to type and serves as a good typical example for all Wordwise commands. <ESCAPE> to Menu Mode and type

*KEY7 OC27,52
*KEY8 OC27,53

As you press <RETURN> at the end of each line, Wordwise will prompt you to 'Press any key'. Use the space bar for this purpose and then enter the next command. Function keys *f7* and *f8* have now been programmed with the OC commands. Once this has been done return to Edit Mode and type as follows:

<*f1*><SHIFT-CTRL-*f7*><*f2*>
This text is underlined
<*f1*><SHIFT-CTRL-*f8*><*f1*>
This text is not underlined

As you can see, the command typing time has been drastically reduced since the OC string is entered with a single keystroke!

However, each embedded command still requires three actions to enter it; these are

<*f1*>
<SHIFT-CTRL-*fn*>
<*f2*>

It would be nice if the *f1* and *f2* key actions could also be included in the one CTRL-SHIFT-*fn* sequence. Well they can, for now I'll tell you that *f1* and *f2* are obtained as follows:

f1=¦!!
f2=¦!"

The reasoning behind these somewhat weird key combinations will be revealed shortly. So, combining the three actions into a single command, the *KEY lines to obtain and cancel underlined text become

```
*KEY7 ¦!!OC27,52¦!"
*KEY8 ¦!!OC27,53¦!"
```

Now go back to Edit Mode, and the earlier example becomes

<SHIFT-CTRL-*f7*>
This text is underlined
<SHIFT-CTRL-*f8*>
And this text is not!

The code

How did I obtain the code to generate the *f1* and *f2* keys above? The answer is that each of the function keys, and indeed each of the keyboard keys, has a code number associated with it. To generate this code number it is necessary to add several keys together. For example, if I wanted to obtain the number 15 and I could use only single digit numbers in the range 1 to 9, one way would be to add the following together:

9+1+5=15

Now if 15 represented the character @, and 9, 1 and 5 were represented by the letters A, B and C we could say that

A+B+C=@

The value of the key *f1* is 161; to obtain this we add the characters ¦ and ! and ! together. The values of these characters are

¦ ! = 128
! = 33

Adding 128 to 33 gives 161, the code for *f1*. 33 is the ASCII code for "!" and 128 is ¦!. Likewise *f2* has the code 162. To obtain this we can subtract 128 (as we know this is ¦!) to leave 34. The character with the ASCII code 34 is " (see Appendix C), therefore the key stroke is

¦!"

Rather than having to sit down and work out the codes for each of the keys as you need them I have done the work for you and placed them in Table 9.1. for ease of reference.

Clever clogs

Now if you want to be clever you can even make up your own command strings to perform tasks that you would like to do regularly. Here are a few examples.

There is no Wordwise command that will generate a new paragraph for you with a single key press. How you start your own paragraphs is a matter of style; I like to use the following sequence

RETURN
RETURN
<*f1*TI4*f2*>

Each paragraph starts off indented by four characters. Convert each keystoke into key strings by referring to Table 9.1 and we have:

RETURN = ¦M
RETURN = ¦M
<*f1*TI4*f2*>= ¦!!TI4¦!”

Key	Code	Key string	Key	Code	Key string
f0	160	¦! (SPACE)	CTRL-←	156	¦!¦\
f1	161	¦!!	CTRL-→	157	¦!¦}
f2	162	¦!”	CTRL-↓	158	¦!¦^
f3	163	¦!#	CTRL-↑	159	¦!¦_
f4	164	¦!$			
f5	165	¦!%	SHIFT-←	140	¦!¦L
f6	166	¦!&	SHIFT-→	141	¦!¦M
f7	167	¦!’	SHIFT-↓	142	¦!¦N
f8	168	¦!(	SHIFT-↑	143	¦!¦O
f9	169	¦!)			
←	172	¦!,	CTRL-A	1	¦A
→	173	¦!-	CTRL-S	19	¦S
↓	174	¦!.	CTRL-D	4	¦D
↑	175	¦!/			
TAB	9	¦I	ESC	27	¦[
RETURN	13	¦M			

Table 9.1. Control codes for the various Wordwise control keys.

So placing this in *f0* we arrive at the command line

```
*KEY0 ¦M¦M¦!!TI4¦!"
```

Being able to delete a line of text is useful. It would be nice if you could move to the line you wished to delete, press a function key and have the line removed for you. We could do this by moving to each end of the line, inserting a marker at each end and then deleting the marked text. Normally we would do this with:

<SHIFT←>
<*f3*>
<SHIFT→>
<*f3*>
<*f7*>

Refering to Table 9.1 we obtain:

<SHIFT←> = ¦!¦L
<*f3*> = ¦!#
<SHIFT→> = ¦!¦M
<*f3*> = ¦!#
<*f7*> = ¦!’

Putting it all together into *f9* we obtain:

```
*KEY9 ¦!¦L¦!#¦!¦M!#¦!'
```

This could be adapted slightly to copy the current line to the bottom of your text thus:

<SHIFT←> = ¦!¦L
<*f3*> = ¦!#
<SHIFT→> = ¦!¦M
<*f3*> = ¦!#
<SHIFT↓> = ¦!¦N
<*f9*> = ¦!)

Putting this into *f8* would give:

```
*KEY8 ¦!¦L¦!#¦!¦M¦!#¦!¦N¦!)
```

Being able to delete text to the end of the line from the current cursor position is useful; the following definition does just this:

```
*KEY5 ¦!#¦!¦M¦!#¦!'¦!¦M
```

Disassembling this we obtain:

¦!# = <*f3*>
¦!¦M = <SHIFT→>
¦!# = <*f3*>
¦!' = <*f7*>
¦!¦M = <SHIFT→>

This works by placing a marker at the current cursor position, moving to the end of the line, inserting a marker and then deleting the marked text.

Wordwise Plus allows the use of CTRL-R to remove markers from text; there is no such facility in the standard Wordwise. However, a little thought allows the problem to be solved with the aid of a function key definition thus:

<SHIFT↑> – Move to top of text
<*f4*> – Cursor to?
<*f3*> – Marker
CTRL-A> – Delete character above cursor
<*f4*> – Cursor to?
<*f3*> – Marker
CTRL-A> – Delete character above cursor

This returns the key definition:

```
*KEY4 ¦!¦O¦!$¦!#¦A¦!$¦!#¦A
```

The drawback here is that the cursor is moved from its current position to the position of the last marker. One way around this would be to leave a DIY marker, perhaps an @, and then return to this after the removal of the markers with *f4*. The revised key definition would become:

```
*KEY4 ¦!¦O¦!$¦!#¦A¦!$¦!#¦A¦!¦O¦!$@
```

This also includes a <SHIFT↑> to ensure that it will work should the cursor have been positioned later in the text than the markers. If you wish to use a DIY marker other than @, simply change the last character in the key string above to the one you wish to use.

Another way of removing markers, albeit more complex, is

```
*KEY4 @@¦!¦O¦!$¦!#¦A¦!$¦!$#¦A¦!¦O¦[5G@@¦M¦M¦[
```

The @@ in this definition is used as a place marker but is deleted at the end by using a global search with menu option 5. See if you can work through this one and fathom out how it works! If you are having trouble, remember that you can switch between Edit and Menu Mode through <ESCAPE> which is generated with [with the function keys.

As you can see, there is a lot you can do with the function keys. If there is a particular action you want, first sit down and decide how you would achieve it without using the key strings and then use Table 9.1 to convert it into a key string!

Removing the tedium

Defining key strings is fine providing you don't have to redefine them every time you want to use Wordwise. The thought of spending ten minutes at the start of every word processing session to type in awkward key strings that make you go boss-eyed is not very appealing. There is an easier method, however – make Wordwise do the work for you!

Having worked out exactly what you wish your key definitions to hold, switch to a clean Edit Mode; there should be no text or embedded commands present at all. Now type in your key definitions one by one. Each key definition should start on a new line and be terminated by a single RETURN. I like to set up my own function keys in the following manner:

f0 – New paragraph
f1 – Double-sized characters on
f2 – Double-sized characters off
f3 – Underlining on
f4 – Underlining off
f5 – Emphasised printing on
f6 – Emphasised printing off
f7 – Italic printing on
f8 – Italic printing off
f9 – Delete line
f11 – Remove markers

You can see that I have included an extra function key, *f11* in my definition. The red function keys, *f0* to *f9* are at the top of the keyboard, however there are an additional five function keys defined as follows:

f10 – BREAK
f11 – COPY
f12 – left arrow
f13 – right arrow
f14 – down arrow
f15 – up arrow

These keys, *except* for the BREAK key *f10*, can all be used to hold key strings for use in combination with SHIFT-CTRL. Figure 9.3 shows their position on the keyboard.

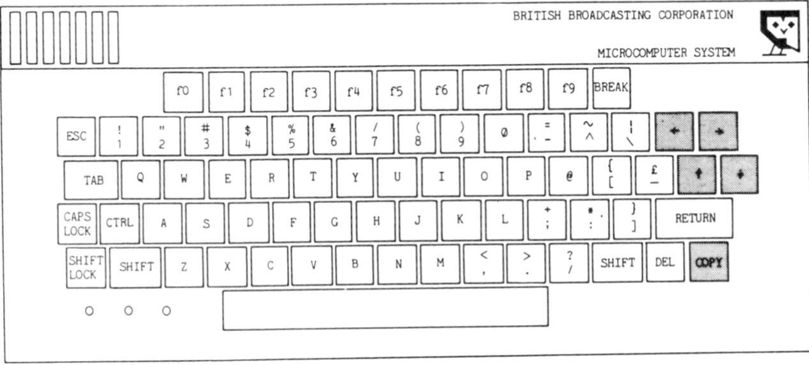

Figure 9.3. Function keys *f11* to *f15*.

To define the keys as I suggest above, type the following in Edit Mode:

```
*KEY0 |M|M|!!TI4|!"
*KEY1 |!!OC14|!"
*KEY2 |!!OC20|!"
*KEY3 |!!OC27,45,1|!"
*KEY4 |!!OC27,45,0|!"
*KEY5 |!!OC27,69|!"
*KEY6 |!!OC27,70|!"
*KEY7 |!!OC27,52|!"
*KEY8 |!!OC27,53|!"
*KEY9 |!|L|!#|!|M|!#|!"
*KEY11 |!|O|!$|!#|A|!$|!#|A|!|O|!$@
```

Figure 9.4 shows how the Edit Mode screen should look at this stage. These key definitions will work on both Wordwise Plus and the standard Wordwise. Of course, you could adapt them to take advantage of the new embedded commands in Wordwise Plus if you wish.

```
Words-33          Characters free-23570 I
Start

*KEY0  |M|M|!!TI4|!"
*KEY1  |!!OC14|!"
*KEY2  |!!OC20|!"
*KEY3  |!!OC27,45,1|!"
*KEY4  |!!OC27,45,0|!"
*KEY5  |!!OC27,69|!"
*KEY6  |!!OC27,70|!"
*KEY7  |!!OC27,52|!"
*KEY8  |!!OC27,53|!"
*KEY9  |!|L|!#|!|M|!#|!"
*KEY11 |!|O|!$|!#|A|!$|!#|A|!|O|!$@
End
```

Figure 9.4. The function key definitions displayed in Menu Mode.

The next thing to do is to save these key definitions to tape or disc using option 1 on the main menu; use a suitable filename such as KEYS. Each time you switch on Wordwise the first thing to do is to execute these commands stored on tape or disc as an ASCII file. To do this enter Menu Mode and type in the command

*EXEC KEYS

or more simply

*E. KEYS

As the file loads from tape or disc it will set up the function keys as already described. To see that it works switch into Edit Mode and then go through pressing CTRL-SHIFT with each of the function keys in turn. Should you wish to change or edit the function keys' actions at any stage you can do this simply by using option 2 on the menu to load in the text file!

Now that you have set up your function keys for additional action it is worth making up a keystrip to place under the keystrip plastic at the top of your micro. In Appendix D you'll find such a keystrip that you can cut out and use directly, replacing your existing one. There is also a blank version should you wish to change the definitions. If you do not wish to cut the book then you could obtain a photocopy of the page in question.

Chapter Ten
Wordwise Utilities

In this chapter I'll be presenting three utility programs that I have found invaluable when using Wordwise and Wordwise Plus. The programs are as follows:

1. Catalogue : details the contents of each Wordwise text file if it has been suitably commented.
2. Memory Dump : allows you to restore part of an accidentally deleted file.
3. Keystrip : allows you to print your own customised function keystrips.

Catalogue

The problem with saving text files on disc is that you are limited to a measly 7 characters for the filename of your document. Filenames such as LETTER1, LETTER2, MEMOCC, although meaningful to you at the time of saving the file, creep into oblivion as the days pass by. Then a week or two later you find that you cannot remember what name you gave to what file, and the only way you can locate what you want is to load each file in turn until you come across it! Of course, purists will say that you should keep a list of the contents of each file on a disc – but I'm a sinner in this respect, as are the majority of people, I suspect!

When run, the Catalogue program will look at each file on the disc in the specified drive and, in particular, at the very first line in the file. If this line conforms to a special format comment line it will display the file's name, the comment itself and the length of the file. If the file does not contain a comment it will ignore the file. The comment itself can be up to a line in length, which should be more than enough space to place a more detailed description of the file contents. In addition, Catalogue will allow you to enter directly into Wordwise either with or without defining the function keys.

Figure 10.1 shows the screen output for the file comments. Each file is given its full directory filename in addition to a file number. This is followed by the comment line itself and finally the length of the file to the nearest

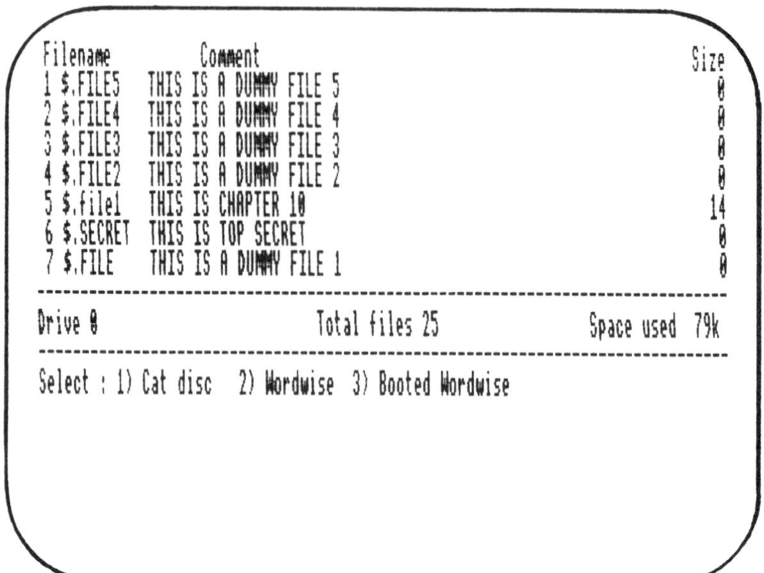

Figure 10.1. Files are clearly distinguishable using the CAT program.

kilobyte. In addition, the total number of files and the space used on the disc are supplied.

Inserting a COmment into a file is quite simple and makes use of the pseudo embedded command CO. The comment must be specified on the *very first* line of the document, which should include no other embedded

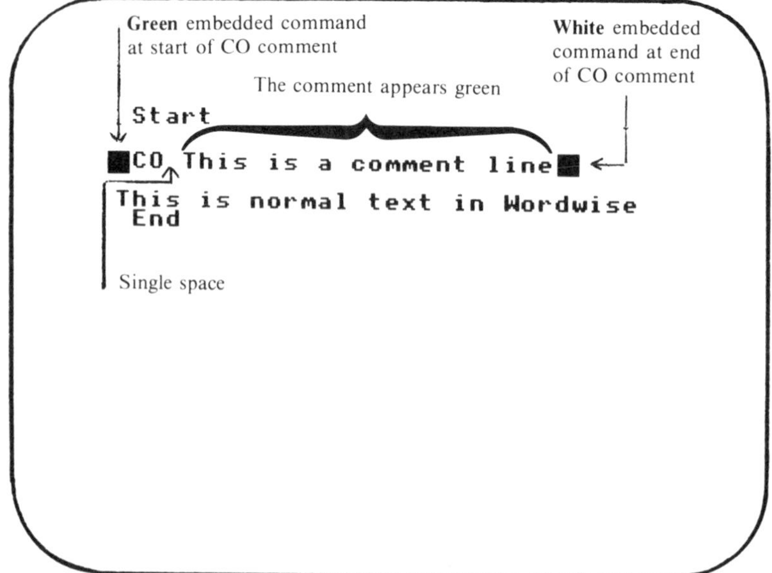

Figure 10.2. How a COmment line should be set up.

commands. It *must* also start at the front of the line; ideally, it is worth inserting a couple of <RETURN>s after the comment line. The following syntax is used to insert a comment:

<*f1*CO This is the comment line *f2*>

Figure 10.2 shows how this might appear on the Edit Mode screen; note that the comment itself should be separated from CO by a space and that it appears in green. The comment line will be ignored when previewing or printing text. Other than inserting the comment line there is nothing else to do to your files; simply use them as normal. Once again I would stress that for CAT to work correctly the first three bytes in your document must be:

f1 , C, and O

This is because the CAT program looks for these three characters in the first three bytes of the file. In case you're wondering, the *f1* is stored as the number 2 in the file.

Listing 10.1 provides the Catalogue program which is written in Basic.

```
 10 REM Wordwise Boot Menu
 20 REM (c) Bruce Smith
 30 REM Wordwise/Wordwise Plus
 40 REM WW+ A User's Guide
 50 :
 60 ON ERROR GOTO 1380
 70 MODE 3
 80 DIM buffer% 50,B%&200,catalogue&50
 90 oscli%=&FFF7
100 *FX18
110 *FX12
120 D%=0
130 :
140 PROCscreen
150 PROCassemble
160 CALLcatalogue
170 PROCreadblk
180 PROCdisplay
190 PROCselect
200 IF key=49 THEN RUN
210 IF key=50 THEN *WORDWISE
220 PROCexec
230 END
240 :
250 DEF PROCdisplay
260 PROCoscli("DR."+STR$(D%))
270 @%=2
```

Listing 10.1. The CAT program.

```
  280 number%=0
  290 size%=0
  300 PRINT
  310 FOR N%=0 TO E%-1
  320 filesize%=OPENUP filename$(N%)
  330 size%=size%+EXT#filesize%
  340 byteone%=BGET#filesize%
  350 bytetwo%=BGET#filesize%:bytethree%=
BGET#filesize%
  360 IF byteone%=2 AND bytetwo%=ASC"C" A
ND bytethree%=ASC"O"  THEN PROCprint
  370 CLOSE #filesize%
  380 NEXT
  390 PRINT STRING$(79,"-")'"Drive ";D%;
  400 PRINTTAB(32)"Total files ";E% TAB(6
3)"Space used  ";(size%+500)DIV1000;"k"
  410 CLOSE#0
  420 PRINTSTRING$(79,"-")
  430 ENDPROC
  440 :
  450 DEF PROCscreen
  460 CLS
  470 PRINTTAB(28,3)"Wordwise Boot Menu"
  480 PRINTTAB(28,4);STRING$(18,"-")
  490 PRINTTAB(26,8)"1) Catalogue of File
s"
  500 PRINTTAB(26,10)"2) Booted Wordwise"
  510 PRINTTAB(26,12)"3) Wordwise"
  520 PRINTTAB(28,15)"which option ... ";
  530 K%=GET
  540 IF K%=51 THEN *WORDWISE
  550 IF K%=50 THEN PROCexec:END
  560 PRINTTAB(24,8)SPC(5)"Catalogue of F
iles"
  570 PRINTTAB(29,9)STRING$(18,"_")
  580 PRINTTAB(24,10)SPC(20)
  590 PRINTTAB(29,11)"Current drive"SPC(4
);D%;
  600 PRINTTAB(24,12)SPC(20)
  610 PRINTTAB(28,15)SPC(20)
  620 PRINTTAB(23,13)SPC(6)"New drive"SPC
(8);
  630 drive%=GET-48
  640 IF drive%>-1 AND drive%<4 THEN D%=d
rive%:PRINT;D%:PROCoscli("DR."+STR$(D%))E
LSE PRINT;D%
```

Listing 10.1 (contd)

```
  650 PRINTTAB(25,21)"~~ compiling  catal
ogue ~~"
  660 ENDPROC
  670 :
  680 DEF PROCselect
  690 PRINT"Select : 1) Cat disc   2) Wor
dwise  3) Booted Wordwise"
  700 key=GET
  710 ENDPROC
  720 :
  730 DEF PROCoscli(cline$)
  740 $buffer%=cline$
  750 X%=buffer%
  760 Y%=buffer% DIV 256
  770 CALL oscli%
  780 ENDPROC
  790 :
  800 DEF PROCassemble
  810 osword=&FFF1
  820 FOR pass=0 TO 2 STEP 2
  830 P%=catalogue
  840 [OPT pass
  850 LDA #&7F
  860 LDX #blk MOD 256
  870 LDY #blk DIV 256
  880 JMP osword
  890 .blk
  900 ]
  910 ?P%=D%
  920 P%!1=B%
  930 P%?5=3
  940 P%?6=&53
  950 P%?7=0
  960 P%?8=0
  970 P%?9=&22
  980 P%?10=0
  990 NEXT
 1000 ENDPROC
 1010 :
 1020 DEF PROCreadblk
 1030 E%=(B%?&105)/8
 1040 DIM filename$(E%-1)
 1050 FOR N%=0 TO E%-1
 1060 FOR Y%=0 TO 6
 1070 filename$(N%)=filename$(N%)+CHR$(B%
?(Y%+8*(N%+1)))
```

Listing 10.1 (contd)

```
 1080 NEXT
 1090 G%=B%?(Y%+8*(N%+1))
 1100 IF G%>127 THEN G%=G% AND &7F
 1110 filename$(N%)=CHR$(G%)+"."+filename
$(N%)
 1120 NEXT
 1130 ENDPROC
 1140 :
 1150 DEF PROCprint
 1160 IF number%=0 THEN PROCheading
 1170 filename$(number%)=filename$(N%)
 1180 PRINT number%+1 TAB(3)filename$(num
ber%)TAB(13);
 1190 PTR#filesize%=PTR#filesize%+1
 1200 FOR C%=1 TO 63
 1210 byteone%=BGET#filesize%
 1220 IF byteone%=13 THEN C%=64 ELSE PRIN
T CHR$(byteone%);
 1230 NEXT
 1240 PRINTTAB(77)(EXT#filesize%+500)DIV
1000
 1250 number%=number%+1
 1260 IF number%=20 THEN VDU7:PRINT'".. A
NY key to CONTINUE ..":IF GET THEN VDU11:
PRINTSPC(27):VDU11,11
 1270 ENDPROC
 1280 :
 1290 DEF PROCheading
 1300 CLS
 1310 PRINT" Filename"SPC(10)"Comment"SPC
(49)"Size"
 1320 ENDPROC
 1330 :
 1340 DEF PROCexec
 1350 *EXEC KEYS
 1360 ENDPROC
 1370 :
 1380 ON ERROR OFF
 1390 CLOSE#0
 1400 MODE 7
 1410 REPORT:PRINT" at line ";ERL
 1420 *FX12
 1430 END
```

Listing 10.1 (contd)

Using Catalogue

Once you have typed in Catalogue save it to a newly formatted disc using the command

SAVE "CAT"

It's a good idea to mark your disc

WORDWISE UTILITIES

I tend to place CAT on each of my Wordwise text file discs as well so that they become quite easy to use.

Now you must create a !BOOT file on your disc. To do this ensure that your disc is in the logged on drive (drive 0 probably) and type

*BUILD !BOOT

*BUILD is a command that is included in the Disc Filing System and will be there whether you are using the Acorn DFS or any other make. Once you have typed in this command the disc will whirl and you will be prompted with a number as follows:

```
*BUILD !BOOT
 1
```

Some DFSs will include leading zeros. Directly after the 1 type

CHAIN "CAT"

The screen will look like this:

```
*BUILD !BOOT
 1 CHAIN "CAT"
```

Now press <RETURN>, after which line number 2 will be displayed. At this stage press <ESCAPE>. Once more the disc will whirl in the drive and the Basic prompt will reappear. Now type

*OPT 4,3

Again the disc drive will come to life.

In creating a !BOOT file we have now made it very easy to chain in our CAT program simply by pressing the SHIFT and BREAK keys together. However, before you try this, switch into Wordwise and create two or three text files for the CAT program, using a comment line at the top. In fact, the files can simply be comment lines if you so wish. Save each one to your disc in turn using different filenames for each.

The next stage is to transfer the KEYS program presented in Chapter 9. You should have this saved safely on disc so load it in using option 2. Move the cursor to the bottom of the key definitions and add the following two lines of text:

*FX202,176,79
*WORDWISE

Now save the file to your utilities disc, using option 1, under the filename KEYS.

The CAT program is now ready to use. First switch to Basic by typing *BASIC or pressing CTRL-BREAK. Now with the disc in the drive hold down the SHIFT key and then press BREAK, after which you can release both keys together. The drive will come to life and will CHAIN in the CAT program. The screen will clear and present you with the three options shown in Figure 10.3.

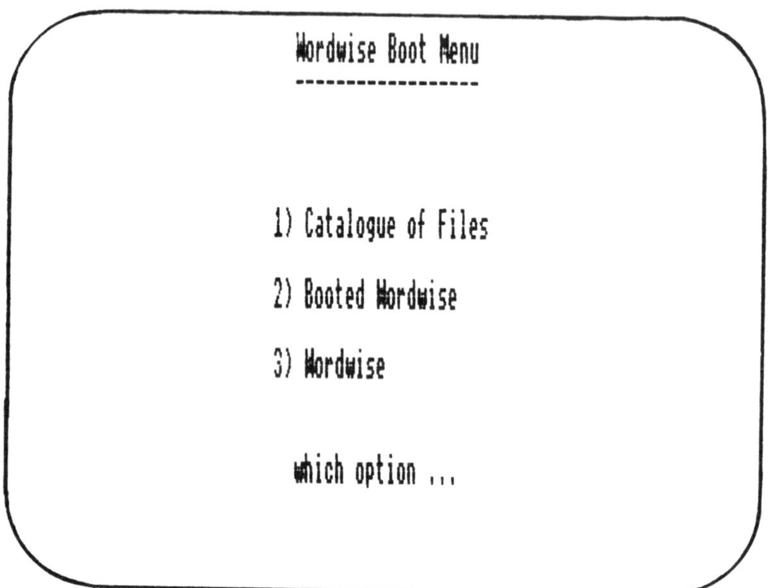

Figure 10.3. The CAT program supplies three options.

The function of each option is as follows:

1) Lists any comment files found in Wordwise files.
2) Performs *EXEC KEYS, entering Wordwise and setting up the function keys as described in Chapter 9. In addition the extra *FX call inserted will switch the keys so they will produce lower-case letters and SHIFT will give upper-case characters.
3) Performs *WORDWISE, and does not define function keys.

Selecting options 2 or 3 will execute them directly. If you select option 1 you will be asked to specify the disc drive that you wish to catalogue. Enter 0,1,2 or 3 as required.

Line by line

You should be able to adapt the CAT program to suit your own requirements without too much trouble. To help, a description of the program follows.

Line 60 : Set up error handling
Line 70 : Screen display is performed in Mode 3
Lines 80 to 120 : Set up arrays and variables
Line 140 : Select option
Line 150 : Set up OSWORD parameter block
Line 160 : Read disc catalogue
Line 170 : Read parameter block
Line 180 : Display options
Line 190 : Get option choice
Line 200 : If 1 then reRUN
Line 210 : If 2 then enter Wordwise
Line 220 : If 3 then *EXEC KEYS
Line 230 : End of program
Line 250 : Start of PROCdisplay
Line 260 : Select drive
Lines 270 to 300 : Set variables
Line 310 : File reading loop
Line 320 : Get size of current file
Line 330 : Update total space used
Line 340 : Read first file byte
Line 350 : Read second and third bytes of file
Line 360 : Are the first three bytes 2, "C" and "O"? If so, goto PROCprint
Line 370 : Close current file
Line 380 : Do next file
Lines 390 to 420 : Print disc details
Line 430 : End of procedure
Line 450 : Start of PROCscreen
Lines 460 to 520 : Print options on screen
Line 530 : Get option choice
Line 540 : If 2 then select Wordwise
Line 550: If 3 then do *EXEC KEYS
Lines 560 to 630 : Get choice of drive to catalogue
Line 640 : Select drive
Line 650 : Issue compiling message
Line 660 : End of procedure
Lines 680 to 710 : Post catalogue option selection routine.
Lines 730 to 780 : Simulates OSCLI for Basic I users
Lines 800 to 1000 : Define catalogue reading OSWORD parameter block.
Lines 1020 to 1130 : Read each filename from parameter block.

Lines 1150 to 1270 : Read each comment line from each commented file and print it to the screen.
Lines 1340 to 1360 : Perform *EXEC KEYS
Lines 1380 to 1430 : Error handling routine.

Memory dump

I can say with all certainty that there will come a time when you accidentally delete the text you are currently working on from Wordwise, supposedly losing it forever. The chances of this happening using Wordwise Plus are somewhat less than with the standard Wordwise, as it is only likely to happen if you load new text by accident. Whatever the cause this following utility will be of great comfort, as it allows you to locate your Wordwise text in memory so that you can resave it ready for reloading into Wordwise.

When you type text into Wordwise it stores each character in memory. If you should accidentally lose this for some reason, your text is not erased from memory; it is simply that Wordwise has reset its pointers so that it has no idea where the text is. If, on the other hand, you happen to load in new text, it is quite probable that the new text will be placed over the old 'lost' text. If this is the case you can only hope that the new text is considerably shorter than the old text so that you can at least restore some of the former text – which will save you some retyping.

Listing 10.2 shows the DUMP program which is written mainly in assembly language – though a knowledge of machine code programming is definitely not required. Just type in the program as you see it. If you make

```
   10 REM Wordwise Restore
   20 REM by Bruce Smith
   30 REM Wordwise Plus
   40 REM A User's Guide
   50 :
   60 address=&70
   70 lines=73
   80 oswrch=&FFEE
   90 FOR pass=0 TO 3 STEP 3
  100 P%=&C00
  110 [OPT pass
  120 LDA #22
  130 JSR &FFEE
  140 LDA #7
  150 JSR &FFEE
  160 LDA #24
  170 STA lines
  180 LDA &18
```

Listing 10.2. The DUMP program.

```
190 STA address+1
200 LDA #0
210 STA address
220 :
230 .memory_dump
240 JSR address_print
250 :
260 .hex_bytes
270 LDX #7
280 LDY #0
290 :
300 .hex_loop
310 LDA(address),Y
320 JSR hexprint
330 JSR space
340 INY
350 DEX
360 BPL hex_loop
370 JSR space
380 :
390 .asçii_bytes
400 LDX #7
410 LDY #0
420 :
430 .ascii_loop
440 LDA(address),Y
450 CMP #&20
460 BMI full_stop
470 CMP #&80
480 BCC leap_frog
490 :
500 .full_stop
510 LDA #ASC"."
520 :
530 .leap_frog
540 JSR oswrch
550 INY
560 DEX
570 BPL ascii_loop
580 LDA #13
590 JSR &FFE3
600 CLC
610 LDA address
620 ADC #8
630 STA address
```

Listing 10.2 (contd)

```
 640 BCC no_carry
 650 INC address+1
 660 :
 670 .no_carry
 680 DEC lines
 690 BNE memory_dump
 700 JSR &FFE0
 710 CMP #27
 720 BEQ escape
 730 LDA #23
 740 STA lines
 750 JMP memory_dump
 760 :
 770 .escape
 780 LDA #&7E
 790 JSR &FFF4
 800 RTS
 810 :
 820 .space
 830 LDA #32
 840 JMP oswrch
 850 :
 860 .address_print
 870 LDX #address
 880 LDA 1,X
 890 JSR hexprint
 900 LDA 0,X
 910 JSR hexprint
 920 JSR space
 930 JSR space
 940 RTS
 950 :
 960 .hexprint
 970 PHA
 980 LSR A : LSR A
 990 LSR A : LSR A
1000 JSR first
1010 PLA
1020 :
1030 .first
1040 AND #&0F
1050 CMP #10
1060 BCC over
1070 ADC #6
1080 :
```

Listing 10.2 (contd)

```
1090 .over
1100 ADC #48
1110 JMP oswrch
1120 ] NEXT
1130 :
1140 A%=0
1150 FOR N%=&C00 TO &C98
1160 A%=A%+?N%
1170 NEXT
1180 IF A%<>16338 PRINT"Checksum error"
:END
1190 *SAVE WDUMP C00 C99 C00
```

Listing 10.2 (contd)

any errors these will be reported. If, after running, the program gives the message

Checksum error

recheck the listing carefully. Once the program has run correctly it will automatically save the machine code it generates onto your Wordwise utilities disc or cassette tape, which should be positioned appropriately. The filename used is WDUMP. You should now save the program listing itself using the filename DUMP.

It is well worth a practise run with the program at this stage, so that you have an idea how to use the program when you need to do so at a later date. If you are using the standard Wordwise, just enter a couple of lines of distinctive text in Edit Mode, then press <BREAK> and type N in response to the prompt

Old text? (Y/N)

Users of Wordwise Plus might find it useful to enter a couple of words in Edit Mode and then save these using option 1. Now delete the text and enter a few lines of new text. Now reload the original couple of words from tape or disc using option 2. In both cases the aim is to restore the original text.

In the demonstration that follows I have entered the following text into Wordwise Plus:

> This is some text that I have typed into Wordwise Plus as part of the *WDUMP demonstration program. Now I will accidentally load in a new, but shorter file over it to show how some text can be restored!

The file that was subsequently loaded over consisted of a single word – MISTAKE!

A dry run

The first thing to do or rather not to do when you 'lose' some text is to panic! First locate the disc or tape with the WDUMP routine on it. Then return to Basic by typing

*BASIC

Once the familiar prompt appears run the machine code of WDUMP. If you are using disc this can be performed simply by typing the command

*WDUMP

Tape users will need to use

*RUN WDUMP

Once the machine code has loaded, the screen will clear to show a row of numbers, as illustrated in Figure 10.4. The left-hand column is the memory address currently being displayed. This will be the address of PAGE, which on my micro is &1900 – yours may be different. After the line address follow eight memory bytes – their contents are expressed in hexadecimal notation. After this follow a further eight characters. If the memory contents are ASCII characters then these bytes will show the ASCII characters, otherwise a full-stop will be shown.

At present the screen display shows 24 lines of memory; pressing the space bar once will display the next 23 lines of memory. The idea is to keep

```
1900  0D FF 00 00 00 00 00 00   ........
1908  00 00 00 00 00 00 00 00   ........
1910  00 00 00 00 00 00 00 00   ........
1918  00 00 00 00 00 00 00 00   ........
1920  00 00 00 00 00 00 00 00   ........
1928  00 00 00 00 00 00 00 00   ........
1930  00 00 00 00 00 00 00 00   ........
1938  00 00 00 00 00 00 00 00   ........
1940  00 00 00 00 00 00 00 00   ........
1948  00 00 00 00 00 00 00 00   ........
1950  00 00 00 00 00 00 00 00   ........
1958  00 00 00 00 00 00 00 00   ........
1960  00 00 00 00 00 00 00 00   ........
1968  00 00 00 00 00 00 00 00   ........
1970  00 00 00 00 00 00 00 00   ........
1978  00 00 00 00 00 00 00 00   ........
1980  00 00 00 00 00 00 00 00   ........
1988  00 00 00 00 00 00 00 00   ........
1990  00 00 00 00 00 00 00 00   ........
1998  00 00 00 00 00 00 00 00   ........
19A0  00 00 00 00 00 00 00 00   ........
```

Figure 10.4. *WDUMP – a typical first screen.

displaying memory until you come across your text. Figure 10.5 shows this in the case of Wordwise Plus. Ignore the SEG..ENDSEG sequences if you are using Wordwise Plus; we require to look at the end of these for the familiar 'Start'. This can be clearly seen in the tenth line of the dump. The important thing to do now is to note where the very first letter we wish to save is located. In this case it is the letter 's' from 'some' in line 11. The address of this letter must be calculated (it is &1DDE) and noted.

```
1D78   36 0D 0D 81 45 4E 44 53   6...ENDS
1D80   45 47 20 0D 00 00 81 53   EG ....S
1D88   45 47 20 37 0D 0D 81 45   EG 7...E
1D90   4E 44 53 45 47 20 0D 00   NDSEG ..
1D98   00 81 53 45 47 20 38 0D   ..SEG 8.
1DA0   0D 81 45 4E 44 53 45 47   ..ENDSEG
1DA8   20 0D 00 00 81 53 45 47    ....SEG
1DB0   20 39 0D 0D 81 45 4E 44    9...END
1DB8   53 45 47 20 0D 00 00 81   SEG ....
1DC0   53 74 61 72 74 0D FF 49   Start..I
1DC8   53 54 41 4B 45 21 73 6F   STAKE!so
1DD0   6D 65 20 74 65 78 74 20   me text
1DD8   74 68 61 74 20 49 20 68   that I h
1DE0   61 76 65 20 74 79 70 65   ave type
1DE8   64 20 8D 69 6E 74 6F 20   d .into
1DF0   57 6F 72 64 77 69 73 65   Wordwise
1DF8   20 50 6C 75 73 20 61 73    Plus as
1E00   20 70 61 72 74 20 6F 66    part of
1E08   20 74 68 65 20 8D 2A 57    the .*W
1E10   44 55 4D 50 20 64 65 6D   DUMP dem
1E18   6F 6E 73 74 72 61 74 69   onstrati
1E20   6F 6E 20 70 72 6F 67 72   on progr
1E28   61 6D 2E 0D 4E 6F 77 20   am..Now
```

Figure 10.5. The start of the 'lost' text is located and its address noted.

The next step is to find the end of the text. Again, this just requires you to step through memory until you find it, as shown in Figure 10.6. Again calculate the address of the last character you wish to save. Here it is the <RETURN> character signified by the 0D byte whose address is &1E97. Now that we know the start and end addresses of the text to be restored we can leave the WDUMP program. To do this press <ESCAPE>.

The penultimate step of the restoration process is to save the text. Do this with

```
*SAVE TEXT 1DDE 1E97
```

Of course you substitute your own start and end addresses if they differ. You have now safely restored your text; all that remains to be done is to re-enter Wordwise and load the TEXT using option 1!

```
1E18   6F 6E 73 74 72 61 74 69   onstrati
1E20   6F 6E 20 70 72 6F 67 72   on progr
1E28   61 6D 2E 0D 4E 6F 77 20   am..Now 
1E30   49 20 77 69 6C 6C 20 61   I will a
1E38   63 63 69 64 65 6E 74 6C   ccidentl
1E40   79 20 6C 6F 61 64 20 69   y load i
1E48   6E 20 61 20 6E 65 77 2C   n a new,
1E50   20 8D 62 75 74 20 73 68    .but sh
1E58   6F 72 74 65 72 20 74 65   orter te
1E60   78 74 20 66 69 6C 65 20   xt file 
1E68   6F 76 65 72 20 69 74 20   over it 
1E70   74 6F 20 73 68 6F 77 20   to show 
1E78   8D 68 6F 77 20 73 6F 6D   .how som
1E80   65 20 74 65 78 74 20 63   e text c
1E88   61 6E 20 62 65 20 72 65   an be re
1E90   73 74 6F 72 65 64 21 0D   stored!.
1E98   81 00 00 00 00 00 00 00   ........
1EA0   00 00 00 00 00 00 00 00   ........
1EA8   00 00 00 00 00 00 00 00   ........
1EB0   00 00 00 00 00 00 00 00   ........
```

Figure 10.6. Step on until the end of the 'lost' text is found.

Keystrip printer

The next program is quite simply a keystrip printer. It should work on all Epson-compatible printers and should require only the minimum of adaptation to get it performing satisfactorily on other types of printer.

Listing 10.3 contains the program which is written in Basic. Using the

```
 10 REM Keystrip printer
 20 REM Bruce Smith
 30 REM Wordwise Plus
 40 REM A User's Guide
 50 :
 60 MODE 7
 70 PRINT CHR$(141);CHR$(131);SPC(3);
 80 PRINT"Function key strip printer"
 90 PRINT CHR$(141);CHR$(131);SPC(3);
100 PRINT"Function key strip printer"
110 PRINT''CHR$(130);SPC(8);
120 PRINT"Bruce Smith  1985"
130 PRINT''"Turn on printer then ";
140 PRINT"press <RETURN>"
150 *FX21,0
160 REPEAT UNTIL GET=13
170 :
```

Listing 10.3. The keystrip printer program.

```
180  MODE 0
190  chrs=12
200  VDU 2
210  VDU 1,27,1,64
220  VDU 1,15
230  VDU 1,27,1,85,1,1
240  VDU 1,27,1,51,1,16
250  PRINT''
260  :
270  FOR key%=1 TO 10
280  PRINT "+";STRING$(chrs,"-");
290  NEXT
300  PRINT "+"
310  :
320  FOR loop%=1 TO 2
330  PROCprint
340  FOR key%=1 TO 10
350  PRINT "+";STRING$(chrs,"-");
360  NEXT
370  PRINT "+"
380  NEXT
390  PRINT''
400  VDU 3
410  END
420  :
430  DEF PROCprint
440  FOR lines%=1 TO 3
450  FOR N%=1 TO 10
460  READ text$
470  PRINT "!";text$;
480  PRINTSPC(chrs-LEN(text$));
490  NEXT
500  PRINT "!"
510  NEXT
520  ENDPROC
530  :
540  REM Wordwise keys
550
560  DATA INSERT,GREEN,WHITE,MARKER,CUR
SOR,WORD,DELETE,DELETE,MOVE,COPY
570  DATA or,EMBEDDED,EMBEDDED, ,TO?,CO
UNT,TO?,MARKED,MARKED,MARKED
580  DATA OVERWRITE,COMMAND,COMMAND, ,
, TO?, , TEXT,TEXT,TEXT
590  :
```

Listing 10.3 (contd)

```
600  REM insert definitions here
610  DATA ,,,,,,,,,,
620  DATA ,,,,,,,,,,
630  DATA ,,,,,,,,,,
```

Listing 10.3 (contd)

program is straightforward enough. As it stands it will print out two rows to contain the key definitions. By default the top row of definitions hold the standard Wordwise functions – these will not change under normal circumstances. The bottom row provides room for you to add the arrangement of keys for use with CTRL-SHIFT.

To print your own comments here you will need to adapt lines 610, 620 and 630 of the listing. As it stands there are three lines of ten commas. To insert your particular comment in a specific box simply place the comment before the appropriate comma – do not remove any commas; there should be ten per line at all times. To add two or three lines of comment to a single box the appropriate comments should be placed in lines 610, 620 and 630 which relate directly to lines 1, 2 and 3 of the printed text. For example, to add the definitions, TOP and BOTTOM to keys *f0* and *f1* we would need to change only line 610 as follows:

```
610 DATA TOP,BOTTOM,,,,,,,,
```

If we wished to place these comments to relate to keys *f8* and *f9* line 610 would become

```
610 DATA,,,,,,,,,TOP,BOTTOM
```

If, however, we wished to place two lines of comments in the *f0* and *f1* boxes we would need to change lines 610 and 620 as follows:

```
610 DATA TOP,BOTTOM,,,,,,,,
620 DATA LINE,LINE,,,,,,,,
```

When the key strip is printed it would appear in boxes 1 and 2 as

TOP
LINE

and

BOTTOM
LINE

respectively.

Figure 10.7 shows how a basic keystrip will look when printed out.

INSERT or OVERWRITE	GREEN EMBEDDED COMMAND	WHITE EMBEDDED COMMAND	MARKER	CURSOR TO?	WORD COUNT TO?	DELETE TO?	DELETE MARKED TEXT	MOVE MARKED TEXT	COPY MARKED TEXT

Figure 10.7. The function keystrip produced by Listing 10.3.

Chapter Eleven
Wordwise Programs

It may seem daft at first sight, but one of the best applications for Wordwise is to use it to write programs! Before you fall about laughing just think about it: Wordwise offers program editing facilities vastly superior to that of the very simple line editor of Basic. All the word processing facilities are available. These include search and replace, block move, copy and delete, line insertion and deletion, and tabbing to allow you to format your programs neatly and easily. The fact that you have the ability to scroll backwards and forwards through listings is a boon in itself. Just think of it; to insert an extra command here and there just scroll to the appropriate point in Insert Mode and type away – no need to recopy the whole line. If you decide to change a variable name, then use the search and replace facilities. Who's laughing now!

How to do it!

Enter Wordwise in the normal manner and type your Basic or assembly language program. The nice part about doing this is that you don't have to use line numbers! Simply type in the commands. Those of you who like to program using GOTOs and GOSUBs will now be punished for your wicked ways – you can't use line numbers because there aren't any! PROCedures and FNs make admirable substitutes for GOSUBs, and GOTO is easily simulated using EVAL and a function, thus:

```
INPUT X$
X$=EVAL("FN_"+X$)
```

which is much more desirable than:

```
INPUT A
ON A GOTO 100,200,300
```

As a practise run enter the following 'program' into Edit Mode of Wordwise:

```
REM A program written in Wordwise
MODE 7
PRINT CHR$(141);SPC(7);"Wordwise Plus"
PRINT CHR$(141);SPC(7);"Wordwise Plus"
PRINT ''
PRINT SPC(9);"A test program"
END
```

Once the program is ready there is one more thing to do. Although it matters not that there are no line numbers while the program text is in Wordwise, they must be added when the program is to be loaded into Basic itself. To do this simply move the cursor to the top of the program text, press <RETURN> to insert a blank line, and type here:

AUTO

Figure 11.1 shows just how the Edit Mode screen will look at this time. AUTO is, of course, the command that tells Basic to perform its automatic line numbering sequence, and this gives some indication of how we actually convert the program to a Basic format.

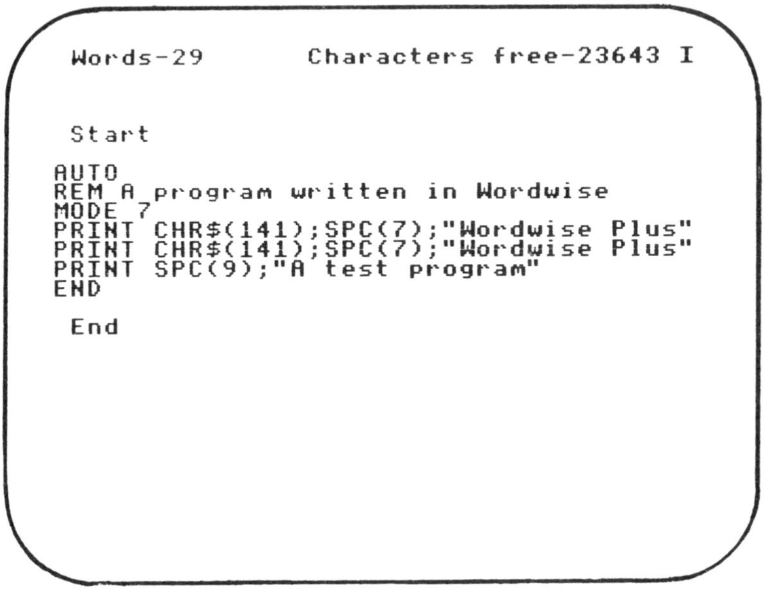

```
 Words-29        Characters free-23643 I

 Start
AUTO
REM A program written in Wordwise
MODE 7
PRINT CHR$(141);SPC(7);"Wordwise Plus"
PRINT CHR$(141);SPC(7);"Wordwise Plus"
PRINT SPC(9);"A test program"
END
 End
```

Figure 11.1. Writing a Basic program in Wordwise.

The procedure is like this. First save the file onto tape or disc as normal using option 1. In the above case use the filename

BASTEST

Once the file has been saved, revert to Basic by issuing the command

```
*BASIC
```

from the Menu Mode. We must now *EXEC the file in using the command

```
*EXEC BASTEST
```

The first command in the file is AUTO, so as soon as Basic encounters this it will initiate the automatic line numbering sequence. Then each line will in turn be read in from the file and onto the end of a line number. The <RETURN> character at the end of each line will ensure that the Basic line is inserted into memory, while generating the next line number. When all the lines of text have been read in a final line number will be prompted but with no text to be placed on it – simply press <ESCAPE> to leave the AUTO facility and you are ready to RUN the program.

Basic to Wordwise

Reversing the process is relatively straightforward – that is, converting a Basic program into a Wordwise text file. What we need to do is to create an ASCII text file using Basic's *SPOOL facility. This is done by issuing the following three commands one after the other:

```
*SPOOL PROG
LIST
*SPOOL
```

where PROG is the program name. Try it with the demo program now in Basic memory. When you type LIST the program will list to the tape or disc file you have opened with *SPOOL. The last *SPOOL command closes this.

Switch to Wordwise and load in the PROG file using option 2 on the main menu. <ESCAPE> to Edit Mode. As you can see we have some unwanted goodies. Most obvious are line numbers! These are really no good now and can be deleted, as can the superfluous *SPOOL at the end of the file.

A number rubout

The line numbers which become part of the text file when creating a text file from a Basic program are a nuisance and really need to be removed before the program can be edited correctly. One way of doing this is to hand delete all the numbers from the text one by one, but this is laborious. The following program called MCLINE (Listing 11.1) will actually perform the task for you with no problems – unless you use tape, which unfortunately does not support the filing system calls required to handle the reading and writing of two files simultaneously.

```
10 REM Number Stripper
20 REM Bruce Smith
30 REM Wordwise Plus
40 REM A User's Guide
50 :
60 PROCsetup
70 PROCassemble
80 PROCchecksum
90 END
100 :
110 DEF PROCsetup
120 gsinit=&FFC2
130 gsread=&FFC5
140 osfind=&FFCE
150 osbget=&FFD7
160 osbput=&FFD4
170 osargs=&FFDA
180 ENDPROC
190 :
200 DEF PROCassemble
210 FOR pass=0 TO 3 STEP 3
220 P%=&C00
230 [OPT pass
240 .read%
250 OPT FNequs ("          ",pass)
260 .write%
270 OPT FNequs ("          ",pass)
280 .start
290 LDA #1
300 LDX #112
310 LDY #0
320 JSR osargs
330 LDA &71
340 STA &F3
350 LDA &70
360 STA &F2
370 CLC
380 JSR gsinit
390 BNE over1
400 .error1
410 BRK
420 OPT FNequb (16,pass)
430 OPT FNequs ("Syntax:- *MCLINE <sou
rce file> <destination file>",pass)
440 BRK
```

Listing 11.1. The MCLINE program.

```
450 .over1
460 LDX #0
470 .leap1
480 JSR gsread
490 BCS over2
500 STA read%,X
510 INX
520 CPX #11
530 BNE leap1
540 .error2
550 BRK
560 OPT FNequb (&CC,pass)
570 OPT FNequs ("Bad filename",pass)
580 BRK
590 .over2
600 CLC
610 JSR gsinit
620 BEQ error1
630 LDX #0
640 .leap2
650 JSR gsread
660 BCS over3
670 STA write%,X
680 INX
690 CPX #11
700 BNE leap2
710 BEQ error2
720 .over3
730 LDA #64
740 LDX #(read% MOD &100)
750 LDY #(read% DIV &100)
760 JSR osfind
770 STA &70
780 BEQ error3
790 LDA #128
800 LDX #(write% MOD &100)
810 LDY #(write% DIV &100)
820 JSR osfind
830 STA &71
840 BEQ error4
850 .entry
860 LDY &70
870 JSR osbget
880 BCS exit
890 LDY &71
```

Listing 11.1 (contd)

```
 900 JSR osbput
 910 CMP #13
 920 BNE entry
 930 .leap3
 940 LDY &70
 950 JSR osbget
 960 BCS exit
 970 CMP #32
 980 BEQ leap3
 990 CMP #48
1000 BMI leap4
1010 CMP #58
1020 BCC leap3
1030 .leap4
1040 LDY &71
1050 JSR osbput
1060 SEC
1070 BCS entry
1080 .exit
1090 LDY #0
1100 TYA
1110 JSR osfind
1120 RTS
1130 \
1140 .error3
1150 BRK
1160 OPT FNequb (&D6,pass)
1170 OPT FNequs ("File not found",pass)
1180 BRK
1190 .error4
1200 BRK
1210 OPT FNequb (&C0,pass)
1220 OPT FNequs ("Can't open file",pass)
1230 BRK
1240 ]
1250 NEXT
1260 ENDPROC
1270 :
1280 DEF FNequs (string$,opt)
1290 $P%=string$
1300 P%=P%+LEN(string$)
1310 =opt
1320 :
1330 DEF FNequb (byte%,opt)
```

Listing 11.1 (contd)

```
1340 ?P%=byte%
1350 P%=P%+1
1360 =opt
1370 :
1380 DEF PROCchecksum
1390 A%=0
1400 FOR N%=&C00 TO &CFC
1410 A%=A%+?N%
1420 NEXT
1430 IF A%<>28065 PRINT"Checksum Error"
:VDU7:END
1440 PRINT"Checksum Correct!"
1450 *SAVE MCLINE C00 CFC C0E
1460 ENDPROC
```

Listing 11.1 (contd)

Type in the program run it. If all is well the program will save itself to the current filing medium. The program incorporates a checksum evaluator and will therefore stop and notify you if the checksum is incorrect. The machine code generated is assembled into page &C, the area usually reserved for the user definable characters. If you wish to assemble the machine code elsewhere then simply change the destination setting in line 220. Note, however, that the checksum will not be correct in this case, so assemble it as shown first to ensure that the listing has been entered correctly. Then delete lines 80, and 1380 to 1460 inclusive before adapting line 220 to suit. Line 1450 will also require altering to suit the new assembly area.

Using MCLINE is a simple task. The syntax is

*MCLINE <source> <destination>

The first thing to do is to create a *SPOOL file of the listing that you wish to strip of numbers. This is done thus:

```
*SPOOL PROG
LIST
*SPOOL
```

where PROG is the name of the source file. MCLINE will not work correctly if the source file is not a source file – you will end up with gibberish!

The next stage is to issue the complete command line

*MCLINE PROG WPROG

Once MCLINE loads it will look for the file called PROG, then read it, erasing line numbers and writing the resulting data to the file called WPROG. Be careful that you get the source and destination files in the correct order – if the destination filename is extant and you swap them around by accident you could wipe your source file. The moral here is:

always save a copy of the program as well as the *SPOOLed version.

Once the transfer is complete, enter Wordwise and load the WPROG file with option 2. When you <ESCAPE> into Edit Mode you should find your program intact and depleted of line numbers! You will, however, find an extra character at the end of each line. This is the ¦ character which is the control code for <RETURN>. This are superfluous and can be stripped by using the global search and replace. Switch to Menu Mode and press 5 followed by G. Type a ¦ as the search string and simply hit <RETURN> when asked for the replace string. Now all you require to do is to delete the *SPOOL and L. words that you will find at the top and bottom of the listing respectively. You can now insert AUTO at the top of the listing ready for *EXECing at a later stage when you have carried out any editing or changes.

Chapter Twelve
Hints and Tips

This chapter is devoted to a whole variety of subjects grouped together under the general heading of hints and tips. Most apply to both Wordwise and Wordwise Plus, though some are specific to the latter and this is stated in the appropriate sections. In this chapter you will find information of the more esoteric operations and effects of both Wordwise Plus and standard Wordwise. In addition, memory expansion to gain more Edit Mode space is examined.

Controlling wraparound W+

There is a CTRL function that we have not yet covered that is available in Wordwise Plus only; this is CTRL-F which controls the action or non-action of the how the text is displayed on the Edit Mode screen.

Normally when using Wordwise Plus, if you are in Edit Mode and you enter a word that is too long to fit onto the end of the line, it is moved down onto the next line in its entirety. This is called on-screen formatting. This formatting can be turned on and off by pressing CTRL-F, i.e. the CTRL and F keys together. Press them once and the screen formatting is turned off; press them again and the screen formatting is turned back on – the procedure known as 'toggling' between states. Figure 12.1 shows what happens when we type Wordwise Plus across the screen in Edit Mode. Normally as you hit the 'u' in the third occurrence of 'Plus', the word moves down onto the second line – not so when CTRL-F is used (while in Edit Mode); the 'u' stays on the first line and the 's' is printed on the second line.

Note that you can happily toggle states as you go down the screen, leaving what you have typed before unaltered. However, if you scroll up the screen with formatting on, past unformatted text, Wordwise Plus will reformat it for you!

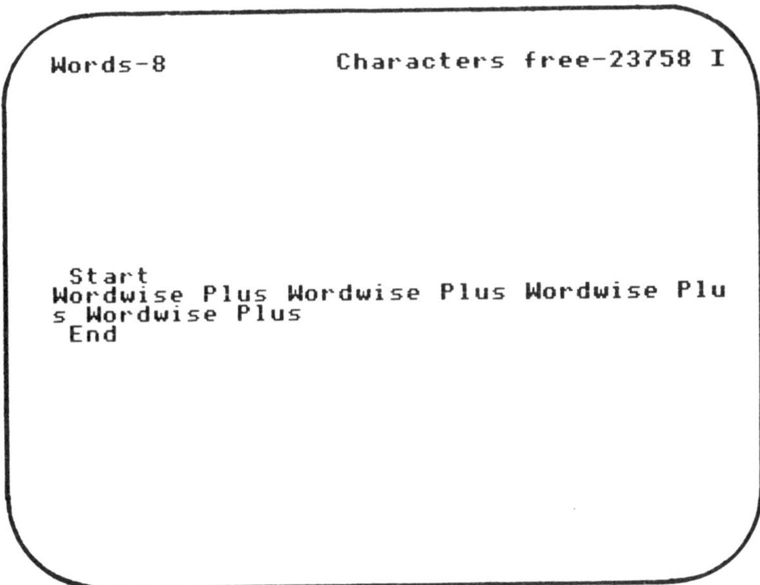

Figure 12.1. Words wrap around when formatting is turned off.

CTRL-D revisited

As we have seen, CTRL-D is used to delete the word and space before the word under which the editing cursor sits. Like all the keys in Wordwise, CTRL-D has an auto-repeat facility – in other words, if you hold it down it will keep performing the task to which it is assigned. One way to delete a section of text is to place the cursor at the first word to be deleted and then hold down CTRL-D; the words distal (i.e. to the 'end' of the text) will be erased. However, when you get to the end of a paragraph the cursor will 'jump' back to the paragraph above the one you have just deleted and effectively start deleting in the opposite direction! So take care when using CTRL-D to delete larger sections of text – better still, use markers and *f7*.

OC who?

It can happen that when you print out your document you find that an OC embedded command which you inserted into a section of text has not been sent to the printer by Wordwise. This normally occurs at the start of a document when you are setting up the various embedded command parameters. For example, you might be expecting italics at the start of a section of text only to find that your printer is still churning out normal text.

This non-occurrence normally happens when you are defining an indent after the OC command, which subsequently gets 'lost', eaten up by the indent command, i.e.:

<*f1*OC27,52>
<*f1*IN5>

The remedy is quite simple – place the INdent embedded command before any embedded OC commands:

<*f1*IN5>
<*f1*OC27,52>

White spaces

Another regular occurrence is that two words appear joined together (concatenated) when you preview or print your text, but when you examine them in Edit Mode there is a space between them. This 'space' is, in fact, not a space but a superflous white embedded command, *f2*, which, although it shows as a character space in Edit Mode, is ignored by any preview or printing of your text. The simple way out of this is to delete the white space and add a proper space, or just tap the space key where the words are being 'joined' together.

The underlining problem

Underlining text can create problems for the first time user, particularly when it comes to handling text that is to be centred as well as underlined. For example, the text:

<*f1*CE*f1*US*f2*Underline text*f1*UE*f2*>

would produce this output:

Underlined Text

in Wordwise Plus. The reason for this is in the way that the CE command works. CE will act upon all embedded commands until it finds the first character of the text to be centred. It then prints the required number of spaces to centre the text, followed by the text itself. The solution here is to make sure that the printer codes are 'printed' central as well, and this is done by inserting the pad character after the CE command and before the US code thus:

<*f1*CE*f2*|*f1*US*f2*Underline text*f1*UE*f2*>

will function correctly as:

Underlined Text

The underlining action of dot matrix printers makes it a useful tool for drawing up table top and bottom margins. One way to do this is to generate a blank line that is to be underlined. I do this using tab stops, thus

<*f1*US*f2*(TAB)*f1*UE*f2*>

If you want to produce some text using one of the special printer fonts, such as italics, you might find that it occurs over a page break – resulting in the header being printed in the selected print style. In such cases, use CP to force a conditional page to ensure that the text is printed in its entirety on the same page.

Printer reset

To ensure that your printer is reset before you print any documents, get into the habit of inserting

OC27,64

at the very start of any printer output codes. If you are using headers with Wordwise, then ensure that there is some printing, if only one space, before the first header of a page, otherwise the initalisation will occur *after* the header is printed. Wordwise Plus will not allow you to take any such action before printing a header on the first page, so you cannot initialise if you want a header!

The embedded space

Take care when you enter your embedded codes not to insert any spaces into them; Wordwise will ignore the rest of the command! Wordwise Plus will skip across any spaces within an embedded command and act as expected. For example,

<*f1*LM 8*f2*>

will fail in Wordwise (i.e. the default will be set) but will be effected in Wordwise Plus. Both Wordwise and Wordwise Plus will ignore any embedded command that begins with a space, i.e.

<*f1* LM8*f2*>

Saving and loading function keys

An alternative way to save the function key definitions is to save the memory block in which they are stored – the memory from &B00 to &BFF inclusive. To do this enter and run the key definitions and then save them with

*SAVE FKEYS B00 C00

Reloading them is simple enough in Menu Mode with

*LOAD FKEYS

The disadvantage of using this method is that the function keys cannot be edited simply. However, there is an advantage in that using this method allows you to load in new function key definitions quite easily. To do this, define your first set of function keys ensuring that at least one function key, say *f0*, has the definition

*KEY0 [*LOAD"FKEY1" ¦M[[

and then save this with

*SAVE FKEY1 B00 C00

Now define the next set of keys ensuring that *f0* has the definition

*KEY0 [*LOAD"FKEY2" ¦M[[

and save these keys with

*SAVE FKEY2 B00 C00

Once you have *LOADed the first set of keys, which could be part of your !BOOT file, you can simply load and reload the two sets of key definition as and when you require them simply by pressing *f0*. Of course, both files must be on the currently installed disc or your tape must be positioned accordingly.

Making a hash of it W+

When using option 5 on the main menu to perform a search and replace, it is possible to specify wildcard characters within the search string. A wildcard character is a special character that can be used as an ambiguous character – a sort of wild deuce. The wildcard character is the hash sign, #. For example, suppose we wished to search for the word 'Chapter' but were not sure whether we had spelt it with an upper or lower-case 'C'. The search string could be entered as

#hapter

When the search takes place, Wordwise Plus will try to locate all 7 letter words that have 'hapter' as their last six characters. Similarly, 'T#p' would search for all three letter words that start with 'T' and end with 'p'. Words such as Tap, Top and Tip would then be recognised.

It is possible to use more than one wildcard within a string, thus 'Th##' would search for all words beginning with 'Th'.

Extra lines

The white embedded command, <*f2*> or the <RETURN> key can be used to mark the end of an embedded command. If you use both, then an extra blank line will be printed in the text and to the printer.

No footers W+

Normally when printing or previewing text if a footer is not specified then the page number will be printed. If you wish to remove this facility then set up a dummy footer simply by using a blank DF command and follow it immediately by a RETURN.

<*f1*DF*f2*>

Star care

Before using any * commands with the printer, check the printer itself. If it hangs up when a star command is executed and you subsequently need to press the BREAK key, your text will be lost. The ESCAPE key should be used if possible. If not, use the DUMP utility presented in Chapter 10 to rescue it!

Wordwise aids

If you are typing large amounts of text with any regularity but are not an experienced typist then give some thought to purchasing SPELLCHECK II from Beebugsoft (Figure 12.2). SPELLCHECK II is a ROM-based spelling checker that will search through your text looking for words that it does not recognise and inform you of the fact. What SPELLCHECK cannot do is correct your spelling. I find it an invaluable aid. My typing is relatively fast but prone to errors when my fingers are trying hard to keep up with the words I thought of some five sentences ago! The obvious way around this is to proof read your document for spelling errors when it is complete – but even this results in missing a few. Then, of course, you have to find the incorrectly spelt word and edit it.

With SPELLCHECK II fitted you simply type *SPELL to enter the spellchecker, load your text from disc, and then insert the dictionary disc which contains a base of 6000 words. The words in your text are compared with this base dictionary and SPELLCHECK flags any that it does not recognise. The unknown words can then be edited if they are incorrectly spelt, or added to the base file if they are correct but not in the base dictionary.

There are two modes of operation for SPELLCHECK. The most popular is the automatic check where your entire text is examined first before it takes

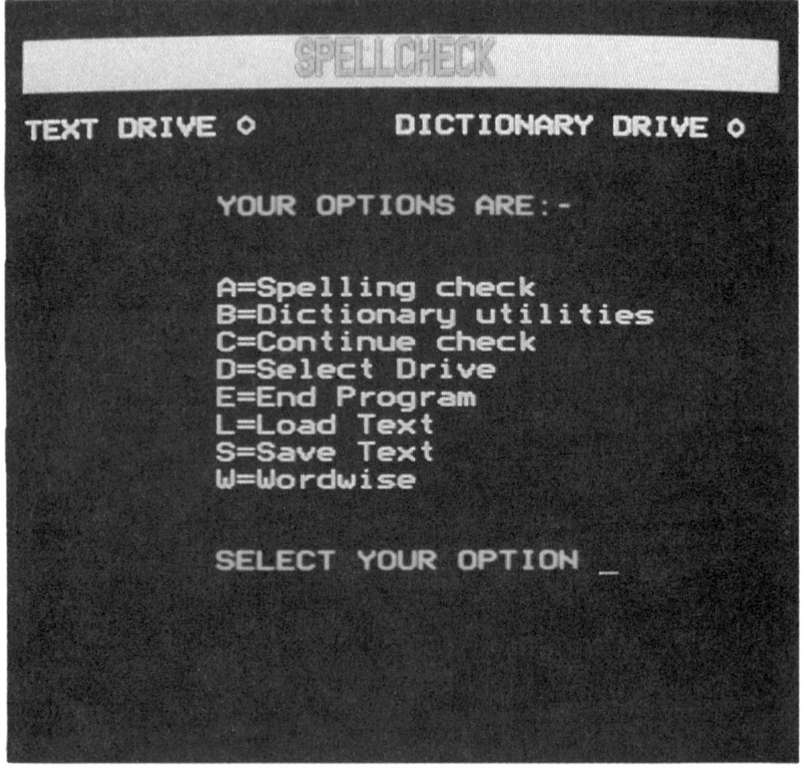

Figure 12.2. The SPELLCHECK II menu.

you through each unrecognised word. Secondly there is the attended check, whereby you correct each word as SPELLCHECK finds it. I prefer the former, which provides a useful, and most welcome, coffee break.

SPELLCHECK II is fully second processor-compatible, and is a worthwhile addition to your word processing suite of firmware. It is also compatible with Acornsoft's View word processor ROM.

Thanks for the memory!

When you switch on Wordwise or Wordwise Plus you have room to enter around 24000 characters, or roughly 4000 words of average book text. For most purposes this is quite adequate, and I make a point of never producing one piece of text more than 3000 words in length – for safety reasons mainly. However, the unforseen problem is that the characters free count also takes into account the space available in the memory normally used to display the Preview Mode screen. This means that as soon as you have less than 1500 characters free, Wordwise is unable to preview your text in a standard 80-

column screen mode. What it does is to step into a lower mode 40-column screen and preview it here. This obviously lacks the clarity of the 80-column screen, however it is still possible to see where indents and page breaks fall.

A way around this problem is to add more memory to the BBC Micro. Such a memory addition could be in the form of a 20K expansion board which supplies all the memory you need to display the Preview Mode screen, thus allowing you to use the full number of character spaces available for text while still previewing in an 80-column mode.

The boards I would recommend here are those produced by Aries Computers of Cambridge. The Aries B20 board supplies 20K of RAM and is very easy to fit and use. Early pre 1.17 versions of Wordwise will not work in conjunction with this board, but it is possible to upgrade to a compatible version (contact Computer Concepts for details). Wordwise Plus is fully compatible. Slightly more expensive is the Aries B32 board which supplies a full 20K of screen RAM in addition to 12K of sideways RAM. This board will only work with Wordwise Plus.

Purchasing the 6502 Second Processor will allow you to gain more memory but at double the price. Wordwise Plus is tube-compatible and will therefore work in the Second Processor. If the Second Processor is switched on and Wordwise Plus is selected then it will copy across straight away, increasing the characters free count to 28420.

Hi-Wordwise Plus is the disc based version aimed at the top of the 6502 Second Processor memory map and frees even more memory for text storage.

Chapter Thirteen

Sideways RAM

Many of you could well have a sideways RAM board installed in your BBC Micro. Alternatively it might be a ROM expansion board that also allows use of sideways RAM after a couple of RAM chips have been fitted (consult your ROM board manual on this). Sideways RAM is a very useful tool as it gives you the ability to customise machine code programs that can sit parallel with Wordwise or Wordwise Plus and as such can be used to enhance its already versatile performance.

Writing utilities

To place utilities in sideways RAM it is necessary to write a sideways ROM header and mini-interpreter to decode and action the selected command. This is not as difficult as it would seem; for full details on how to write your own sideways RAM software have a look at my book, *The BBC Micro ROM Book*.

To show you just how simple the process can be, Listing 13.1 is an example of some sideways software for you to type in and use if you have sideways RAM. Once the machine code is loaded into sideways RAM it adds the printer font software to the MOS. This includes the following new commands:

*DON – Double-sized text ON
*DOFF – Double-sized text OFF
*UON – Underlining ON
*UOFF – Underlining OFF
*EON – Emphasised ON
*EOFF – Emphasised OFF
*ION – Italics ON
*IOFF – Italics OFF
*CON – Condensed ON
*COFF – Condensed OFF
*FORM – Form feed

```
10 REM Printer Fonts
20 REM (c) Bruce Smith 1985
30 REM Wordwise Plus
40 REM A User's Guide
50 :
60 osnewl=&FFE7
70 osasci=&FFE3
80 comline=&F2
90 D%=&3000
100 :
110 FOR PASS=0 TO 3 STEP 3
120 P%=&5000
130 [
140 OPT PASS
150 OPT FNequb (0,PASS)
160 OPT FNequb (0,PASS)
170 OPT FNequb (0,PASS)
180 JMP service_entry+D%
190 OPT FNequb (&82,PASS)
200 OPT FNequb ((offset MOD 256),PASS)
210 OPT FNequb (1,PASS)
220 .title
230 OPT FNequs ("Printer Fonts 1.00",PASS)
240 OPT FNequb (0,PASS)
250 .offset
260 OPT FNequb (0,PASS)
270 EQUS "(C) Love Byte"
280 OPT FNequb (0,PASS)
290 .service_entry
300 PHA
310 CMP #9
320 BEQ help
330 CMP #4
340 BEQ unrecognised
350 PLA
360 RTS
370 .help
380 TYA
390 PHA
400 TXA
410 PHA
420 .over
430 JSR printhelp+D%
440 PLA
450 TAX
```

Listing 13.1. Demonstration program for the sideways RAM font utilities.

```
460 PLA
470 TAY
480 .return
490 PLA
500 RTS
510 .printhelp
520 JSR osnewl
530 LDX #&FF
540 .helploop
550 INX
560 LDA title+D%,X
570 JSR osasci
580 BNE helploop
590 JSR osnewl
600 RTS
610 :
620 .unrecognised
630 TYA
640 PHA
650 TXA
660 PHA
670 LDX #&FF
680 DEY
690 STY &100
700 .ctloop
710 INX
720 INY
730 LDA table+D%,X
740 BMI found
750 CMP (comline),Y
760 BEQ ctloop
770 .again
780 INX
790 LDA table+D%,X
800 BPL again
810 CMP #&FF
820 BEQ out
830 INX
840 LDY &100
850 JMP ctloop+D%
860 :
870 .out
880 .nothisrom
890 PLA
900 TAX
```

Listing 13.1 (contd)

```
 910 PLA
 920 TAY
 930 PLA
 940 RTS
 950 .found
 960 CMP #&FF
 970 BEQ nothisrom
 980 STA &39
 990 INX
1000 LDA table+D%,X
1010 STA &38
1020 JMP (&38)
1030 :
1040 \ set up Command Table
1050 .table
1060 EQUS "EON"
1070 OPT FNequb (((eon+D%)DIV 256),PASS)
1080 OPT FNequb (((eon+D%)MOD 256),PASS)
1090 EQUS "EOFF"
1100 OPT FNequb (((eoff+D%)DIV 256),PASS)
1110 OPT FNequb (((eoff+D%)MOD 256),PASS)
1120 EQUS "DON"
1130 OPT FNequb (((don+D%)DIV 256),PASS)
1140 OPT FNequb (((don+D%)MOD 256),PASS)
1150 EQUS "DOFF"
1160 OPT FNequb (((doff+D%)DIV 256),PASS)
1170 OPT FNequb (((doff+D%)MOD 256),PASS)
1180 EQUS "UON"
1190 OPT FNequb (((uon+D%)DIV 256),PASS)
1200 OPT FNequb (((uon+D%)MOD 256),PASS)
1210 EQUS "UOFF"
1220 OPT FNequb (((uoff+D%)DIV 256),PASS)
1230 OPT FNequb (((uoff+D%)MOD 256),PASS)
1240 EQUS "ION"
1250 OPT FNequb (((ion+D%)DIV 256),PASS)
1260 OPT FNequb (((ion+D%)MOD 256),PASS)
1270 EQUS "IOFF"
1280 OPT FNequb (((ioff+D%)DIV 256),PASS)
1290 OPT FNequb (((ioff+D%)MOD 256),PASS)
1300 EQUS "GB"
1310 OPT FNequb (((gb+D%)DIV 256),PASS)
1320 OPT FNequb (((gb+D%)MOD 256),PASS)
1330 EQUS "USA"
1340 OPT FNequb (((usa+D%)DIV 256),PASS)
1350 OPT FNequb (((usa+D%)MOD 256),PASS)
```

Listing 13.1 (contd)

```
1360 EQUS "FORM"
1370 OPT FNequb (((form+D%)DIV 256),PASS)
1380 OPT FNequb (((form+D%)MOD 256),PASS)
1390 OPT FNequb (&FF,PASS)
1400 :
1410 .commands
1420 :
1430 \ *EON
1440 .eon
1450 .beep
1460 LDA #3:LDX#10
1470 LDY #0:JSR&FFF4
1480 LDA#27:JSR&FFEE
1490 LDA#69:JSR&FFEE
1500 JMP ackback+D%
1510 \
1520 \ *EOFF
1530 .eoff
1540 LDA #3:LDX#10
1550 LDY #0:JSR&FFF4
1560 LDA#27:JSR&FFEE
1570 LDA#70:JSR&FFEE
1580 JMP ackback+D%
1590 \
1600 \ *DON
1610 .don
1620 LDA #3:LDX#10
1630 LDY #0:JSR&FFF4
1640 LDA#14:JSR&FFEE
1650 JMP ackback+D%
1660 \
1670 \ *DOFF
1680 .doff
1690 LDA #3:LDX#10
1700 LDY #0:JSR&FFF4
1710 LDA#20:JSR&FFEE
1720 JMP ackback+D%
1730 \
1740 \ *UON
1750 .uon
1760 LDA #3:LDX#10
1770 LDY #0:JSR&FFF4
1780 LDA#27:JSR&FFEE
1790 LDA#45:JSR&FFEE
1800 LDA #1:JSR&FFEE
```

Listing 13.1 (contd)

```
1810 JMP ackback+D%
1820 \
1830 \ *UOFF
1840 .uoff
1850 LDA #3:LDX#10
1860 LDY #0:JSR&FFF4
1870 LDA#27:JSR&FFEE
1880 LDA#45:JSR&FFEE
1890 LDA #0:JSR&FFEE
1900 JMP ackback+D%
1910 \
1920 \ *ION
1930 .ion
1940 LDA #3:LDX#10
1950 LDY #0:JSR&FFF4
1960 LDA#27:JSR&FFEE
1970 LDA#52:JSR&FFEE
1980 JMP ackback+D%
1990 \
2000 \ *IOFF
2010 .ioff
2020 LDA #3:LDX#10
2030 LDY #0:JSR&FFF4
2040 LDA#27:JSR&FFEE
2050 LDA#53:JSR&FFEE
2060 JMP ackback+D%
2070 \
2080 \ *GB
2090 .gb
2100 LDA #3:LDX#10
2110 LDY #0:JSR&FFF4
2120 LDA#27:JSR&FFEE
2130 LDA#55:JSR&FFEE
2140 LDA #1:JSR&FFEE
2150 JMP ackback+D%
2160 \
2170 \ *USA
2180 .usa
2190 LDA #3:LDX#10
2200 LDY #0:JSR&FFF4
2210 LDA#27:JSR&FFEE
2220 LDA#55:JSR&FFEE
2230 LDA #0:JSR&FFEE
2240 JMP ackback+D%
2250 \
```

Listing 13.1 (contd)

```
2260 \ *FORM
2270 .form
2280 LDA #3:LDX#10
2290 LDY #0:JSR&FFF4
2300 LDA#12:JSR&FFEE
2310 \
2320 .ackback
2330 LDA #3:LDX #0
2340 LDY #0:JSR&FFF4
2350 PLA:PLA:PLA
2360 LDA #0
2370 RTS
2380 ]
2390 NEXT
2400 A%=0
2410 FOR N%=&5000 TO &51CE
2420 A%=A%+?N%
2430 NEXT
2440 IF A%<>56427 PRINT"Checksum Error":END
2450 PRINT"Checksum is correct!"
2460 END
2470 :
2480 DEF FNequs (string$,opt)
2490 $P%=string$
2500 P%=P%+LEN(string$)
2510 =opt
2520 :
2530 DEF FNequb (byte%,opt)
2540 ?P%=byte%
2550 P%=P%+1
2560 =opt
```

Listing 13.1 (contd)

*USA – Select American character set
*GB – Select British character set

Entering and testing

Type in the program as shown and save it; then RUN it correcting any errors that are signalled. When the program assembles correctly it will calculate its own checksum and report if it finds any errors. Save the final corrected assembly listing. Note that the program does not assemble the machine code directly into sideways RAM. Save the machine code with *SAVE FONTS

5000 51CF 8000 8000. This is deliberate as this option is not available on some sideways RAM boards such as the *Acorn User* UserRAM.

Once the machine code has been saved it can be loaded into sideways RAM following the instructions supplied with your sideways RAM board. Next inform the MOS of the new ROM image simply by hitting the <BREAK> key.

Typing *HELP should reveal

```
*HELP

WORDWISE PLUS 1.49

DFS 1.20
  DFS
  UTILS

Printer Font 1.00

OS 1.2
```

You could then RUN the following short program in Basic to test the commands – note that the printer *must* be switched on otherwise the program will 'hang-up'.

```
 10 REM Font Demo
 20 PRINT CHR$2;"This is text";CHR$3
 30 *EON
 40 PRINT CHR$2;"Emphasised text";CHR$3
 50 *EOFF
 60 *DON
 70 PRINT CHR$2;"Double Sized";CHR$3
 80 *DOFF
 90 *UON
100 PRINT CHR$2;"Underlined text";CHR$3
110 *UOFF
120 *ION
130 PRINT CHR$2;"Italic text";CHR$3
140 *IOFF
150 *GB
160 PRINT CHR$2;"Pounds #####";CHR$3
170 *USA
180 PRINT CHR$2;"Hash #####";CHR$3
190 *FORM
```

*FORM will eject a sheet of paper, while *USA and *GB will determine whether you print hashes or pounds when you use the hash character within your text.

If the commands are operating correctly from Basic then they will work in Wordwise and Wordwise Plus. Their use in early versions of Wordwise is limited as they may be typed only in Menu Mode and will thus affect any forthcoming printed text that does not contain resetting OC codes. Their use in Wordwise Plus and later versions of Wordwise, however, is much greater due to the inclusion of the OS embedded command. Thus, rather than using OC27,69 within your text, simply use OS"EON" – much neater! Wordwise Plus also has the * command available as an embedded command and thus even *EON is possible.

The program

As with the other Basic programs within this book, the sideways RAM font is Basic I and Basic II-compatible. Users of Basic II will be able to make use of the EQU functions directly, thus shortening the listing somewhat. For example, lines such as

    OPT FNequs ("FORM",pass)

would shorten to

    EQUS "FORM"

The FN definitions at the end of the program listing would also become redundant.

As it stands the program is a little longwinded and not tightly coded. This is quite deliberate, to ensure that the program has a modular and easy to follow appearance. This should allow users of other printers to insert their own printer output codes into the appropriate places with ease. A line by line description of the program follows to assist you in this.

Line by line

Lines 60 to 90	: Set variables
Lines 110 to 140	: Set assembly parameters
Lines 150 to 170	: Set language entry to zero
Line 180	: Set service entry
Line 190	: Set ROM type
Line 200	: Set copyright pointer
Line 210	: Set ROM version number
Lines 230 to 240	: Assemble ROM title string
Lines 260 to 280	: Assemble copyright string

Line 290	: Service entry point
Line 300	: Save accumulator
Lines 310 to 320	: Branch if *HELP
Lines 330 to 340	: Branch if unrecognised command
Lines 350 to 360	: Not this ROM – restore and return
Lines 370 to 410	: *HELP to push registers
Lines 430 to 600	: Print help string, restore and return
Lines 620 to 690	: Save registers, set X and save Y
Lines 700 to 800	: Search through command table for unrecognised command
Lines 810 to 820	: If &FF then not this ROM
Lines 830 to 850	: Repeat search for command
Lines 870 to 940	: Exit routine – restores registers
Lines 950 to 970	: If &FF the command has not been found
Lines 980 to 1020	: Found command – get address and jump to it
Lines 1050 to 1390	: Command table and execution addresses
Lines 1430 to 2300	: Command execution code
Lines 2330 to 2370	: Restore registers, set accumulator to zero and return
Lines 2380 to 2560	: Checksum calculated and EQU functions

Each command takes the format

*FX3,10 – this disables the VDU but enables the printer irrespective of VDU2 or VDU3

Printer control codes

Jump to ackback

The code at 'ackback' restores VDU status with *FX3,0. This is the default status – to restore the actual status you would need to push the X register onto the hardware stack after issuing the *FX3,10 call. This should be pulled and used as the restoration call, i.e. *FX 3,X.

PART TWO

Chapter Fourteen
Segments

Wordwise Plus has an extra option in Menu Mode. This is option 9, and pressing it will transfer you into the segment menu (Figure 14.1).

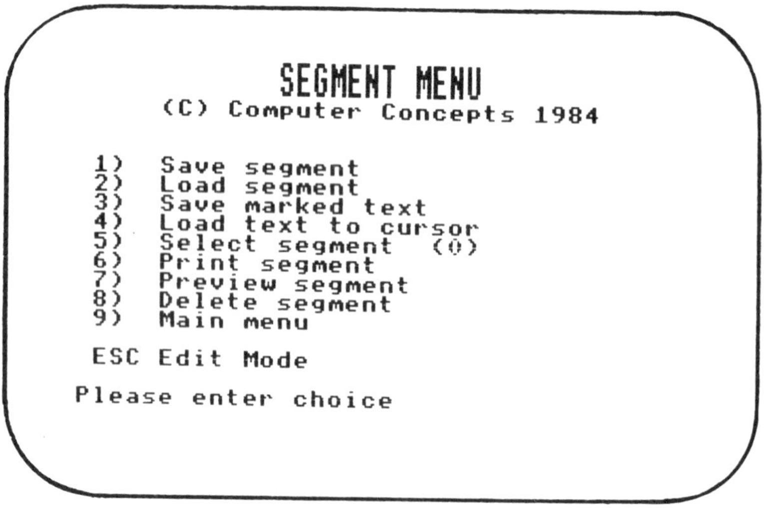

```
                SEGMENT MENU
        (C) Computer Concepts 1984

     1)  Save segment
     2)  Load segment
     3)  Save marked text
     4)  Load text to cursor
     5)  Select segment  (0)
     6)  Print segment
     7)  Preview segment
     8)  Delete segment
     9)  Main menu

     ESC Edit Mode

    Please enter choice
```

Figure 14.1. The segment menu.

Think of the BBC Micro's memory map as a circle, then imagine dividing it up into eleven divisions. In geometric terms these 11 pie slices are called segments (Figure 14.2). The first segment of memory is the Wordwise Plus text segment area into which all your normal document text is typed. The other segments are numbered from 0 to 9 and are referred to as SEG0 to SEG9. Again these can be used to hold text if you wish, for example small memos or notes to yourself that you wish to keep away from the main document. More often than not, though, you will use them to hold 'programs' that are written in the Wordwise Plus programming language; more on this in a while.

Since the memory map of the BBC Micro is finite, as is the size of our imaginary circle, obviously as you add text to a segment or the main text space it expands and the empty space is reduced accordingly.

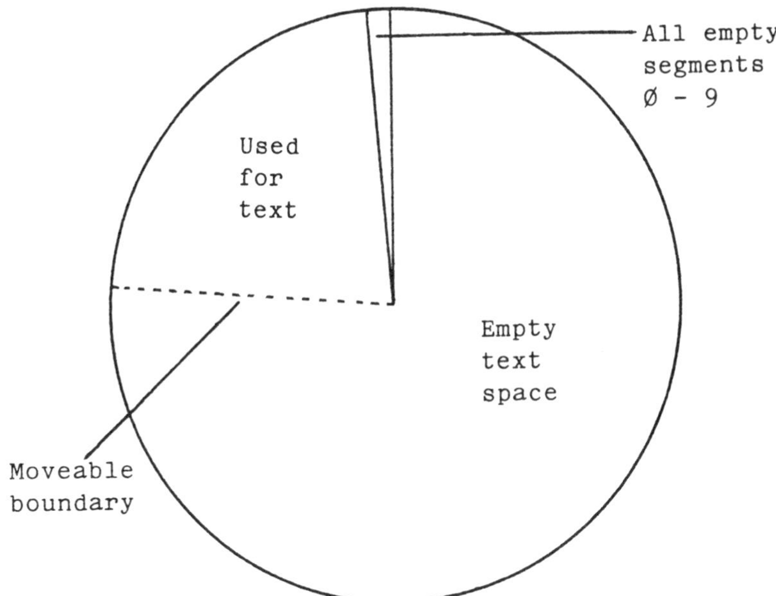

Figure 14.2. The segment arrangement.

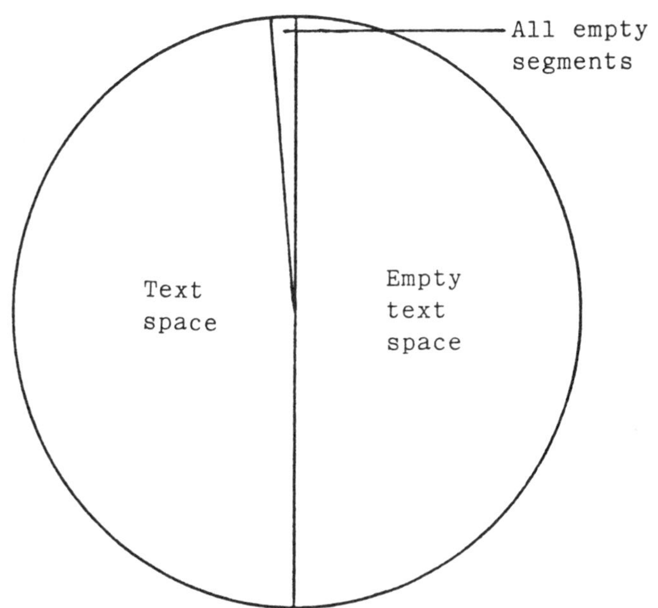

Figure 14.3. Adding text decreases the amount of memory left for use by segment and the text area.

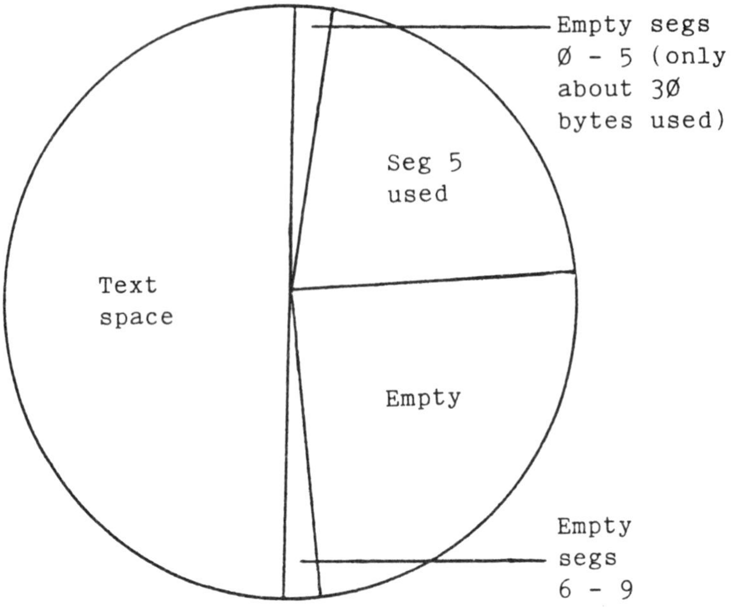

Figure 14.4. Adding text to a segment reduces the total space remaining.

Of course, the main text area need not contain the bulk of the text; as long as there is memory available then segments and text area can be any size. For example you could place all your text in SEG7 and place nothing at all in the other segments, as shown in Figure 14.5.

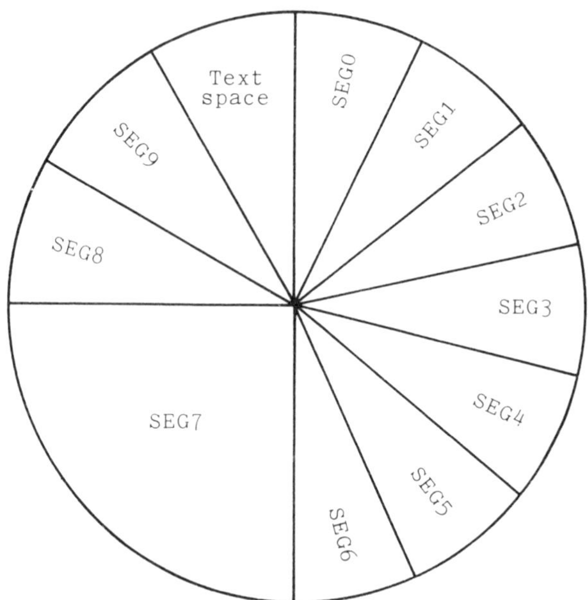

Figure 14.5. Text can be placed in segments alone.

The Segment Menu

The segment menu was illustrated in Figure 14.1. As you can see it is almost identical to the main menu. Options 1 to 4 are the same except that they act on the currently selected segment. Option 5 is different. This allows to you select the segment you wish to use. Options 6 and 7 print and preview the text as normal. Option 8 is new; this will allow you to delete the contents of the current segment. Finally option 9 allows you to transfer back to the main menu.

The <ESCAPE> key can be used to switch between the segment menu and the the SEG itself; try it. Figure 14.6 shows you the sort of layout you should see; in fact, its almost the same as the normal Edit Mode screen except that the *start* is replaced with the word SEG followed by the segment number. The status line reveals the same information. The character count will vary depending on how much text is in the other segments. The word count relates to the particular segment. When in SEG Mode the function keys have the usual functions assigned to them but, of course, operate only on the current segment. Only one set of markers is allocated to the segments; selecting another segment will clear any markers present in the current segment.

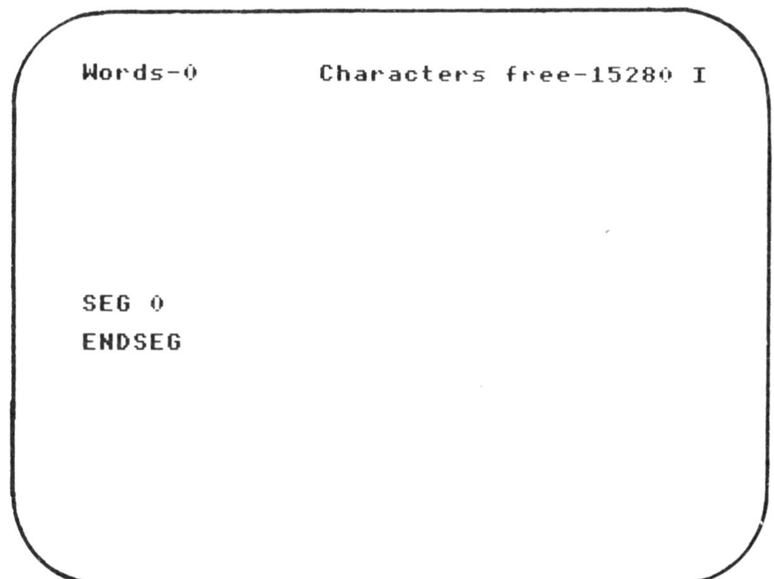

Figure 14.6. The segment Edit Mode screen.

<ESCAPE> back to the segment menu. Moving between segments is quite a simple procedure. First press key 5; the screen will prompt a question as Figure 14.7 shows. You answer this by typing the number of the segment to which you wish to move, so to move to SEG 5 press key 5. You will notice

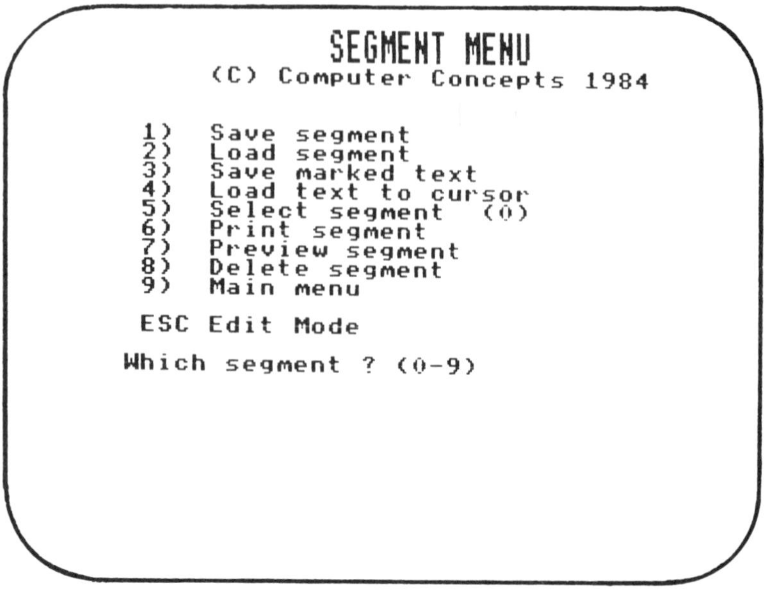

```
SEGMENT MENU
(C) Computer Concepts 1984

1)  Save segment
2)  Load segment
3)  Save marked text
4)  Load text to cursor
5)  Select segment  (0)
6)  Print segment
7)  Preview segment
8)  Delete segment
9)  Main menu

ESC Edit Mode

Which segment ? (0-9)
```

Figure 14.7. Changing segments.

that the yellow number in brackets has changed from a 0 to a 5. This number always reflects the 'current' segment. The current segment is the one that you will always transfer to when you use option 9 to toggle between the main menu and the segment menu.

Deleting segment text

Option 8 on the segment menu allows you to delete all the text within the current segment. This deletion is final, so be very sure that you do want to delete its contents. Try it. First enter some text into the current SEG and then select option 8 from the segment menu. The message

Are you sure? (Y/N)

will appear on the screen – press Y to delete the text. Pressing any other key will abort the deletion.

The programming language

As I have already mentioned, Wordwise Plus incorporates its own programming language. This language is in many repects quite similar to Basic itself, and if you have any Basic programming ability you should find it very easy to write programs in the programming language. But what is the worth of such a programming language? Well in very simple terms it means that Wordwise Plus is almost infinitely extendable – you can perform just about any action of text and words that you wish by writing a driving program in one or several of the segments. We will be looking at the programming language commands during the next few chapters but a few examples might serve as an illustration at this point.

We have seen how useful !BOOT files can be for setting up and initialising Wordwise so that it is ready for you to use with the minimum of fuss. By using the programming language we can also get the !BOOT file to load in some standard text for use – perhaps a letter heading – and then load other text or application programs into some segments. A suitable !BOOT file could be constructed as shown in Figure 14.8. Here the first ten lines define function keys 0 to 9 inclusive and then select *WORDWISE. The LETTER text is then loaded in followed by UTIL0 and DOCUM into SEG0 and SEG9 respectively.

```
*KEY0 |M|M|!!TI4|!"
*KEY1 |!!OC14|!"
*KEY2 |!!OC20|!"
*KEY3 |!!OC27,45,1|!"
*KEY4 |!!OC27,45,0|!"
*KEY5 |!!OC27,69|!"
*KEY6 |!!OC27,70|!"
*KEY7 |!!OC27,52|!"
*KEY8 |!!OC27,53|!"
*KEY9 |!|L|!#|!|M|!#|!"
*WORDWISE
:LOAD TEXT "LETTER"
:SELECT SEGMENT 0
:LOAD TEXT "UTILO"
:SELECT SEGMENT 9
:LOAD TEXT "DOCUM"
```

Figure 14.8. A !BOOT file can use the programming language commands to good effect.

The programming language commands are all prefixed with a colon; this is because they are being used in menu mode. All the programming language commands are available in this way. We have seen that option 8 can be used to delete text from a SEG if so desired; this drastic action is not available in the main menu. However, it can be simulated by entering the following line

:DELETE TEXT

Unlike the segment menu option 8, this does not ask if you are serious about your intention; it just does it! This method can also be used to clear segments as well, if so required.

SEG

The final Wordwise embedded command that we need to examine is SEG. This allows us to call and execute the contents of a segment from within a document. SEG must be followed by the number of the segment concerned. Try the following example. Enter or load a reasonable amount of text into the Edit Mode text area (use markers and *f9* to do this quickly if need be) but place the following command at the very top of the text

<*f1*SEG0*f2*>

Move across into SEG0 and enter

VDU 14

Finally return to the main menu via option 9 and then preview your text. As soon as the SEG0 embedded command is encountered the contents of segment 0 are executed – a VDU 14 is performed to place the Beeb into paged mode. This means that the previewed text is presented a page at a time. Pressing <SHIFT> will display the next page. Simple but very useful!

Executing segment programs

Once you have written a segment program, how do you go about getting it to run? The answer is that you press <SHIFT> and the function key that relates to the number of the segment you wish to run. For example, if a program is placed in SEG0, to execute it press

<SHIFT-*f0*>

Similarly, if a program resides in SEG4 press

<SHIFT-*f4*>

You can execute any segment from any other segment in this way – you do not have to be using that particular segment at the time. Any segment can be executed from any other segment.

Once running a segment can execute another program in another segment. Select SEG0 and enter this short program:

```
CLS
SELECT TEXT
PRINT "THERE ARE ";
PRINT W%;
PRINT " WORDS IN THE TEXT"
PRINT "THE LAST FILENAME WAS: ";
PRINT F$
A%=GET
```

Remember that the variable W% is used to hold the current word count and F$ the last filename used. Now <ESCAPE> to the segment menu and press

<SHIFT-*f0*>

The screen will clear and you will presented with the information about the word count and last filename used! Press any key and you will find yourself back at the main menu.

Chapter Fifteen

Text Processing

In this chapter we'll begin looking at some of the commands available to us in the Wordwise Plus programming language. The commands that we are interested in here are those that act on the text itself, be it in the main text space or within a segment. There are numerous small example programs given throughout this and the remaining chapters; unless otherwise stated enter these in SEG0 and test them by pressing <SHIFT-*f0*>. In most instances you will need some text within the normal Wordwise Plus text space. For the purposes of experimentation it does not matter what this text is, but ideally it should be several hundred words in length. Do experiment with the commands; in this way you will become familiar with them quite quickly.

Cursor control

The cursor is very important. When you enter text into Wordwise Plus the cursor's position determines the position at which the text is entered. It also governs where text is deleted from, copied to or moved from. Its role in applications programs, then, is important, particularly when they are being used to manipulate the text. To this end the CURSOR command is perhaps one of the most important, as it allows the text cursor to be moved around the text. As with all the examples in these forthcoming chapters, commands such as CURSOR will be displayed in upper-case characters. However, the use of lower-case characters is permitted, because 'CURSOR' and 'cursor' are seen as being the same. I like to reserve the lower-case characters for another aspect of the Wordwise Plus programming language that we will discuss soon.

The CURSOR command must always be followed by a directional command, i.e. one that specifies the direction of movement. The CURSOR commands are:

```
CURSOR TOP
CURSOR BOTTOM
CURSOR RIGHT
```

CURSOR LEFT
CURSOR UP
CURSOR DOWN
CURSOR AT

The first six cursor commands are fairly self-explanatory; CURSOR TOP moves the cursor to the extreme left at the very top of the text, CURSOR BOTTOM moves it to the bottom of the text at the extreme right end of the bottom line. CURSOR RIGHT and CURSOR LEFT move it one character position either way, while CURSOR UP and CURSOR DOWN move it one line vertically.

The CURSOR AT command must always be followed by a number or numeric variable in the range 0 to 39. These numbers relate directly to the number of characters that can be displayed across the screen in Edit Mode, the first character being at position 0 and the last at position 39. For example, to place the cursor at the sixth character position on the current line you would use the command

CURSOR AT 5

Remember we start at 0 so the sixth position is number 5!

Like CURSOR AT, the single moving CURSOR commands can be followed by a numeric value to specify the number of units to move in a particular direction. Some examples are:

CURSOR LEFT 5 – move 5 positions left
CURSOR RIGHT 2 – move 2 positions right
CURSOR UP 9 – move 9 lines up
CURSOR DOWN 17 – move 17 lines down

Numeric variables can be used in place of numbers, i.e.

CURSOR LEFT A%

would move the cursor left by the number of positions specified in the variable A%. So if A%=9 the cursor would be moved left 9 character positions.

Choice selection

When you write a segment program one of the first things you will do is select the area of Wordwise Plus where the program is to perform its action. This is done using the command SELECT. Just like CURSOR, SELECT will be followed by a further piece of information that will define either the text area to be selected or the segment and its number. Typical examples are:

SELECT TEXT
SELECT SEGMENT 8
SELECT SEGMENT X%

Enter the following program into SEG0:

```
SELECT TEXT
CURSOR TOP
DISPLAY
A%=GET
CURSOR BOTTOM
DISPLAY
A%=GET
SELECT SEGMENT 0
```

We have two new commands here that are easy to understand. Firstly DISPLAY; this simply places you in Edit Mode. A%=GET is directly equivalent to Basic's GET command – in this case we are just waiting for a key to be pressed, the ASCII value of which is placed into the variable A%.

Breaking down the program we have this:

SELECT TEXT	– select the main text area
CURSOR TOP	– move the cursor to the top of the text
DISPLAY	– display the text in Edit Mode
A%=GET	– wait until you press a key
CURSOR BOTTOM	– now move the cursor to the bottom of the display
DISPLAY	– and show the text again
A%=GET	– wait until a key is pressed
SELECT SEGMENT 0	– and return to SEG0

Execute this program by pressing <SHIFT-*f0*> and see what happens – try experimenting with the positioning of the cursor. It is vital that you gain the ability to move the cursor around the current text if you want to write effective text processing programs.

Simulating functions

The function keys provide a useful set of actions in Edit Mode. The FKEY command allows these to be simulated within the body of a program; FKEY is therefore a very effective command. It must be followed by a number that relates to the function key to be simulated. The command

FKEY 0

would simulate the pressing of *f0* and therefore switch from insert to overwrite mode.

By combining CURSOR and FKEY small but useful utility programs can be built up. With these two commands alone we can write a program to copy the top line of text to the bottom of the text. Enter this in SEG0:

```
SELECT TEXT
PRINT
PRINT
PRINT "Moving line now"
CURSOR TOP
CURSOR AT 0
FKEY 3
CURSOR AT 39
FKEY 3
CURSOR BOTTOM
FKEY 9
DELETE MARKERS
DISPLAY
A%=GET
```

Enter Menu Mode and press <SHIFT-*f0*> to see it work.

Let's look at this program line by line:

SELECT TEXT	– work on main text area
PRINT	– print a line
PRINT	– print a line
PRINT "Moving line now"	– signal action
CURSOR TOP	– move cursor to top of the text
CURSOR AT 0	– ensure it's at the very start
FKEY 3	– insert a marker
CURSOR AT 39	– move to very end of the line
FKEY 3	– and insert second marker
CURSOR BOTTOM	– move to bottom of the text
FKEY 9	– and copy marked text here
DELETE MARKERS	– delete the markers
DISPLAY	– show the result
A%=GET	– until a key is pressed!

The PRINT command works somewhat like its Basic counterpart, however you are restricted to one string per line. The semicolon may be used to ensure that text is kept to a single line but it is not possible to reopen quotes after it. The DELETE command works as it would seem, and is described below.

The program can be readily adapted to suit most needs just by altering either the CURSOR parameters or the FKEY action. For instance, the following program would move lines 10 to 15 in the text area to the bottom of the text.

```
SELECT TEXT
PRINT
PRINT
PRINT "Moving lines 10-15 now"
CURSOR TOP
CURSOR AT 0
CURSOR DOWN 10
FKEY 3
CURSOR AT 39
CURSOR DOWN 5
FKEY 3
CURSOR BOTTOM
FKEY 8
DELETE MARKERS
DISPLAY
A%=GET
```

In this instance you might find it easier to enter a list of, say, twenty line numbers down the right-hand side of the text to make it easier to see the effect this program has on the text.

Function keys *f4* to *f6* normally expect an item of data to work on. In such cases the data can be specified after the command. The example that follows will move the cursor to the first occurrence of the letter 'a' that is below the eighth line.

```
SELECT TEXT
CURSOR TOP
CURSOR AT 0
CURSOR DOWN 8
FKEY 4,"a"
DISPLAY
A%=GET
```

Function key *f5* operates in similar fashion. The following segment program will delete text from the sixth character on the top line to the first occurrence of the letter "o".

```
SELECT TEXT
CURSOR TOP
CURSOR AT 5
FKEY 6,"o"
DISPLAY
A%=GET
```

For most applications the FKEY command is similar to pressing the corresponding function key in an Edit Mode. There are two differences, however, that should be remembered. The most important of these is the use of the command

FKEY 7

This deletes the marked text. Unlike the function key, pressing it does *not* prompt you with the safety net question

Are you sure? (Y/N)

It simply carries out the command, as the following program demonstrates. (Do ensure that the text you're deleting in this instance has been safely saved already!)

```
REM fkey 7 demo
REM deletes 20 lines
SELECT TEXT
CURSOR TOP
FKEY 3
CURSOR DOWN 20
FKEY 3
FKEY 7
DISPLAY
A%=GET
```

The short listing also shows the use of the REM command. REM is short for REMark and allows REMinding comments to be inserted without affecting the operation of the segment program itself. It's a good idea always to start a program with a REM, but remember they do eat up the Characters free count.

The second point to remember when using the FKEY command is that you cannot specify a marker as an argument, for example, using *f4* to move the cursor to a marker. Instead this must be performed in a different manner, which will be described shortly.

Deleting text

We encountered the DELETE command in the program to move lines given earlier. Like the CURSOR command it must be followed by one of five parameters that define exactly what is to be deleted. The five commands are:

DELETE AT
DELETE LEFT
DELETE MARKED
DELETE MARKERS
DELETE WORD

The first of these, DELETE AT, acts just like <CTRL-A> in that it deletes the character above the cursor. The following example will delete the tenth character in the bottom line of text.

```
REM DELETE AT demo
SELECT TEXT
CURSOR BOTTOM
CURSOR AT 9
DELETE AT
DISPLAY
A%=GET
```

DELETE AT can be followed by a numeric value, either directly or in a numeric variable. In this case the characters up to that value will be deleted.

This segment program will erase the tenth to eighteenth characters from the bottom line of text.

```
REM DELETE AT num demo
SELECT TEXT
CURSOR BOTTOM
CURSOR AT 9
DELETE AT 9
DISPLAY
A%=GET
```

Figure 15.1 shows how the program works on the text.

DELETE WORD is, in effect, <CTRL-D> in Edit Mode; it deletes the word which the cursor is currently under. If it is followed by a number then it will delete that number of words from and including the word at which the cursor is positioned. The segment program below demonstrates the use of DELETE WORD by erasing the first five words from the text area. This time a numeric variable is used to hold the number of words to be deleted.

```
REM DELETE WORD demo
SELECT TEXT
B%=5
CURSOR TOP
DELETE WORD B%
DISPLAY
A%=GET
```

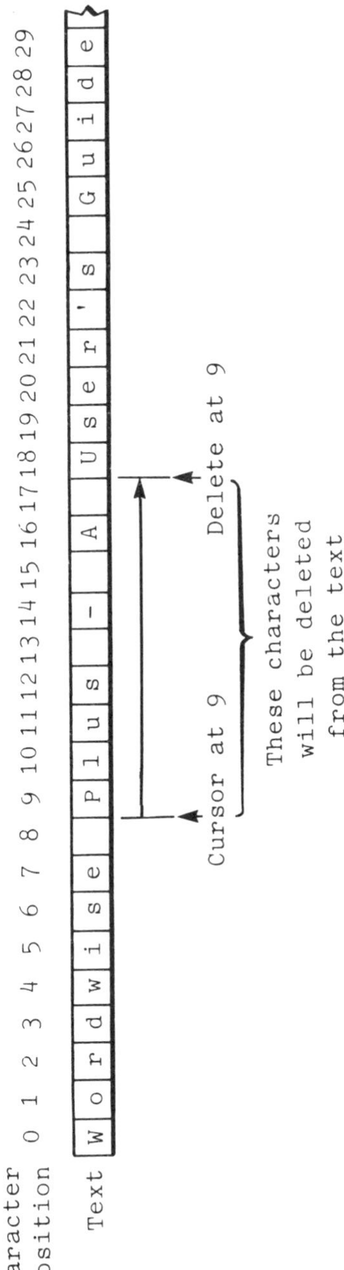

Figure 15.1. How to calculate what text is deleted.

DELETE MARKERS erases markers from within the selected text or segment space, acting as <CTRL-R>, while DELETE MARKED will rub out all text held between two markers, and acts as FKEY 7. If you want to erase all text completely from within Wordwise Plus then the command

DELETE TEXT

which can be entered as

:DELETE TEXT

in Menu Mode will perform the task admirably!

Finders Keepers

Any letters, numbers, word or phrase can be located with the aid of the FIND command, be it in the text space or a segment. FIND is normally followed by one of three parameters:

FIND "Word or phrase"
FIND A$
FIND MARKERS

The first command allows you to specify exactly the word or series of words that you are looking for. The following program will locate the first use of 'and' within a document in the main text space.

```
REM FIND "" demo
SELECT TEXT
CURSOR TOP
FIND "and"
DISPLAY
A%=GET
```

Note that the string of characters is case dependent in this instance, thus 'and', 'AND', 'ANd' are all seen as being different. Also the command starts working from the current position of the cursor. This is useful as it means that we can either restrict the search to the lower portion of the text or find the second (or third, fourth etc.) occurrence of a word. The following program would find the second use of 'the' in a piece of text.

```
REM FIND 2nd "the"
SELECT TEXT
CURSOR TOP
FIND "the"
CURSOR RIGHT
FIND "the"
DISPLAY
A%=GET
```

The program simply uses the

FIND "the"

command twice. Note, though, the inclusion of the CURSOR RIGHT command to split them. When FIND locates the word or words it is looking for it places the cursor under the first character in the word. The CURSOR RIGHT moves the cursor one place to the right otherwise FIND will locate the word it is sitting under the second time around!

Using a string variable as the FIND parameter is straightforward. All that is required is that the string parameter is defined before the use of the command. If A$ held the string "for" then FIND A$ would search the text locating the next occurrence of 'for', as shown below,

```
REM FIND A$
SELECT TEXT
A$="for"
CURSOR TOP
FIND A$
DISPLAY
A%=GET
```

Finally, FIND MARKERS overcomes the deficit in the FKEY command. When used this will place the cursor under the first marker that is located.

As with all the FIND commands, if the item being sought is not found the cursor is left at the very end of the text, no matter where it was placed prior to use of the command.

Getting into print

The PRINT command has already been used in one of the earlier segment programs to show how text can be displayed on the screen. In that example the PRINT command was followed by a string of characters enclosed within quotes:

PRINT "Hello there"

However, PRINT can be used in other ways. For example, it can be used to print out string variables or numbers, some examples of which follow:

```
REM PRINT demo
CLS
PRINT "Hello there!"
A$="string variable"
PRINT "This is a ";
PRINT A$
PRINT
```

```
PRINT "The result of 3+5 is :";
PRINT 3+5
PRINT
PRINT "There are ";
PRINT W%;
PRINT " words"
A%=GET
```

CLS is the command to CLear Screen, which effectively gives you a blank screen to print on. By using a semicolon at the end of the PRINT string we ensure that the next piece of text is printed on the same line. Similarly, inserting PRINT on its own will print a blank line.

The PRINT command can also act rather like option 6 on the main menu, used to send your text to a printer. This is determined if PR[illegible]is followed by a specialist command. The special PRINT comman[illegible]

PRINT TEXT
PRINT PAGE
PRINT MARKED
PRINT FILE

The whole of the text space or selected segment can be printed using the command PRINT TEXT. If a specific page of the text is required then PRINT PAGE followed by the page number will suffice, i.e.

PRINT PAGE 6

which will dump page 6 of your document to the printer. PRINT MARKED will print just a marked section of text. The following program would print the first 30 lines of some text in the main text space to the printer.

```
REM PRINT MARKED demo
SELECT TEXT
CURSOR TOP
FKEY 3
CURSOR DOWN 29
FKEY 3
PRINT MARKED
DISPLAY
A%=GET
```

The final command PRINT FILE takes the file specified and prints it to the printer, i.e.

PRINT FILE "CHAP15"

This would print the file called 'CHAP15' to the printer. Obviously this file must be on the current disc or tape so that it can be read in and printed. If there are any embedded commands within the text these will be acted upon.

Wordwise Plus sees each character you type in at the keyboard as a number, which is a standard number known as its ASCII value (ASCII being American Standard Code for Information Interchange!). The ASCII value of any character can be found using the function ASC. For example, to print the ASCII code for the letter 'W', <ESCAPE> into Menu Mode and type

:PRINT ASC("W")

On pressing <RETURN> the number 87 will appear, 87 being the ASCII value for the letter 'W'. The real usefulness of ASC comes when using string variables. In such cases it can be used to return the ASCII value of the first character in a string, as the following segment program shows:

```
REM ASC demo
CLS
A$="Wordwise"
B$="Plus"
PRINT "ASC W=";
PRINT ASC(A$)
PRINT "ASC P=";
PRINT ASC("B$)
A%=GET
```

A command that works in the opposite way from ASC is CHR$. Given a number CHR$ will convert it into the equivalent ASCII character. We saw above that the ASCII code for 'W' was 87. Enter Menu Mode and type

:PRINT CHR$(87)

The letter 'W' will be displayed. By using the addition function, i.e. a +, it is possible to use CHR$ to add together letters to form a string variable, as the following program shows:

```
REM CHR$ demo
CLS
A$=CHR$(66)+CHR$(66)+CHR$(67)
PRINT A$
A%=GET
```

Execute this segment program and see that the letters 'BBC' are displayed; 66 is the ASCII code for 'B' and 67 the ASCII code for 'C'.

Seeing is believing

A command that is similar in action to the PRINT command is PREVIEW. In this case, however, the file is printed onto the screen. The PREVIEW commands are:

PREVIEW TEXT
PREVIEW PAGE
PREVIEW MARKED
PREVIEW FILE

These act just as their PRINT counterparts and any existing document is not destroyed in any way.

New for old

The FIND command is useful for locating a particular word within text. Option 5 on the Wordwise Plus menu provides a search and replace facility, and this exists in the command REPLACE. Unlike option 5, however, REPLACE will only substitute the old word with the new word on the first occasion.

The command can be used either with the words specified in strings or by means of string variables. The following two programs show how both can be used to REPLACE 'when' for 'with' and 'two' for 'too'

```
REM REPLACE demo 1
SELECT TEXT
CURSOR TOP
REPLACE "when", "with"
DISPLAY
A%=GET
```

```
REM REPLACE demo 2
SELECT TEXT
CURSOR TOP
A$="two"
B$="too"
REPLACE B$,A$
DISPLAY
A%=GET
```

It is, of course, possible to mix character strings with variable strings thus:

REPLACE A$, "silly"
REPLACE "silly", A$

The REPLACE will always start from the position of the cursor, so to find a first occurrence the cursor must first be placed at the top of the screen with CURSOR TOP.

A good swap

Changing a character from lower-case to upper-case and vice versa is straightforward in Edit Mode using CTRL-S. It is just as simple from a segment program using the SWAP command. Like CTRL-S this works on the character immediately above the cursor. To change the case of the 7th character on the third line you could use:

```
REM SWAP demo
SELECT TEXT
CURSOR TOP
CURSOR DOWN 2
CURSOR RIGHT 6
SWAP
DISPLAY
A%=GET
```

SWAP can be followed by a number or number variable. In such instances it will act by swapping the case of that number of letters to the right of the cursor. After any SWAP the cursor is left at the character after the last one swapped.

Type writing

A command that I find very useful is the TYPE command. This allows you to insert text into your current document, at the position of the cursor, in a variety of ways. The simplest way is to return to the main menu and enter

:TYPE "This is extra text"

If you now <ESCAPE> to Edit Mode you'll see that this text has been entered.

Text can be typed in from string variables using segment programs. Try this:

```
REM TYPE demo
A$="Wordwise Plus"
A$=A$+CHR$(13)
B$="A User's Guide"
SELECT TEXT
CURSOR BOTTOM
TYPE A$
TYPE B$
DISPLAY
A%=GET
```

When this program is executed A$ and B$ will be TYPEd to the bottom of the text in Edit Mode. Note, in the defintion of A$ above, that CHR$(13) has been added to the end of 'Wordwise Plus'. CHR$(13) is the ASCII code for the RETURN character, and this ensures that B$ is printed on the line below A$.

Finally, we can even type the entire contents of one segment into another! Enter the following segment program into SEG0:

```
REM TYPE demo2
SELECT TEXT
CURSOR BOTTOM
TYPE SEGMENT 1
DISPLAY
A%=GET
```

Now type some text into SEG1, any amount you like. Once this is completed execute SEG0, and the text just placed into SEG1 will be copied across to the bottom of the main text area! Of course, you don't need a program to do this for you. If you just want to copy a segment, such as segment 1, into the text space, simply enter the main menu and type

:TYPE SEGMENT 1

String functions

There are several functions with the Wordwise Plus programming language that act directly on strings. In alphabetical order these functions are:

GCK$
GCT$
GLK$
GLT$
LEN
STR$
VAL

The first four of these pair off neatly, so let us look at each pair in turn first of all.

Getting text

The GCT$ and GLT$ functions both work on text currently held within the bounds of Wordwise Plus. The meaning of each is

GCT$ – Get Character from Text
GLT$ – Get Line from Text

The following segment program shows how we can use GCT$ to read and then display the first character on the first ten lines in a document held within the main text space:

```
REM GCT$ demo

SELECT TEXT
CLS
CURSOR TOP

DOTHIS
C$=GCT$
PRINT C$
CURSOR DOWN
CURSOR AT 0
TIMES 10

A%=GET
```

GCT$ returns as a string the character under which the cursor is currently sitting. The cursor is then moved one space to the right. As GCT$ returns a string it must be read into a string, variable C$ in this instant. The CURSOR DOWN moves the cursor down one line while CURSOR AT 0 ensures that it is positioned on the very first character on that line.

The next program looks very similar to the one above but in this instance it uses GLT$ to read a line of text into C$. A line of text is defined here as being either 255 characters long or until a <RETURN> character is located – whichever is the shorter. Note that embedded commands tend to confuse the command, when printing causing it to bleep and hang up on you – so only use it away from embedded codes or on spooled text.

```
REM GLT$ demo

SELECT TEXT
CLS
CURSOR TOP

DOTHIS
C$=GLT$
PRINT C$
CURSOR DOWN
CURSOR AT 0
TIMES 2

A%=GET
```

If at the end of the text the last line does not contain either the 255 characters or a <RETURN>, then a bleep will be made but the line will be read into the defined string variable.

Keyboard capers

The commands GCK$ and GLK$ are almost identical to those just described, but instead of getting the character or line from the text it is obtained from the keyboard. The two commands are therefore

GCK$ – Get Character from Keyboard
GLK$ – Get Line from Keyboard

It would seem at first sight that GCK$ is identical to GET. There is a difference, though, in that GCK$ returns the key pressed as a string variable and not merely as a number. The following program sets up a loop that will only exit when you press "F".

```
REM GCK$ demo

CLS

REPEAT
C$=GCK$
IF C$<>"F" THEN PRINT "Try again!"
UNTIL C$="F"
```

Unlike GCK$, when you use GLK$ the characters you enter are printed onto the screen. You can enter up to 120 characters, but a line of text can be terminated at any time simply by pressing <RETURN>. This program uses GLK$ to wait for the correct entry of a password.

```
REM GLK$ demo

CLS
PRINT "Guess the password"
PRINT
W$="PASSWORD"

REPEAT
PRINT "Enter password :";
C$=GLK$
IF C$<>W$ THEN PRINT "Wrong!"
UNTIL C$=W$

PRINT "Correct!"
A%=GET
```

Lengths and things

Once a string has been assimilated in one way or another it is often useful to calculate its length, and this is where the LEN command comes into action. LEN will count the number of characters in a given string and then return the result. The following segment program uses GLK$ to read in a string and LEN to find the number of characters the string contains:

```
REM LEN demo

CLS

REPEAT
PRINT "Enter a string :";
C$=GLK$
A%=LEN C$
PRINT "That string has ";
PRINT A%;
PRINT " characters"
UNTIL C$=""
```

The loop here is completed when a null string is entered. A null string is when you simply press <RETURN> and C$ has nothing deposited in it.

The STR$ function allows you to convert a number held within a numeric variable into its ASCII counterpart. For example if Z%=12345 then STR$ would convert Z% into the string "12345". This program shows how an incrementing number can be added to a string.

```
REM STR$ demo

CLS
Z%=0

REPEAT
B$="The current number is :"
A$=STR$(Z%)
B$=B$+A$
PRINT B$
Z%=Z%+5
UNTIL Z%=200

A%=GET
```

The command VAL works in the opposite way from STR$. VAL takes a string as its argument and tries to convert it into a number. For instance, the program:

```
REM VAL demo1

A$="12345"
X%=VAL (A$)
PRINT X%

A%=GET
```

will convert A$ into a number and place it into the numeric variable X%. If A$ were changed to

A$="12345hello there!"

then it would still return 12345 in X%. VAL cannot cause an error; it will simply convert as many numeric characters as it can and exit on the first non-numeric character. This means that if a string starts with a letter as opposed to a number it will return 0. Both the following will return 0:

PRINT VAL "−23"
PRINT VAL "+9"

This is because − and + are both non-numeric.

Chapter Sixteen
Structures

The Wordwise Plus programming language contains within it a number of structures that allow you to write programs more effectively. These structures include loops, procedures and conditionals. Let's look at loops first of all.

Repetitive programs

The REPLACE command detailed earlier will only replace a single occurrence of a word. This is not particularly useful unless you can, say, change all the occurrences of a word within a document. One way of doing this would be to count the occurrences and then insert enough REPLACE commands within a segment program to do it. This is both time wasting and long-winded. This is where loops come in. A loop is simply a control command that allows a section of program to be executed a predetermined number of times. The command that needs to be repeated is placed within the two commands that mark the start and end of the loop.

One such loop structure is the DOTHIS ... TIMES loop. The command DOTHIS marks the start of the loop, while TIMES is the end. TIMES itself must be followed by a number or numeric variable to determine the number of times a loop is executed. As an example, suppose we wished to replace the first 6 occurrences of the word "stupid" with "silly". The next program would do the job:

```
REM DOTHIS demo
SELECT TEXT
CURSOR TOP

DOTHIS
REPLACE "stupid","silly"
TIMES 6

DISPLAY
A%=GET
```

Although I have only used one command inside the DOTHIS ... TIMES loop, it is quite permissible to add as many as you wish. It is also possible to embed loops within one another so that you have loops within loops, just like this:

```
REM DOTHIS demo2
CLS
K%=1

DOTHIS
PRINT K%

DOTHIS
PRINT  "Hello!"
A%=GET
TIMES 6

K%=K%+1
TIMES 6
```

Can you see what is happening here – try running the program to see!

Note how I clearly identify the loop by inserting a blank line – this is good programming style. Another way of emphasising a loop structure is to indent its contents slightly, just like this:

```
DOTHIS
 FIND "Buy "
 REPLACE "one","two"
TIMES 6
```

However, I feel that this can make a program look somewhat messy, particularly if you are placing loops within loops because the indents become more severe.

Another type of loop that can be used in segment programs is the REPEAT ... UNTIL loop. As its name suggests, this loop repeats until a certain condition is met. Quite often it is used in conjunction with a numeric variable that is being used as a *loop counter*. The next program shows how the numbers 1 to 10 can be printed onto the screen using a REPEAT ... UNTIL loop.

```
REM REPEAT demo
CLS
K%=0

REPEAT
K%=K%+1
PRINT K%
UNTIL K%=10

A%=GET
```

If we examine the program closely we can see more clearly what is going on.

```
REM REPEAT demo – program name
CLS             – CLear the Screen
K%=0            – set K% equal to 0
REPEAT          – start of REPEAT loop
K%=K%+1         – add 1 to the value of K%
PRINT K%        – print value of K%
UNTIL K%=10     – perform from REPEAT until K%=10
A%=GET          – press a key to finish
```

We have still to solve the problem of being able to perform a global REPLACE within a document. In both the loops examined so far it has still been necessary to define the number of times the loop is executed. To start work from the top of the text, the CURSOR TOP command is used. A special function allows us to perform loops until the end of text is reached – this function is EOT, which stands for End Of Text. By placing this after the UNTIL part of a loop we can REPLACE until the EOT is reached:

```
REM UNTIL EOT
SELECT TEXT
CURSOR TOP

REPEAT
REPLACE "stupid", "silly"
UNTIL EOT
```

Another example of the use of the REPEAT ... UNTIL loop with EOT follows. This time the program is counting the number of letter 'a's within the text:

```
REM UNTIL EOT 2
SELECT TEXT
CURSOR TOP
A%=0

REPEAT
FIND "a"
A%=A%+1
PRINT A%
CURSOR RIGHT
UNTIL EOT

PRINT "The number is :";
PRINT A%
X%=GET
```

You can place REPEAT ... UNTIL loops within one another, so that it is possible to have these loops controlling other REPEAT ... UNTIL loops. There is a restriction on the number that can be 'nested' in this way, however – the maximum is seven.

The correct procedure

There might be a section of program that you find is cropping up several times within the body of your main program. Rather than keep entering it every time it is needed, you can write it as a procedure that you can simply call by name when it is required. Obviously the procedure call will require a command, so it is only worth writing a section of program as a procedure if it is more than a few lines in length.

Procedures are given names. This is an advantage because it means that you can name a procedure so that it reflects its operation. For example, you might have a procedure that calculates the VAT on a figure. An ideal name for this procedure would be 'vat'. Note that I have used lower-case characters in this case – it is permissible to use upper-case, but if you keep to the rule of upper-case for commands and lower-case for procedure names you will find your program easier to read and neater in presentation. Once you have decided upon the name for your procedure, mark the start of the procedure with its name prefixed with a full stop, thus:

```
.vat
```

The end of the procedure is marked by the command ENDPROC, thus:

```
.vat
REM commands placed
REM here
ENDPROC
```

You call a procedure at any time with the command PROC followed directly by the name of the procedure, i.e.

```
PROCvat
```

Once the procedure has been completed control is returned to the command after the PROC.

The following program uses a procedure to print the character after the key you press at the keyboard. If you press 'A' it will type 'B', if you type 'd' it will type 'e' and so forth, and will stop only when the <RETURN> key is pressed. Look at how the procedure is implemented:

```
REM PROC demo
CLS
PRINT "ASCII +1 CONVERTER"
PRINT
```

```
PRINT

REPEAT
PROCconvert
UNTIL A%=14

PRINT "END"
A%=GET
END

.convert
A%=GET
A%=A%+1
PRINT CHR$(A%)
ENDPROC
```

The 'convert' procedure is placed at the end of the segment program. Since it does not form part of the main program this is the correct place for it. So that the main program does not run into the procedure it is stopped with the command END. The call to the procedure is embedded within the REPEAT ... UNTIL loop. It is quite legitimate to have more than one procedure within a program – in fact, you can have as many as you like. A second procedure has been added to the segment program to print the total number of characters printed to the screen:

```
REM 2 PROC demo
CLS
PRINT "ASCII +1 CONVERTER"
PRINT
PRINT
C%=0

REPEAT
PROCconvert
PROCupdate
UNTIL A%=14

PRINT "END"
A%=GET
END

.convert
A%=GET
A%=A%+1
PRINT CHR$(A%)
ENDPROC
```

```
.update
C%=C%+1
ENDPROC
```

In this example the PROC only encompasses a single command, which is somewhat wasteful of space. It illustrates the point however.

IF ...

There will be times when you want a command or procedure executed only if a certain condition prevails. This can be performed using the IF ... THEN construct. The command works like this:

IF <test> THEN <do this>

In other words IF the condition you are testing for is met THEN do the command after THEN. If, on the other hand, the condition is not met, then the rest of the line is skipped. The following segment program uses two different PROCs to print a key pressed and then states whether it was a number or a letter.

```
REM IF..THEN demo
CLS

REPEAT
A%=GET
IF A% >=ASC("A") THEN PROCletter
IF A% <=ASC("9") THEN PROCnumber
UNTIL A%=13
END

.letter
PRINT CHR$(A%);
PRINT " is a letter"
ENDPROC

.number
PRINT CHR$(A%);
PRINT " is a number"
ENDPROC
```

The >= sign means 'greater than or equal to', while the <= sign means 'less than or equal too'.

Going to

The GOTO command allows you effectively to go to another part of your segment program. You'll probably use this command in association with the IF ... THEN construct, when you might want to go to another point in your program if a certain condition is met. The destination of the GOTO is defined by a label, similar in style to the one used by procedures. The following example segment program will move the cursor to the top or bottom of your program depending on your keyboard response.

```
REM GOTO demo
SELECT TEXT
CLS

PRINT "Cursor Mover"
PRINT
PRINT "Press T to goto top"
PRINT "Press B to goto bottom"
PRINT
PRINT "Please enter choice";

REPEAT
A%=GET
UNTIL A%=ASC("T") OR A%=ASC("B")

IF A%=ASC("T") THEN GOTO top
IF A%=ASC("B") THEN GOTO bottom
.end
END

.top
CURSOR TOP
GOTO end

.bottom
CURSOR BOTTOM
GOTO end
```

As with the procedural label, I have chosen to use lower-case characters throughout. Upper-case characters are permissible should you wish to use them. The labels themselves are used on three occasions to mark 'top', 'bottom' and 'end'. The UNTIL part of the loop that tests for a key press actually tests to see if you pressed 'T' OR 'B', and will not complete until you do so. Remember that 'B' is different from 'b'!

True or false

There are two functions which are often used as REPEAT ... UNTIL and

IF ... THEN arguments; these are TRUE and FALSE. In simple terms, if a value of 0 is returned by a text it is said to be FALSE. If, on the other hand, the value is equal to 65535, then it is said to be TRUE! This segment program tests for a counter variable reaching 65535:

```
REM TRUE demo

A%=65530

REPEAT
A%=A%+1
PRINT A%
UNTIL A%=TRUE

PRINT A%
B%=GET
```

When A%=65535 then A% will be TRUE and the REPEAT ... UNTIL loop will be finished.

In a similar fashion this next segment program tests for a TRUE value to detect when A% reaches 0.

```
REM FALSE demo

A%=25

REPEAT
A%=A%-1
PRINT A%
UNTIL A%=FALSE

PRINT A%
B%=GET
```

Many of the other functions within the Wordwise Plus programming language will return TRUE and FALSE depending on their state. For example, if the cursor is at the top of a document then EOT will be FALSE, but when the cursor is at the bottom of the document EOT will be TRUE. The Reference Manual contains more details on which functions return TRUE and FALSE – do consult this if the need to know arises.

Chapter Seventeen
File Processing

In addition to being able to manipulate text stored within Wordwise, segment program commands are also provided to allow you to access your disc or tape to read information from it or conversely to write data to it. Basic programmers will already be familiar with many of these, but for those of you who are not, the following descriptions contain segment program examples.

Regular stuff

Perhaps the most obvious commands available for segment program use are LOAD and SAVE. These work as one would expect but with a few additions: First let's look at SAVE.

The SAVE command must always be followed by one of three parameters which will determine exactly how your text is saved to tape or disc. The three possible options are:

SAVE TEXT
SAVE MARKED
SAVE PARAMS

In all instances the parameter must be followed by the filename itself, either as a string of characters within quotes, i.e.

SAVE TEXT "file"

or specified via a string variable e.g.

SAVE TEXT A$

SAVE TEXT just saves the whole document in the currently selected text area; it is, in fact, identical to option 1 on the menu. For example, to save the text in the main text area from a segment program held in any segment you would use

```
REM SAVE demo1
```

```
SELECT TEXT
SAVE TEXT "TESTER"
```

You can choose to save any segment simply by selecting the relevant segment before saving, such as

SELECT SEGMENT 5

Unlike option 1, however, disc users should beware, as SAVE does not check to see that the file already exists – if it does it will be overwritten – so take care!

SAVE MARKED imitates option 3 on the text or segment menu in that it will only save the marked text. If there are no markers present the error message

MARKERS!

will be displayed. The following segment program will save the first twenty lines of a document.

```
REM SAVE demo2
SELECT TEXT
A$="TESTER"
CURSOR TOP
FKEY 3
CURSOR DOWN 19
FKEY 3
SAVE MARKED A$
FKEY 1
CURSOR TOP
DELETE MARKERS
```

The final SAVE command is SAVE PARAMS. Wordwise Plus contains an area of memory which holds all the values of its dynamic commands. A *dynamic command* is one that can be varied. For example, the line margin can be varied to any value with the embedded command LM. Its default value is 0, but you can assign your own value to this, e.g. LM8. The area where these details are stored is called the *parameter area*. In addition, the parameter area holds any printer definitions you may have set up with RPS.

Rather than keep setting these up each time you wish to use Wordwise Plus, you can save the parameter block for future use. Since a filename is required for the parameter block you could define a whole library of them depending on your personal needs, and your segment program could use the relevant one should you be performing any form of continual file processing, i.e. previewing or printing a whole series of files to form a single document. Once you have defined your set up sequence, execute the set up by printing the null file (i.e. no text other than that forming the parameter set) with option 6 and then use

SAVE PARAMS "file"

to save the parameter block, where 'file' is the chosen filename.

To complement the SAVE commands the LOAD command can also be used in three different ways. These are:

LOAD TEXT
LOAD TTC
LOAD PARAMS

LOAD TEXT will load a new file into the currently selected text area or segment, i.e.

```
REM LOAD demo1
SELECT TEXT
LOAD TEXT "TESTER"
```

LOAD will not test to see if there is already text within the currently selected text area; it will simply overwrite whatever is there.

LOAD TTC means LOAD Text To Cursor, and is therefore simply option 4 of the main menu.

```
REM LOAD TTC demo
SELECT TEXT
CURSOR BOTTOM
LOAD TTC "SECTION"
```

The segment program above will load a file to the bottom of the main text.

LOAD PARAMS is the counterpart of SAVE PARAMS. As such, this is used to load the parameter file. It will only load a parameter file which is saved in a special format, and will return a

Bad Params

error if the file is not a parameter file. The following program shows how three files could all be printed using different parameters,

```
REM LOAD PARAM demo
SELECT TEXT
DEFAULTS
LOAD PARAM "start"
LOAD TEXT "intro"
PRINT TEXT
LOAD PARAM "emphas"
LOAD TEXT "middle"
PRINT TEXT
LOAD PARAM "elite"
LOAD TEXT "end"
PRINT TEXT
```

Files can also be saved by spooling them using option 8 on the menu. SPOOL is also available as a command for use in segment programs. SPOOL takes four different formats which define its operation. These are:

SPOOL TEXT
SPOOL PAGE
SPOOL MARKED
SPOOL FILE

As usual, each of these commands must be followed by a filename string or a filename in the guise of a string variable.

SPOOL TEXT simply spools the current selected text in its formatted state, just as option 8 would be used from the main or segment menu, i.e.

SPOOL TEXT "TESTER"

SPOOL PAGE will spool a specified page of text. This command therefore expects to find two separate items of information. In addition to the filename of the spooled page, the page number must also be specified. The following program will spool page 3 of a document in Wordwise Plus:

```
REM SPOOL PAGE demo
SELECT TEXT
DEFAULTS
SPOOL PAGE "TESTER",3
```

We have inserted a new command in the program here; DEFAULTS. This command is used to reset all changeable parameters within Wordwise Plus to their default values, i.e. those defined when Wordwise Plus is first switched on. Examples include printer parameters, line length, headers and tab stops. This need only be done if you have previously previewed, printed or spooled the file, as Wordwise Plus will have incremented a special page pointer within its own special parameter block – this will reflect the last page number it encountered. If you now try to spool a page within your current document Wordwise Plus will assume that it has already gone, as its current page number is higher than the one you have asked to spool. This is not a fault within Wordwise Plus; in fact, it is a useful feature as it allows you to spool pages from files one after the other as they are read in from disc. So if you wish to spool a current page, always execute DEFAULTS first of all.

SPOOL MARKED allows you to spool to tape or disc a marked section of text. Spooling the first twenty lines of the text space is quite straightforward, as the following segment program proves:

```
REM SPOOL MARKED

SELECT TEXT
CLS
CURSOR TOP
```

```
FKEY 3
CURSOR DOWN 20
FKEY 3
SPOOL MARKED "PAGE"
CURSOR TOP
DELETE MARKERS
```

The final SPOOL command is SPOOL FILE. This command will read in from tape or disc a file that has been saved as text, i.e. either with option 1 on the main or segment menu or with the command SAVE TEXT. It will then make a spool file from it and save this to tape or disc in a formatted state. The command expects to be followed by two filenames. The first is the name of the Wordwise file and the second is the destination name of the file it is to be spooled into, i.e.

SPOOL FILE “source” “destin”

Open all hours

The remaining file acting commands in the Wordwise Plus programming language all act on getting either single characters or lines of characters from the disc, or conversely putting them there in the first place!

Before you can place a series of characters onto disc or tape you must first inform the computer that you wish to do so. This is done by using a function called OPENOUT. This function must be followed by a filename of the file that you wish to open out to. Because of the high speed random access ability of discs this command is really only suitable for use with discs, though it certainly can be used to a limited extent on tape-based systems. The drawback here is that you can only really have a single file open at any one time to read to or write from. This is not the case on a disc-based system when you can have up to five files open for reading to and writing from.

As you open out to a file the computer gives that file a number – and this number must be noted and saved in a numeric variable for future use. A typical example of the OPENOUT command in use is

A%=OPENOUT (“file1”)

Here the file we are opening out to is called ‘file1’. The number given to the file ‘file1’ is placed into the variable A%. This number is called the ‘channel’ number, channel meaning that this is what the data flows through.

Once a file has been opened for output it can be written to at any time using the BPUT# command. BPUT# must be followed by two values; the first is the channel number of the file, and the second is the value to be written to the file. The channel number is saved in a numeric variable at the time of OPENOUT, and for obvious reasons now. The program below uses both of these commands to write 255 Xs to a file called XTEST.

```
REM Write to file
A%=OPENOUT ("XTEST")

DOTHIS
BPUT# A%,ASC("X")
TIMES 255

CLOSE# A%
```

This type of operation is not so straightforward, so let us examine the action of each line in turn.

A%=OPENOUT ("XTEST")	– this opens a file on disc called "XTEST". The channel number of the XTEST file is placed in the variable A%
DOTHIS	– set up a loop
BPUT# A%,ASC("X")	– write the ASCII character "X" to the file whose channel number is in A%
TIMES 255	– do the loop 256 times
CLOSE #A%	– close the file whose channel is A%

The last command is new, but fairly self-explanatory. When a file has been finished with it must be closed. A particular file can be closed by specifying its channel number, or alternatively all of the files can be closed with the blanket command

CLOSE #0

The next program takes the BPUT# command and shows how it can be used within a loop to allow you to write an ASCII file, typed in at the keyboard, to a disc file:

```
REM BGET demo
CLS
A%=OPENOUT ("TESTER")

REPEAT
D%=GET
PRINT CHR$(D%);
BPUT# A%,D%
UNTIL D%=13

CLOSE #A%
```

Ensure that you have a disc in the selected disc drive and then execute the segment holding the program. The screen will clear, and then the disc will whirl as a file called "TESTER" is opened. Now type in just half a dozen words or so, pressing RETURN to end. The file will then be closed. What you have just typed will have been written character for character to the file.

Coming back in

Now that we have written some data to a disc how do we go about reading it back? Well, OPENOUT and BPUT# have their own counterparts to do this. These are the commands OPENIN and BGET#. OPENIN allows you to OPEN an existing file to read it IN, while BGET# allows you to GET a single byte from the file. If the term byte is confusing, don't worry – think of it as meaning a single character. The following program will read in the data just written by the program above.

```
REM BGET demo
CLS
A%=OPENIN ("TESTER")

REPEAT
D%=BGET# A%
PRINT CHR$ (D%);
UNTIL D%=13

CLOSE #A%
G%=GET
```

Like its counterpart, OPENIN will return a channel number which must be saved in a numeric variable. The file that is being opened must, of course, be specified. Once the channel has been ascertained bytes of information can be read into a numeric variable ready for printing. The action of each command in the program is explained more fully below,

CLS	– Clear screen
A%=OPENIN ("TESTER")	– Open the file called TESTER ready to be read in; Save channel number in A%
REPEAT	– Set up loop
D%=BGET# A%	– Get byte from channel A% and save it in D%
PRINT CHR$ (D%);	– Print the ASCII value of the byte
UNTIL D%=13	– Repeat until a <RETURN> character is found
CLOSE #A%	– Close the file whose channel number is in A%
G%=GET	– Display results until a key is pressed

The BGET# function works by reading a byte from a file and returning the number of that byte. This is fine for reading actual numbers from files, but means than an extra command must be incorporated into the program if we wish to translate the number into an ASCII character, i.e. by using the CHR$ function. A function is provided that will perform the equivalent of a BGET# but it will return the byte as the actual character and thus must be read into a string variable. The function is GCK$# – the Get Character from File function.

Using the above program as an example we can replace two functions with one so that the program becomes

```
REM GCF$# demo
CLS
A%=OPENIN ("TESTER")

REPEAT
D$=GCF$# A%
PRINT D$;
UNTIL D$=""

CLOSE #A%
G%=GET
```

A further change has occured in the program; the UNTIL line now reads

UNTIL D$=""

The double quotes are used to signify a <RETURN> character which is ASCII 13. This is rather a clumsy way of reading a file in, particularly as it will simply end on encountering the very first <RETURN>. One way round this would be to find the length of the file and use this value as the control variable in a DOTHIS ... TIME loop. The length of a file can be ascertained with the function EXT#.

To read the length of a file, which must already be opened, the syntax of the function is simply

L%=EXT# A%

where A% is the channel and L% the variable into which the file length will be placed. By adding a couple of extra line to the GCF$ demo above we can also return the length of the file:

```
REM EXT# demo
CLS
A%=OPENIN ("TESTER")
L%=EXT#A%
PRINT "length is :";
PRINT L%
```

```
REPEAT
D$=GCF$#A%
PRINT D$;
UNTIL D$=""

CLOSE #A%
G%=GET
```

All that is required to slim down the program is to adjust the arrangement of the loop thus:

```
REM EXT# demo2
CLS
A%=OPENIN ("TESTER")
L%=EXT#A%

DOTHIS
D$=GCF$#A%
PRINT D$;
TIMES L%

CLOSE #A%
G%=GET
```

Just like the other get character functions, GCF$# also has a line counterpart, GLF$#, which stands for Get Line from File. As with GCF$# this must be read into a string variable. A line in this instance is determined as all text up to a <RETURN> character or 255 characters, whichever comes first.

```
REM GLF# demo
CLS
A%=OPENIN ("TESTER")

D$=GLF$#A%
PRINT D$

CLOSE #A%
G%=GET
```

The above segment program reads just a single line from the TESTER file.

The problem now arises as to how to read in, say, a whole file using the GLF$# function. In this instance EXT# is of no real use; it would be useful if there were a function that would test to see if the end of the file had been reached. This function does exist and is called EOF# – End Of File. The segment program below uses it to read in a file, which should contain no embedded commands and ideally will be a spool file.

```
REM EOF# demo
CLS
A%=OPENIN ("TESTER")

REPEAT
D$=GLF$#A%
PRINT D$
UNTIL EOF#A%

CLOSE #A%
G%=GET
```

As with all file acting functions, the channel number plays an integral role in the EOF# function. A line by line account of the program is detailed below.

CLS	– Clear screen
A%=OPENIN ("TESTER")	– Open the file to be read in; place channel number in A%
REPEAT	– Set up loop
D$=GLF$#A%	– Place line from file A% in D$
PRINT D$	– Print D$
UNTIL EOF#A%	– Repeat until the end of file A% is reached
CLOSE #A%	– Close file A%

Getting the point

The final file acting command is PTR#. This function affects the file pointer and determines just which character is to be read next from the file. In normal use the file pointer is incremented by one, but by using PTR# the increment value will be changed as the following program demonstrates. Here PTR# is used to increment the file pointer so that it reads only every other character in a file.

```
REM PTR# demo
CLS
A%=OPENIN ("tester")

REPEAT
L%=EXT#A%
IF PTR#A%=L%-1 THEN GOTO end
D$=GCF$#A%
PRINT D$;
PTR#A%=PTR#A%+1
.end
UNTIL EOF#A%
```

```
CLOSE #A%
G%=GET
```

The IF ... THEN statement is used to ensure that PTR# is not pushed beyond the end of the file, which would otherwise result in a 'read only' error.

In addition to moving the 'reading' pointer along, PTR# can also act to put bytes to disc. In other words it can be used to position just where in a file a byte will be placed. The final program in this chapter demonstrates this. First it will wait for you to enter a line of text. Then it will write an asterisk over every other character on the file which has just been established, before reading it back!

```
REM PTR# demo2

CLS
A%=OPENOUT ("TESTER")

REPEAT
D%=GET
PRINT CHR$(D%);
BPUT# A%,D%
UNTIL D%=13

PTR#A%=0

L%=EXT#A%
L%=L%/2
L%=L%-1

DOTHIS
BPUT# A%,ASC("*")
PTR# A%=PTR# A%+1
TIMES L%

CLOSE #A%

A%=OPENIN ("TESTER")

REPEAT
D$=GCF$# A%
PRINT D$;
UNTIL EOF# A%

CLOSE #A%
G%=GET
```

Chapter Eighteen

And Finally ...

There are a few more commands available in the Wordwise Plus programming language that remain to be discussed; in alphabetical order they are:

CALL	SOT
DOLINE	TIME
FREE	VARFREE
NEW	VDU
OSCLI	WORDS
RECOUNT	

We can remedy this by looking at each.

Using machine code

For those of you that understand the delights (or otherwise!) of machine code programming, the CALL command will prove of great use. It acts like its Basic counterpart and allows you to execute a small machine code routine that has been prewritten and loaded in.

The niche into which you tuck any code must be chosen with care as it will either be corrupted by Wordwise Plus or could even cause Wordwise Plus itself to crash if loaded in after Wordwise Plus has been selected. The user defined character buffer from &C00 to &CFF can be considered a safe area. Disc users can also make use of the cassette input and output buffers from &900 to &AFF inclusive. My advice is, be safe and use &C00 to &CFF.

Your reasons for using machine code routines with Wordwise Plus will, of course, vary. However, one routine I have found invaluable is a very short one indeed. When previewing a file from disc using PREVIEW the normal Edit Mode screen is in use, as opposed to the normal Mode 3 screen for a preview. The section of machine code I use selects Mode 3 before you preview your file. One very important point I must stress here is that *no* check is made to see if you can actually change to Mode 3. If you have a document in memory, save it *first* to be safe. If you don't and the document is using the

Mode 3 screen memory then you will certainly lose your current text. Users of screen RAM boards such as the Aries B20 or B32 need not worry as the screen RAM is always available.

```
 10 REM Mode 3
 20 REM for Wordwise Plus
 30 :
 40 P%=&C00
 50 [
 60 LDA #22
 70 JSR &FFEE
 80 LDA #3
 90 JSR &FFEE
100 RTS
110 ]
```

Listing 18.1. Mode 3 selection.

I'll describe how you set about installing a machine code routine using the Mode 3 example. First, once you have your idea, enter Basic and write your assembly listing program. The Mode 3 selection program is shown in Listing 18.1. If you can test the program at this stage then do so. In the case of a Mode 3 selection this is possible; simply CALL to the start address from Basic by typing, in this case

CALL &C00

The next step is to save the machine code itself. Look at the assembly listing (Figure 18.1) and note the start, end and execution addresses, and then *SAVE the code. In this example it would be

*SAVE MODE3 C00 COB C00

It is wise to keep a copy of your assembly listing as well, so SAVE this in the normal way.

Now that the machine code has been saved (and possibly tested) it is ready for use. The segment program below shows a typical use:

```
REM using machine code
*LOAD MODE3 C00
CALL &C00
PREVIEW FILE "CH18"
PRINT
PRINT
PRINT "Press any key"
A%=GET
```

The program begins by *LOADing the machine code and then executing it. The appropriate file is then PREVIEWed and a 'Press any key' prompt issued. Just substitute your own filename for "CH18". If you are using this

```
0C00
0C00 A9 16     LDA #22
0C02 20 EE FF JSR &FFEE
0C05 A9 03     LDA #3
0C07 20 EE FF JSR &FFEE
0C0A 60        RTS
```

Figure 18.1. The Mode 3 assembly listing.

machine code patch regularly there is no need to reload it every time you need it. Once it is loaded it should remain intact until you switch off Wordwise Plus.

A slightly safer program that will first save and then reload your current text is given below:

```
REM save before MODE3
SELECT TEXT
CLS
PRINT
PRINT
PRINT"Save current file? (Y/N)";
G$=GCK$
IF G$="Y" THEN GOTO yes
IF G$="y" THEN GOTO yes
END

.yes
PRINT
PRINT "Please enter filename ";
F$=GLK$
PRINT
PRINT "Saving file ";
PRINT F$
SAVE TEXT F$
*LOAD MODE3 C00
CALL &C00
PREVIEW FILE "CH18"
PRINT
PRINT
PRINT "Press any key"
A%=GET
```

The three main registers of the 6502 microprocessor registers can be set to specific values before using CALL, by seeding the numeric variables A%, X% and Y%. The low byte of these variables is passed into the accumulator, X and Y registers respectively. The carry flag may also be set or cleared by setting C% to 1 or 0.

It is possible to select Mode 3 for use with Preview File from the main menu, if you have the extra RAM available either through a B20 or B32 board or the 6502 Second Processor. This is done by typing

:<CTRL-V>3 PREVIEW FILE "file"

Commands can be passed to the operating system from segment programs using OSCLI, followed by the command enclosed within quotes. To perform a *HELP in this manner simply enter

OSCLI "HELP"

I said do this

The DOLINE command will take the line of text following it and print it onto the screen. So what? PRINT can do that as well, you may say. Well the difference is that you can also use it to perform an embedded command!

To print the embedded command it is necessary to precede and suffix the command with G and W respectively, which relate to the green and white embedded commands. For example, the following segment would cause some text to be centred:

```
REM DOLINE demo1
CLS
PRINT
PRINT "This text is not centred!"
PRINT
DOLINE "|GCE|WBut this text is!"
A%=GET
```

If you still have the MODE3 routine installed try this demonstration which uses underlined text:

```
REM DOLINE demo2
CALL &C00
DOLINE "|GUS|WThis is underlined|GUE|W"
A%=GET
```

Note that, unlike PRINT, DOLINE does not generate a line feed so the cursor remains positioned after the last printed character.

Lucky numbers

When you are using any of the Edit Mode screens the right-hand side of the status line displays the total number of characters free. This value can be ascertained at any time from within a segment program using the function FREE. The value returned must either be printed or placed into a numeric variable thus:

```
PRINT FREE
V%=FREE
```

The function VARFREE acts in a similar way but returns the number of bytes free in the variable string buffer.

Complementing FREE is WORDS, which returns the number of words within Wordwise Plus. Similarly, this should be printed or saved in a numeric variable, i.e.

```
PRINT WORDS
X%=WORDS
```

The value of WORDS can actually be changed, however. This is done by setting the numeric variable W%, which is used to hold the current word count. To set the word count to 50 use

```
W%=50
```

If you use this at all and wish to restore the actual number of words in your text then simply use the command RECOUNT.

Goodbye text

We saw in an earlier chapter that the command DELETE TEXT used in menu mode could be used to delete the document held in the text space. If you wish to clear all of the text in Wordwise Plus completely and reset all the parameters then the command to use is NEW. The NEW command must be treated with respect. However, if you do use it absentmindedly then the previously described DUMP program can be used to locate the text within memory.

Start of text

Just as EOT can be used to determine whether the cursor is at the End Of text, the function SOT can be used to test if the cursor is at the Start Of Text. If the cursor is at the start of text then SOT will return a TRUE value (i.e. 65535). If it is not the case then a FALSE value (i.e. 0) will be returned.

Counting out time

If you wish to display text for a period of time then the TIME function will be of use. TIME counts in intervals of one hundredth of a second; 1 second, therefore, is when TIME reaches 100. TIME is a special variable and can therefore be set to a determined value. The segment program below shows the technique for getting TIME to tick away the hours!

```
REM TIME demo
CLS
A%=0

REPEAT
TIME =0
REPEAT
UNTIL TIME=100
A%=A%+1
PRINT "TIME GONE :";
PRINT A%;
PRINT " SECONDS"
UNTIL FALSE
```

Monitoring VDUs

Many of the BBC Micro's functions are available to you from within a Wordwise Plus segment program via the VDU command. The command must be used sensibly however; VDU22, for example, could lose your text for you as it is used to change the screen mode. This technique was described at the beginning of this chapter.

The User Guide supplied with your BBC Microcomputer details the VDU commands and the code sequences needed; Chapter 33 to be precise. I would refer you to it for details of each. Some VDU sequences that you might find useful to be going on with are:

VDU 1	– send next character to printer
VDU 2	– turn printer on
VDU 3	– turn printer off
VDU 7	– sound a bleep
VDU 14	– paged mode on
VDU 15	– paged mode off
VDU 23,1,0;0;0;0;	– turn cursor off
VDU 23,1,1;0;0;0;	– turn cursor on
VDU 31,X%,Y%	– move cursor to position X%,Y%

Smooth operators

In many of the examples in this section of the book I have used operators such as + to add, and = to test for equality. There are a number of these operators, as they are known, within Wordwise Plus and they provide a large variety of operations. The operators are divided into groups of precedence. This is important to remember when you are dealing with several operators within an equation. An operator in group 1 will always be evaluated before an operator from group 2, likewise an operator in group 3 has precedence over any in groups below it, and so on.

Group 1
This group contains just two operators:

( ) – brackets
? – peek

Any operators enclosed within brackets will be evaluated before those without. For example, in the line

```
A%=B%+(W%-1)
```

the 1 will be subtracted from W% before the result is added to B%.

The peek operator, ?, also known by the more exotic title of indirection operator, allows you to 'look into' memory locations of the BBC Micro. It can be used in conjunction with a PRINT command or by assignment to a numeric variable, i.e.

```
PRINT ?123 – print contents of location 123
A%=?123    – place contents of location 123 into A%
```

Group 2
Wordwise Plus has no operators assigned to this group.

Group 3
This group contains

* – multiply
/ – divide
DIV – DIVide modulo 8
MOD – MODulus of DIV

The first two items are straightforward enough, and can be used in PRINT or a variable assignment, i.e.

```
PRINT 4*3
A%=100/20
```

DIV and MOD can be used to ascertain the integer result of number division. For example

```
PRINT 345 DIV 255
PRINT 345 MOD 255
```

would return values of 1 and 9 respectively, since 345 DIVided by 255 is 1. The MOD operator will effectively return the remainder, i.e. 90.

Group 4
This group contains just two operators

+ – addition
− – subtraction

These have both been encountered before.

Group 5
The group 5 operators test for equality or otherwise. The operators are:

= – equals
<> – not equal
< – less than
> – greater than
<= – less than or equal to
>= – greater than or equal to

Group 6
The AND operator is included here. This is used to test for more than one condition. For example

```
IF A%=0 AND B%=1 AND C%=2 THEN PRINT "Yes"
```

Here the word "Yes" will only be printed if A%, B% and C% are equal to 0, 1 and 2 respectively.

AND can also be used as a bitwise operator between two numbers. Here only the resultant bit will be set if the corresponding bits are both 1, i.e,

```
a)          0111
            0111
      AND   0111

b)          1010
            1001
      AND   1000
```

In a) the first three bits are set in both numbers therefore the result is three set bits. In b), however, only 1 bit is set commonly to both and is reflected in the result.

Group 7
The OR and EOR operators are included here. OR will test to see if any condition is fulfilled. For example

IF A%=0 OR B%=1 THEN PRINT "No"

"No" will be printed if either A% is equal to 0 or B% is equal to 1. Only one of the two conditions need be true.

OR may be used at bit level where the resultant bit is set, if either of the bits are a 1, i.e.

```
a)           0101
             1010
        OR   1111

b)           1001
             1100
        OR   1101
```

EOR is slightly more complicated and is really only of use at bit level. Here the resultant bit will only be set if one of the two bits under test is a 1. If the bits are identical then the result is 0. The test is said to be Exclusive to the OR (EOR). Two examples follow:

```
a)           1010
             1100
       EOR   0110

b)           1100
             0100
       EOR   1000
```

Numbers

Numbers may be expressed in four ways. The most familiar way is to express a number as a decimal value. All numbers are taken to be decimal unless they are preceded with '&', '@' or '%'. A number preceded with '&' is taken to be a hexadecimal number, i.e. to a base of 16. A number preceded with '@' is taken to be an octal number, that is to a base of 8. A number preceded by '%' is taken to be a binary number. Examples of each are:

```
123        – decimal
&FF        – hexadecimal
@12        – octal
%10001111  – binary
```

PART THREE
Segment Programs

In the pages that follow you will find sixteen segment programs that I hope will be of use. No doubt as you key them in you will get other ideas on ways in which they can be used and adapted. It seems reasonable that an original idea for a segment program will ultimately give birth to at least one or two more!

1: Delete to end of line

Program 1 will delete text from the current position of the cursor to the end of the line. Line, in this instance, is defined as the end of the Edit Mode line, at cursor position 39. The program can be loaded into any segment. To use the program, position the cursor at the relevant point in the line, and then execute the segment.

```
REM Segment Program 1
REM Delete to end of line from
REM current cursor position

SELECT TEXT
DELETE AT 1
FKEY 3
CURSOR AT 39

IF EOT THEN GOTO leap
CURSOR AT 0
CURSOR DOWN

.leap

FKEY 3
FKEY 7

RECOUNT
DISPLAY
```

2: Delete entire line

This program is an extension to the one above in that it will delete all of the line where the cursor sits, i.e. from cursor position 0 to cursor position 39.

```
REM Segment Program 2
REM Delete whole of line on
REM which the cursor is sitting

SELECT TEXT
CURSOR AT 0

IF EOT THEN END

IF SOT THEN GOTO skipleft

CURSOR LEFT 1
G$=GCT$
G%=ASC(G$)

IF G$<>" " AND G%<>13 THEN TYPE" "

.skipleft
DELETE AT 1
FKEY 3
CURSOR AT 39

IF EOT THEN GOTO end

CURSOR AT 0
CURSOR DOWN 1

.end

FKEY 3
FKEY 7

RECOUNT
DISPLAY
```

3: Delete REMs

I'm a great one for putting plenty of REMs at the start of segment programs, as they remind you what is going on. The problem occurs when you are processing a lot of text, when you could really do without the REMs as they eat up valuable text space. Program 3 solves that by deleting any REMs found in a specified segment range. The program should be loaded into segment 0 or 9. Once run it will request you to input the start and end segments to be stripped.

```
REM Segment Program 3
REM Delete all REMs from segments
REM Will remove REM's and rem's

CLS
PRINT
PRINT "REM Stripper"
PRINT
PRINT "Please enter start SEG :";
S$=GCK$
PRINT S$
S%=ASC(S$)
S%=S%-48
PRINT "Please enter end SEG   :";
E$=GCK$
PRINT E$
E%=ASC(E$)
E%=E%-48

REPEAT

SELECT SEGMENT S%
CURSOR TOP

REPEAT
FIND "REM"

DELETE AT 1
FKEY 3
CURSOR AT 39

IF EOT THEN GOTO leap
CURSOR AT 0
CURSOR DOWN

.leap

FKEY 3
FKEY 7
```

```
UNTIL EOT

REM find rem's
CURSOR TOP

REPEAT
FIND "rem"

DELETE AT 1
FKEY 3
CURSOR AT 39

IF EOT THEN GOTO again
CURSOR AT 0
CURSOR DOWN

.again

FKEY 3
FKEY 7

UNTIL EOT

RECOUNT
DISPLAY

S%=S%+1

UNTIL S%=(E%+1)
```

4: Delete pad characters

This program will remove the default pad characters from a Wordwise Plus text file. It will be of use with the RUBOUT program described in Chapter 11.

```
REM Segment Program 4
REM Delete pad characters

SELECT TEXT
CURSOR TOP

REPEAT
REPLACE "|"," "
UNTIL EOT
```

```
CURSOR TOP

REPEAT
F%=FREE
CURSOR TOP

REPEAT
REPLACE "  "," "
UNTIL EOT
Z%=FREE
UNTIL Z%=F%
```

5: Delete OC from text

The operation of program 5 is straightforward. It will strip all embedded OC commands from text currently stored in Wordwise Plus. The program can be placed into any segment.

```
REM Segment Program 5
REM OC embedded command stripper

SELECT TEXT

CURSOR TOP

REPEAT
REPLACE "|W","|R"
UNTIL EOT

CURSOR TOP

REPEAT
REPLACE "|GOC","~"
UNTIL EOT

CURSOR TOP

REPEAT
REPLACE "|Goc","~"
UNTIL EOT

CURSOR TOP
TYPE CHR$(13)
```

```
REPEAT
CURSOR UP
FKEY 4,"~"
FKEY 3
FKEY 4,CHR$(13)
FKEY 3
FKEY 7
CURSOR AT 0
DELETE AT 1
UNTIL EOT
```

6: Delete all format commands from text

This program takes Program 5 a step further in that it will delete all formatting commands from a Wordwise Plus document, thus leaving it in its bare state. In addition, all double spaces will be halved to a single space.

The pad character should be placed in P$ (P for pad). If you redefine this in your text then this string assignment towards the start of the program should be adjusted. Note that as this program can take several moments to execute, on large documents a message is displayed to assure the user that the program is indeed in operation! As with Program 5, Program 6 can be loaded into any segment.

```
REM Segment Program 6
REM Delete all formatting commands

CLS
PRINT
PRINT
PRINT "Please wait - ";
PRINT "processing your text"

SELECT TEXT

P$="|"
CURSOR TOP

REPEAT
REPLACE P$," "
UNTIL EOT

CURSOR TOP
```

```
REPEAT
REPLACE "|T"," "
UNTIL EOT

CURSOR TOP

REPEAT
F%=FREE
CURSOR TOP

REPEAT
REPLACE "  "," "
UNTIL EOT

X%=FREE

UNTIL X%=F%

CURSOR TOP

REPEAT
REPLACE "|W","|R"
UNTIL EOT

CURSOR TOP
TYPE CHR$(13)
CURSOR TOP
REPEAT
CURSOR UP
FKEY 4,"|G"
FKEY 3
FKEY 4,CHR$(13)
FKEY 3
DELETE AT 1
FKEY 7
UNTIL EOT

CURSOR TOP

REPEAT
REPLACE "|R ","|R"
UNTIL EOT
```

7: Line counter

I find Program 7 most useful. Often you are more interested in the number of lines within a document than the number of words; this program counts the total number of lines. It does so by counting the number of <RETURN>s in the document. The program can be loaded into any segment.

```
REM Segment Program 7
REM Count number of lines
REM within document

SELECT TEXT
CURSOR TOP
L%=0

REPEAT
FIND "|R"
L%=L%+1
CURSOR RIGHT
UNTIL EOT

VDU 7
PRINT
PRINT
PRINT "There are ";
PRINT L%;
PRINT " lines"
PRINT
PRINT "Press any key";
A%=GET
```

8: Segment catalogue

To enable you to keep track of precisely what you have loaded into each segment; Program 8 will be of help. It will list the contents of the first REM in each segment. All that you need do is ensure that the title of each program is contained in the very first REM. The program should be loaded into segment 0.

```
REM Segment Program 8
REM Segment catalogue program
REM Place in SEG0
```

```
A%=1
CLS
PRINT
PRINT
PRINT "Segment Cataloguer"
PRINT

REPEAT
SELECT SEGMENT A%
CURSOR TOP
FIND "REM"
CURSOR RIGHT 3
L$=GLT$
PRINT A%;
PRINT " : ";
PRINT L$
A%=A%+1
UNTIL A%=10

A%=GET
SELECT TEXT
```

9: Document updater

Another program that I find useful is Program 9. It simply updates a version number placed in the text. Thus at any time you know just what version or draft of a document you have. All you need do is ensure that at a convenient point in your text (I usually place it near the start) the following is entered exactly as shown:

<*f1*Version No.1*f2*>

The text 'Version No.1' will appear in green. After each save simply execute the segment which contains this program and the current version number will be incremented by 1.

I find it useful to combine this program with Program 10 described next.

```
REM Segment Program 9
REM Update document number
REM Document should contain
REM <f1Version No.1f2>

SELECT TEXT
CURSOR TOP

FIND "|GVersion No."
```

```
CURSOR RIGHT 12

V$=GLT$
V%=VAL(V$)+1

CURSOR LEFT
DELETE LEFT (LEN(V$))

TYPE STR$(V%)
```

10: File test

When saving text with SAVE TEXT no safety net check is made to see if the file already exists on disc. This program solves that problem. The program can be loaded into any segment and is useful when used in conjunction with Program 9.

```
REM Segment Program 10
REM Test for existing file
REM use within body of
REM a segment program

CLS
PRINT
PRINT "Please Enter Filename :";
F$=GLK$
F$="W."+F$

F%=OPENIN(F$)
CLOSE #F%

IF F%=0 THEN GOTO save

PRINT
VDU 7

PRINT "Replace old file? (Y/N)";
T$=GCK$

IF T$="Y" OR T$="y" THEN GOTO save

PRINT
PRINT
PRINT "File not saved"
```

```
PRINT
PRINT "Press any key";
A%=GET

END

.save
SELECT TEXT
SAVE TEXT F$
```

11: Multiple copy printer

Program 11 will allow you to print multiple copies of a text file either from disc or directly from the text area. It can be placed into any segment and is capable of printing up to 65535 documents continuously – that is if you have the paper!

```
REM Segment Program 11
REM Multi copy printer

SELECT TEXT
CLS
VDU 31,7,2
PRINT "Multiple Copy Printer"
PRINT
PRINT
PRINT "Number of copies? ";

N$=GLK$
N%=VAL(N$)

PRINT "Is document in text area? ";
A$=GCK$

IF A$="Y" OR A$="y" THEN GOTO skip
PRINT

PRINT "Please enter filename ";
F$=GLK$


DOTHIS
DEFAULTS
PRINT FILE F$
TIMES N%
```

```
END

.skip

DOTHIS
DEFAULTS
PRINT TEXT
TIMES N%
```

12: Multi file printing

This program should be loaded into segment 0. It allows you to print a series of different files from disc, in addition to making any necessary drive changes and prompting for disc changes. The files to be printed should be loaded into segment 1. The disc drive is selected by prefixing its number with a colon, while a prompt is specified by a ~.

If the following text was placed into segment 1:

```
:0
INTRO
CHAP1
CHAP2
CHAP3
:2
CHAP4
CHAP5
CHAP6
^Figures disc
SEG0
SEG1
SEG2
SEG3
:0
```

the files INTRO, CHAP1, CHAP2 and CHAP3 would be printed from drive 0. This would be followed by the files CHAP4, CHAP5, and CHAP6 from drive 2. The program would then prompt for the 'figures disc', after which SEG0, SEG1, SEG2 and SEG3 would be printed. Finally drive 0 would be reselected.

```
REM Segment Program 12
REM Multi file printing
REM will take files from
```

```
REM specified drives and
REM print them
REM File details in SEG 9
REM thanks to Patrick Quick
REM and Acorn User


REM place this in SEG 0

SELECT SEGMENT 9
DEFAULTS
P%=0
CURSOR TOP

REPEAT
A$=GCT$

IF A$ =":" THEN GOTO drive
IF A$ ="^" THEN GOTO disk

.file
B$=A$+GLT$
PREVIEW FILE B$
GOTO finline

.drive
OSCLI "DRIVE "+GLT$
GOTO finline

.disk
B$=GCT$
C$=GLT$
CLS
PRINT "Insert ";
PRINT C$;
PRINT " disk into drive ";
PRINT B$
PRINT "and then press RETURN ";
REPEAT
UNTIL GET=13
OSCLI "DRIVE "+B$

.finline

UNTIL EOT

END
```

13: Select page printer

This program will allow you to print specific pages from the current text. Paging must, of course, be enabled at the start of that document. The program can be loaded into any segment for use.

```
REM Segment Program 13
REM Place in any segment
REM Select page printer
REM with thanks to Patrick Quick
REM and Acorn User

REM text to be in text area
REM Paging must be enabled with EP

CLS
PRINT
PRINT "Print - first page ? ";
A%=VAL(GLK$)
PRINT "         last page ? ";
B%=VAL(GLK$)

REPEAT
SELECT TEXT
DEFAULTS
P%=0
PRINT PAGE A%
A%=A%+1
UNTILA%>B%
```

14: Embedded command help

This program provides an immediate help sheet of the embedded commands for Wordwise Plus, listing their mnemonics and meaning in two neat columns on the screen. It shows how VDU31 can be used to good effect. The program should be placed into segment 0 and the list of commands into segment 1.

```
REM Segment Program 14
REM Wordwise Plus HELP page
REM Place in Segment 0
REM Commands in Segment 1
```

```
CLS
VDU 31,2,0
PRINT "** Embedded Command Summary **"
PRINT

SELECT SEGMENT 1
CURSOR TOP

Y%=1
REPEAT
C$=GLT$
VDU 31,0,Y%
PRINT C$;
C$=GLT$
VDU 31,20,Y%
PRINT C$;
Y%=Y%+1
UNTIL EOT

PRINT "  Press any key";

A%=GET
select segment 0

END
```

The following list of embedded commands should be entered as shown into segment 1.

```
BP - Begin Page         FI - Fully Inden
BS - Bottom Spc         FP - Footing Pos
CE - Centre             GF - Get File
CI - Cancel Ind         HP - Heading Pos
CO - Contin Out         IN - Indent
CP - Cond  Page         JO - Justify On
DE - Strike End         LL - Line Length
DF - Def. Foot          LM - Left Margin
DH - Def. Head          LNE- Line Num End
DM - Diable Mess        LNS- Line Num Sta
DP - Def Pound          LS - Line space
DS - strk start         NJ - No Justify
DT - Def. Tabs          OC - Output Code
EM - Enable Mess        OPS- Out Print Seq
EP - Enable Page        OS - OS call
ES - Escape Seq         PA - Pause
```

```
PC - Pad Char def.       SEG- call SEGment
PF - Print File          SP - SPace lines
PL - Page Length         SS - Single Space
PN - Page Number         TI - Temp. Indent
PP - Print Page No       TS - Top Space
PS - Print String        UE - Underline End
RPS- def.Print Seq.      US - Underline Start
```

Figure A shows the screen display when the program in segment 0 is executed.

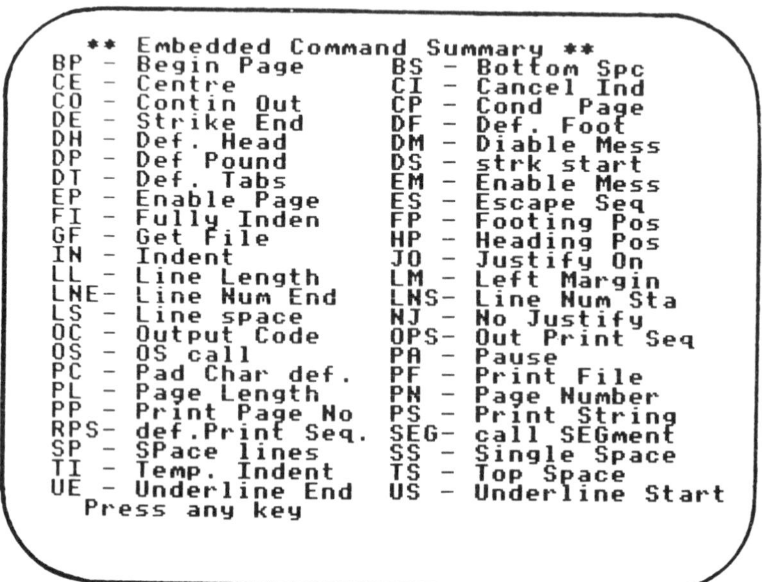

Figure A. Embedded command summary.

15: Command and function help

Program 15 is similar to Program 14 but provides help sheets of the Wordwise Plus programming language commands and functions in three columns (Figure B). Program 15 should be loaded into segment 2 and the list of commands and functions into segment 3.

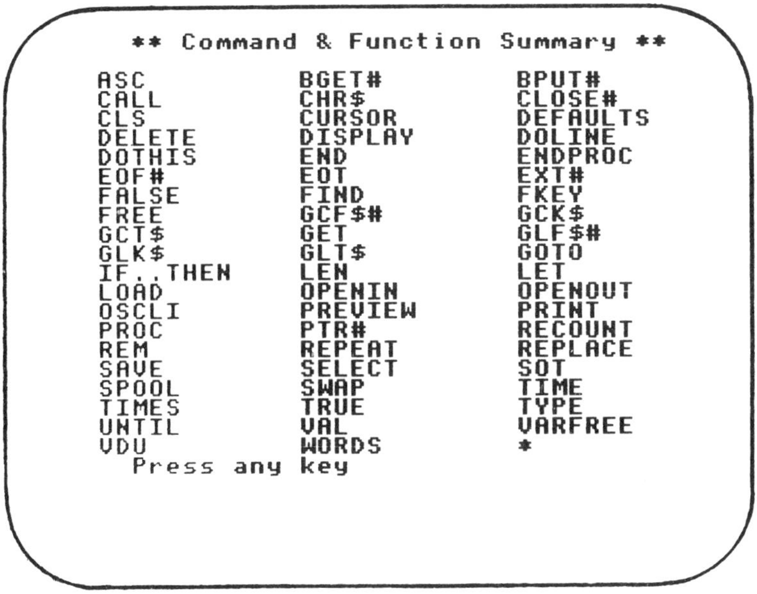

```
   ** Command & Function Summary **

ASC            BGET#          BPUT#
CALL           CHR$           CLOSE#
CLS            CURSOR         DEFAULTS
DELETE         DISPLAY        DOLINE
DOTHIS         END            ENDPROC
EOF#           EOT            EXT#
FALSE          FIND           FKEY
FREE           GCF$#          GCK$
GCT$           GET            GLF$#
GLK$           GLT$           GOTO
IF..THEN       LEN            LET
LOAD           OPENIN         OPENOUT
OSCLI          PREVIEW        PRINT
PROC           PTR#           RECOUNT
REM            REPEAT         REPLACE
SAVE           SELECT         SOT
SPOOL          SWAP           TIME
TIMES          TRUE           TYPE
UNTIL          VAL            VARFREE
VDU            WORDS          *
  Press any key
```

Figure B. Command and function summary.

```
REM Segment Program 15
REM Command & Function HELP page
REM Place in segment 2

CLS
VDU 31,2,0
PRINT "** Command & Function Summary **"
PRINT

SELECT SEGMENT 3
CURSOR TOP

Y%=2
REPEAT
C$=GLT$
VDU 31,0,Y%
PRINT C$;
C$=GLT$
VDU 31,12,Y%
PRINT C$;
C$=GLT$
VDU 31,25,Y%
PRINT C$
```

```
Y%=Y%+1
UNTIL EOT

PRINT "  Press any key";

A%=GET
select segment 0

END
```

The following list comprises the commands and functions to be placed into segment 3.

```
ASC
BGET#
BPUT#
CALL
CHR$
CLOSE#
CLS
CURSOR
DEFAULTS
DELETE
DISPLAY
DOLINE
DOTHIS
END
ENDPROC
EOF#
EOT
EXT#
FALSE
FIND
FKEY
FREE
GCF$#
GCK$
GCT$
GET
GLF$#
GLK$
GLT$
GOTO
IF..THEN
LEN
LET
```

```
LOAD
OPENIN
OPENOUT
OSCLI
PREVIEW
PRINT
PROC
PTR#
RECOUNT
REM
REPEAT
REPLACE
SAVE
SELECT
SOT
SPOOL
SWAP
TIME
TIMES
TRUE
TYPE
UNTIL
VAL
VARFREE
VDU
WORDS
*
```

16: Continuous search

This final segment program is a continuous search program. It uses a list of files stored in segment to search through for an occurrence of a particular word. I find it useful for searching through looking for Appendix or Figure references, to ensure that I obtain a full list prior to compiling them! The program can be placed into any segment, and the list of filenames as well as providing the segment selection is altered accordingly at the front of the program.

As it stands, the program will search for the word 'Appendix' or 'appendix'. The list of filenames placed in segment 1 should be terminated with END, thus:

CHAP1
CHAP2

CHAP3
CHAP4
END

Segment Program 16 is listed below.

```
REM Segment Program 16
REM continuous search

CLS
Z%=1

REPEAT

SELECT SEGMENT 1
CURSOR TOP

DOTHIS
CURSOR DOWN
TIMES Z%

Z%=Z%+1

D$=GLT$
IF D$="END" THEN END

SELECT TEXT
CLS
PRINT
PRINT "Loading file : ";
PRINT D$

LOAD TEXT D$
CURSOR TOP

REPEAT
FIND "Appendix"
VDU 7
DISPLAY
A%=GET
CURSOR RIGHT
UNTIL EOT

CURSOR TOP
```

```
REPEAT
FIND "appendix"
DISPLAY
CURSOR RIGHT
A%=GET
UNTIL EOT


UNTIL FALSE
```

Appendix A
BBC B+ Fitting

The internal layout of the BBC B+ Micro is somewhat different from that of the BBC B. Remove the case top as described in Chapter 1, but do not remove the keyboard. There are 6 ROM sockets in all, and these should be clearly visible at the back left-hand corner of the computer circuit board. Two of the six sockets will contain ROMs; OSBASIC and the DFS. There will be four free ROM sockets. Wordwise or Wordwise Plus may be fitted into any one of these four ROM sockets. (Refer to Chapter 1 for ROM fitting instructions.) Do *not* try to rearrange the ROMs internally. Reassemble the BBC B+ following the instructions outlined in Chapter 1.

In use

The extra memory available on the BBC B+ when shadow memory is selected is not available for use with Wordwise or Wordwise Plus. However, Wordwise Plus users can gain some advantage in that the shadow memory can be used for the screen display. This means that previewing text is always possible in Mode 3, no matter how much text is held within Wordwise Plus.

The following program should be entered into a segment

```
*SHADOW
DEFAULTS
SELECT TEXT
PREVIEW TEXT
*SHADOW 1
PRINT
PRINT
PRINT "Press any key";
A%=GET
```

Executing the relevant segment will allow the text to be previewed using the shadow memory.

Appendix B
Epson Compatible Printer Codes

The following pages contain details of the control codes for the Epson range of printers. These include the FX printer codes which will be applicable for most Epson-compatible printers. If a code does not function as it is detailed then do consult your own printer manual. Although many printers are sold as being Epson-compatible there are often minor differences.

The control codes are arranged in alphabetical order. To extract the correct command look down the list to find the item you require, extract the figures from the Code column and use these direct. For example, to select elite mode for the FX80 printer, look under Elite to see that the 'Elite Mode set' code is given as 27,77. Use this directly in an OC embedded command.

Occasionally you will need to supply your own information; this is depicted by a series of dots, i.e.

27,94,....

Where various parameters are supplied in the description, the appropriate one should be inserted where specified by a variable within the code, i.e.

27,67,n

FX printer codes

Description	Code	Detail
Backspace	8	backspace one place
Bell	7	sounds bell
Bit image set (8)	27,m,n,o	selects various 8 bit graphics modes
(9)	27,94,....	selects various 9 bit graphics modes
MSB to 0	27,61	sets msb of following 8 bit data to 0
MSB to 1	27,62	sets msb of following 8 bit data to 1
MSB cancel	27,3 5	cancels above codes
normal density	27,75,....	following data printed as bit images
dual density	27,76,....	following data printed as bit images
d.d. double speed	27,89,....	as above but faster and no adjacent dots
quadruple density	27,90,....	as above but darker
Cancel	24	deletes previous data in print buffer
Carriage return	13	carriage return
Condensed Mode on	15	stored and subsequent data printed condensed
on	27,15	as above
off	18	cancels above
Control code select	27,73,n	n=1/49 selects codes 0–31 as printable; n=0/48 selects as unprintable
Delete	127	deletes previous char in print buffer
Double strike set	27,71	sets Double Strike Mode
cancel	27,72	cancels above

Description	Code	Detail
Download def'n.	27,38,....	defines download characters
select	27,37,1,0	selects previously defined set
cancel	27,37,0,0	selects ROM character set
ROM copy	27,58,0,0,0	copies ROM character set to download character set
Elite Mode set	27,77	following data printed in elite size
cancel	27,80	cancels above i.e. returns to normal print
Emphasised Mode set	27,69	all following data printed in emphasized mode
cancel	27,70	cancels above
End of paper on	27,57	selects end of paper detector
off	27,56	deselects end of paper detector
Enlarged Mode set	14	enlarged for one line
set	27,14	as above
set	27,87,n	n=1/49 all following data printed enlarged; n=0/48 cancels
cancel	20	cancels mode set by 14
Expansion on	27,54	codes 128–159 and 255 are set as printable (see download)
off	27,55	cancels above
Form feed	12	executes form feed
length lines	27,67,n	sets form length as n lines
length inches	27,67,0,n	sets form length as n inches
Half speed	27,115,n	n= 1/49 sets half speed print; n=0/48 cancels
Incremental print	27,105,n	n=1/49 sets print and view; n=0/48 cancels
Indent	27,108,n	sets n character left margin

Description	Code	Detail
Initialise	27,64	initialises printer, including clearing buffer
International set	27,82,n	prints following data from n character set
Italics on	27,52	prints all following data in italics
off	27,53	cancels above
Line feed forward	10	executes line feed
reverse	27,106,n	executes $^{n}/_{216}$" reverse feed
Margin set	27,108,n	sets n character left margin
Mode select	27,33,n	selects one of 63 typefaces
On	17	enables printer
Off	19	disables printer
Page width	27,81,n	sets page width to n characters
Paper feed	27,74,n	executes an $^{n}/_{216}$" paper feed (0<=n<=255)
Proportional spacing	27,112,n	n=$^{1}/_{49}$ sets proportional spacing; n=$^{0}/_{48}$ cancels
Reset	27,64	initialises printer, including clearing buffer
Reverse feed	27,106,n	executes $^{n}/_{216}$" reverse feed
Skip over perforation	27,78,n	skips n lines at page bottom
cancel	27,79	cancels above
Slow speed	27,115,n	n=$^{1}/_{49}$ sets half speed print; n=$^{0}/_{48}$ cancels
Spacing $^{1}/_{8}$"	27,48	sets subsequent line spacing to $^{1}/_{8}$"
$^{7}/_{72}$"	27,49	sets subsequent line spacing to $^{7}/_{72}$"

Description	Code	Detail
1/6"	27,50	sets subsequent line spacing to 1/6"
n/216"	27,51,n	sets subsequent line spacing to n/216"
n/72"	27,65,n	sets subsequent line spacing to n/72" i.e. dots width
Subscript set	27,83,	n=1/49 sets subscript mode
cancel	27,84	cancels above
Superscript set	27,83,n	n=0/48 sets superscript
cancel	27,84	cancels above
Tab horizontal	9	executes horizontal tab
horizontal	27,68,....	sets horizontal tabs
vertical	11	executes vertical tab
vertical set	27,98,....	sets 8 channels of vertical tabs
vertical	27,47,n	executes n format vert. tabs e.g.one format for each of seven pages
vertical	27,66,....	defines vertical tab positions
Underline	27,45,n	n=1/49 selects underline;
		n=0/48 deselects underline
Unidirectional print	27,60	prints from left to right for single line
	27,85,n	n=1/49 sets unidirectional print;
		n=0/48 sets bidirectional print

Epson MX80 Type 3 codes

Description	Code	Detail
Backspace	8	backspace one place
Bell	7	sounds bell
Bit image		
normal density	27,75,....	following data printed as bit images
dual density	27,76,....	following data printed as bit images
Carriage return	13	carriage return
Condensed Mode on	15	stored and subsequent data printed condensed
off	18	cancels above
Double strike set	27,71	sets Double Strike Mode
cancel	27,72	cancels above
Emphasised Mode set	27,69	all following data printed in Emphasised Mode
cancel	27,70	cancels above
End of paper on	27,57	selects end of paper detector
off	27,56	deselects end of paper detector
Enlarged Mode set	14	enlarged for one line
set	27,87,n	n=1 all following data printed enlarged; n=0 cancels
cancel	20	cancels mode set by 14
Form feed	12	executes form feed
length lines	27,67,n	sets form length as n lines
length inches	27,67,0,n	sets form length as n inches

Description	Code	Detail
Initialise	27,64	initialises printer
International set	27,82,n	prints following data from n character set
Line feed forward	10	executes line feed
Page width	27,81,n	sets page width to n characters
Paper feed	27,74,n	executes an $^{n}/_{216}$" paper feed ($0<=n<=255$)
Skip over perforation	27,78,n	skips n lines at page bottom
cancel	27,79	cancels above
Spacing $^{1}/_{8}$"	27,48	sets subsequent line spacing to $^{1}/_{8}$"
$^{7}/_{72}$"	27,49	sets subsequent line spacing to $^{7}/_{72}$"
$^{1}/_{6}$"	27,50	sets subsequent line spacing to $^{1}/_{6}$"
$^{n}/_{216}$"	27,51,n	sets subsequent line spacing to $^{n}/_{216}$"
$^{n}/_{72}$"	27,65,n	sets subsequent line spacing to $^{n}/_{72}$" i.e. dots width
Subscript set	27,83,1	sets subscript
cancel	27,84	cancels above
Superscript set	27,83,0	sets superscript
cancel	27,84	cancels above
Tab horizontal	9	executes horizontal tab
horizontal	27,68,....	sets horizontal tabs
vertical	11	executes vertical tab
vertical	27,66,....	defines vertical tab positions
Underline	27,45,n	n=1 selects underline; n=0 deselects underline
Unidirectional print	27,85,n	n=1 sets unidirectional print; n=0 sets bidirectional print

EPSON RX80 CODES

Description	Code	Detail
Backspace	8	backspace one place
Bell	7	sounds bell
Bit image		
normal density	27,75,....	following data printed as bit images
dual density	27,76,....	following data printed as bit images
d.d. double speed	27,89,....	as above but faster and no adjacent dots
quadruple density	27,90,....	as above but darker
Carriage return	13	carriage return
Condensed Mode on	15	stored and subsequent data printed condensed
on	27,15	as above
off	18	cancels above
Delete	127	deletes previous char in print buffer
Double strike set	27,71	sets Double Strike Mode
cancel	27,72	cancels above
Elite mode set	27,77	following data printed in elite size
cancel	27,80	cancels above i.e. returns to normal print
Emphasised Mode set	27,69	all following data printed in Emphasised mode
cancel	27,70	cancels above
End of paper on	27,57	selects end of paper detector
off	27,56	deselects end of paper detector

Description	Code	Detail
Enlarged Mode set	14	enlarged for one line
— set	27,14	as above
set	27,87,n	n= $^1/_{49}$ all following data printed enlarged; n= $^0/_{48}$ cancels
cancel	20	cancels mode set by 14
Form feed	12	executes form feed
length lines	27,67,n	sets form length as n lines
length inches	27,67,0,n	sets form length as n inches
Half speed	27,115,n	n= $^1/_{49}$ sets half speed print; n= $^0/_{48}$ cancels
Indent	27,108,n	sets n character left margin
Initialise	27,64	initialises printer
International set	27,82,n	prints following data from n character set
Italics on	27,52	prints all following data in italics
off	27,53	cancels above
Line feed forward	10	executes line feed
Margin set	27,108,n	sets n character left margin
Page width	27,81,n	sets page width to n characters
Paper feed	27,74,n	executes an $^n/_{216}$" paper feed (0<=n<=255)
Reset	27,64	initialises printer, including clearing buffer
Skip over perforation	27,78,n	skips n lines at page bottom
cancel	27,79	cancels above

Description	Code	Detail
Slow speed	27,115,n	n=$^1/_{49}$ sets half speed print; n=$^0/_{48}$ cancels
Spacing $^1/_8$"	27,48	sets subsequent line spacing to $^1/_8$"
$^7/_{72}$"	27,49	sets subsequent line spacing to $^7/_{72}$"
$^1/_6$"	27,50	sets subsequent line spacing to $^1/_6$"
$^n/_{216}$"	27,51,n	sets subsequent line spacing to $^n/_{216}$"
$^n/_{72}$"	27,65,n	sets subsequent line spacing to $^n/_{72}$" i.e. dots width
Subscript set	27,83,n	n=$^1/_{49}$ sets subscript
cancel	27,84	cancels above
Superscript set	27,83,n	n=$^0/_{48}$ sets superscript
cancel	27,84	cancels above
Tab horizontal	9	executes horizontal tab
vertical	11	executes vertical tab
Underline	27,45,n	n=$^1/_{49}$ selects underline; n=$^0/_{48}$ deselects underline
Unidirectional print	27,60	prints from left to right for single line
	27,85,n	n=$^1/_{49}$ sets unidirectional print; n=$^0/_{48}$ sets bidirectional print

Appendix C
ASCII Codes

Character	Hex	Denary	Character	Hex	Denary
Space	2Ø	32	O	4F	79
!	21	33	P	5Ø	80
”	22	34	Q	51	81
#	23	35	R	52	82
$	24	36	S	53	83
%	25	37	T	54	84
&	26	38	U	55	85
’	27	39	V	56	86
(	28	40	W	57	87
)	29	41	X	58	88
*	2A	42	Y	59	89
+	2B	43	Z	5A	90
,	2C	44	← or [	5B	91
–	2D	45	½ or \	5C	92
.	2E	46	→ or]	5D	93
/	2F	47	↑ or ^	5E	94
0	3Ø	48	- or _	5F	95
1	31	49	£	6Ø	96
2	32	50	a	61	97
3	33	51	b	62	98
4	34	52	c	63	99
5	35	53	d	64	100
6	36	54	e	65	101
7	37	55	f	66	102
8	38	56	g	67	103
9	39	57	h	68	104
:	3A	58	i	69	105
;	3B	59	j	6A	106
<	3C	60	k	6B	107
=	3D	61	l	6C	108

Character	Hex	Denary	Character	Hex	Denary
>	3E	62	m	6D	109
?	3F	63	n	6E	110
@	40	64	o	6F	111
A	41	65	p	70	112
B	42	66	q	71	113
C	43	67	r	72	114
D	44	68	s	73	115
E	45	69	t	74	116
F	46	70	u	75	117
G	47	71	v	76	118
H	48	72	w	77	119
I	49	73	x	78	120
J	4A	74	y	79	121
K	4B	75	z	7A	122
L	4C	76	¼ or {	7B	123
M	4D	77	‖ or ¦	7C	124
N	4E	78	¾ or }	7D	125
			÷ or ~	7E	126

Appendix D

Function Keystrips

NEW PARA	DOUBLE ON	DOUBLE OFF	UNDER-LINE ON	UNDER-LINE OFF	EMPH ON	EMPH CFF	ITALICS ON	ITALICS OFF	DELETE LINE
INSERT OR OVER	GREEN	WHITE	MARKER ■	CURSOR TO?	WORD COUNT TO?	DELETE TO?	DELETE MARKED TEXT	MOVE MARKED TEXT	COPY MARKED TEXT

Index